Worlding Home

Framing the Global

Hilary Kahn and Deborah Piston-Hatlen, *series editors*

Worlding Home

AN URBAN ETHNOGRAPHY OF
PEACEKEEPING CAMPS
IN GOMA, DRC

Maren Larsen

INDIANA UNIVERSITY PRESS

This book is a publication of

Indiana University Press
Herman B Wells Library
1320 East 10th Street
Bloomington, Indiana 47405 USA

iupress.org

The open access edition is available at DOI: https://doi.org/10.2979/18764.0.

Manufactured in the United States of America

First Printing 2025

Cataloging information is available from the Library of Congress.

ISBN 978-0-253-07447-8 (hardback)
ISBN 978-0-253-07448-5 (paperback)
ISBN 978-0-253-07450-8 (ebook)
ISBN 978-0-253-07449-2 (web PDF)

Published with the support of the Swiss National Science Foundation.

THIS BOOK IS DEDICATED TO

Emily Ann (Murphy) Baker

(1958–2021)

My mom. My home. My world.

Contents

Acknowledgments

The cooperation, invitations, support, and trust of multiple contingent, battalion, brigade, and force commanders and officers made this work on military peacekeeping camps possible. To all of the soldiers, NCOs, JCOs, youngsters, and *jawans* of the contingents with whom I worked an incredible debt is also owed. I hope that they would excuse me for any additional duties that may have been assigned to them due to my presence in their camps. Similarly, and beyond the camps, civilian and military personnel working in various staff positions and sections of the UN mission provided friendship, acceptance into their national circles, and several longer conversations about mission dynamics. I've gone to great lengths to protect my interlocutors' anonymity in the text through pseudonyms and intentional omission of dates. I would nonetheless like to acknowledge those who went above and beyond their station to encourage, facilitate, and enrich this research. You know who you are. Thank you for your hospitality, patience, and guidance; for helping me figure out what I was doing; for teaching me about military protocols and how to ask the right questions; and for sitting down and sharing rations or running around with me. I treasure every drink, meal, deep chat, joke, argument, tear, dance, and song we shared.

I do want to acknowledge and honor one person by name. I owe my very first visit to a peacekeeping camp—and hence, everything that followed—to the late Shaza Malik, whose invitation to celebrate Eid together changed the last eight years of my life. May she rest in power.

There would never be enough space here to convey my gratitude to all of the people from Goma who helped make this thesis possible and who make every moment I spend in their city so rich, enlightening, friendly, fun, and safe. Many people graciously responded to my requests for meetings, and I am endlessly grateful to all those who spared their time to speak with me about my research topic. At the same time, I learned more from neighbors, friends, and acquaintances than any interview could have ever afforded. It was their patience that helped me understand the various complexities and complexions of Goma, helped me gain a foothold in Swahili, and helped me build countless relationships, only a few of which I mention here. My Maitrise family includes some of the first people I ever met in Goma and have remained dear friends throughout the years. My Michapi family exemplifies the saying *jirani ni ndugu*—"my neighbor is my brother." The hospitality that they have shown me and show their community every day is unparalleled. *Asante sana kwa yote majirani.* The OK family's hospitality on my final field trip meant the world to me, even if I was seemingly never home. Stewart changed my life through language—*asante mwalimu.* Gracieux was my literal ride or die and made sure I always made it home safely every night. *Nashukuru sana bwan.*

My own camp of compatriots in Goma provided and continue to provide great amounts of emotional support. Thank you to Scott Sroda, Molly McFarland, Catherine Picard, Kevin Wilkins, and Chethana Biliyar for participating in and putting up with a wide range of antics.

Meeting fellow scholars in the field was always an exciting and refreshing experience. My fieldwork, thinking, and sanity benefited from exchanges with Karen Büscher, Maarten Hendriks, Jackson Mughuma, Michel Thill, Peer Schouten, Maryam Rokhideh, Christoph Vogel, and Myfanwy James. I feel lucky to have found such a talented colleague and generous friend in Myf through this experience.

It was an honor and privilege to be part of such a talented team of researchers at Social Anthropology and Urban Studies at the University of Basel during my doctoral studies. The Making the City team of Till Förster, Manuel Herz, Barbara Heer, Silke Oldenburg, and Lotte Knakkergaard Nielsen provided thoughtful exchanges throughout my doctoral studies. This research and the Making the City project as a whole would not have been possible without generous funding from the Swiss National Science Foundation (Grant No. 165625). Sophie Oldfield agreeing to join my doctoral committee was an absolute blessing. Her generosity, support, and enthusiasm have been invaluable to this endeavor, and she has become a dear friend and mentor. Cornell University's College of Architecture, Art, and Planning hosted me in the spring of 2022 while I wrote this book's prospectus, and I am grateful to colleagues there and in Ithaca for their warm welcome. Colleagues at the University of Basel and the University of Cape Town have provided the enduring friendship and rigorous feedback over the years that it took to bring this book into being. Special thanks are owed to Marie-Laure Allain Bonilla, Leslie Braun, Anna Bloom Christen, Kenny Cupers, Alaa Dia, Emilio Distretti, Jennifer Felsenberg, Jacob Gueder, Nadja Imhof, Franziska Jenni, Rita Kesselring, Laura Nkula-Wenz, Jon Schubert, Giulia Scotto, Anna Selmeczi, Andrew Tucker, and Frederik Unseld, for their support from the beginning.

Many thanks to Bethany Mowry, Sophia Herbert, Hilary Kahn, Deborah Piston-Hatlen, Darja Malcolm-Clarke, Sami Heffner, and everybody at Indiana University Press who shepherded this project into a book. Two anonymous reviewers engaged thoughtfully and rigorously to make it a better book. Outstanding errors and shortcomings are mine to bear.

A close community of friends and chosen family in Sturgeon Bay, Wisconsin—the place I call home—supported me through the cumulative grief I experienced between submitting my dissertation and writing this book. None of this would have happened without their support. Through it all, my father, Benjamin Larsen, and my brother, Maxwell Larsen, have been and continue to be my moorings.

Acronyms

AFDL Alliance des Forces Démocratiques pour la Libération du Congo-Zaïre (Alliance of Democratic Forces for the Liberation of Congo)

BANMP Bangladeshi Military Police

BMP *boyevaya mashina pekhoty* (Russian "infantry fighting vehicle")

CDT conduct and discipline team

CHU composite helicopter unit

CIMIC civil-military coordination

CLA community liaison assistant

CNDP Congrès National pour la Défense du Peuple (National Congress for the Defense of the People)

CNR Commission Nationale pour les Réfugiés (National Refugee Commission)

COB company operating base

COE contingent-owned equipment

CSD canteen stores department

DDRRR disarmament, demobilization, repatriation, resettlement, and reintegration

DFS Department of Field Support (UN; dissolved in 2018; see DOS)

DOS Department of Operational Support (UN)

DPKO Department for Peacekeeping Operations (UN; dissolved in 2018)

DRC Democratic Republic of the Congo

FARDC Force Armée de la Republique Démocratique du Congo (Armed Forces of the DRC)

FC force commander

FDLR Forces Démocratique pour la Libération du Rwanda (Democratic Forces for the Liberation of Rwanda)

FIB force intervention brigade

FPU formed police unit

GUASFOR Guatemalan Special Forces

HRV human rights violation

IC individual contractor

ICV infantry carrier vehicle

IDP internally displaced person

INDBATT Indian Battalion

INDRDB Indian Rapidly Deployable Battalion

IPF international peacekeeping force

ITIG Institut Technique Industriel de Goma (Goma Industrial Technical Institute)

JCO junior commissioned officer

LA language assistant

M23 Mouvement de 23 mars (March 23 Movement)

MILOB military observer

MINUSMA Mission Multidimensionnelle Intégrée des Nations Unies pour la Stabilisation au Mali (United Nations Multidimensional Integrated Stabilization Mission in Mali)

MLC Mouvement de Libération du Congo (Movement for the Liberation of the Congo)

MONUC Mission de l'Organisation des Nations Unies en République Démocratique du Congo (United Nations Organization Mission in the Democratic Republic of Congo) (renamed MONUSCO in 2010)

MONUSCO Mission de l'Organisation des Nations Unies pour la Stabilisation en République Démocratique du Congo (United Nations Organization Stabilization Mission in the Democratic Republic of the Congo)

MOU memorandum of understanding

NCO noncommissioned officer

NGO nongovernmental organization

OAU Organization of African Unity

PNC Police Nationale Congolaise (Congolese National Police)

POC protection of civilians

QIP quick impact project

QRF quick reaction force

RCD–Goma Rassemblement Congolais pour la Démocratie–Goma
   (Rally for Congolese Democracy–Goma)

RVA Regie des Voies Aériennes (Airway Authority)

RPF Rwandan Patriotic Front

SAAF South African Air Force

SADC Southern African Development Community

SCD standing combat deployment

SEA sexual exploitation and abuse

SEN-FPU Senegalese Formed Police Unit (used to refer to the contingent)

SRSG special representative of the secretary-general

TMK Transport et Messagerie du Kivu (Kivu Transport and Messaging)

UN United Nations

UNDP United Nations Development Programme

UNFICYP United Nations Peacekeeping Force in Cyprus

UNGA United Nations General Assembly

UNHCR United Nations High Commissioner for Refugees

UNIGOM Université de Goma (University of Goma)

UNOPS United Nations Office for Project Services

UNOSOM United Nations Operation in Somalia (I and II)

UNMAS United Nations Mine Action Service

UNMISS United Nations Mission in South Sudan

UNSC United Nations Security Council

URUBATT Uruguayan Battalion

WHAM Winning hearts and minds

Worlding Home

Introduction

The City as Elsewhere

I realized then that I am constantly leaving, trying to discover new places, both imaginatively and physically, and yet always coming closer to home

—Colum McCann, *An Imagined Elsewhere: The City of Cities,* 1

David is not from Goma. For nearly ten years, David has worked as a language assistant with URUBATT, the Uruguayan battalion serving the force of the United Nations Organization Stabilization Mission in the Democratic Republic of Congo (MONUSCO). When he first arrived in Goma to find a job with the peacekeeping mission, he lived with other men from his hometown of Kindu in central Maniema province. He describes this early living situation as a *gîte*, a term I had only ever heard before in reference to vacation rentals in France. The etymology of *gîte* is linked to the French verb *gésir*—to lie or to be located—and it is this sense that the young men from Kindu seize on to describe their living situation: as soon as five people from Kindu colocate elsewhere, they tell me, a *gîte* is born. In July 2019, David invited me to visit the *gîte kindusien*. We hopped into his Toyota Noah minivan around midday to travel to one of the most popular neighborhoods in Goma—Birere. Crawling and bobbing along through winding dirt roads, we eventually reached a two-story building and adjacent courtyard bound by corrugated steel sheets. The property was nestled so close to the airport stopway that departing aircrafts carrying travelers and troops deafened the sounds of the bustling neighborhood below. Some of the men from Kindu that David lived with over ten years ago were still living at the *gîte* and greeted us in Kitetela when we arrived. We settled in downstairs and I asked the men to tell me a bit about how life and accommodation are organized in their *gîte*. An older gentleman paused his card game and related their living situation to that of UN personnel: *In the MONUSCO mission, military personnel from the same country stay together, and when someone leaves, another takes his place.*[1] It seems an obvious comparison to him—the men from Kindu are accommodated like UN soldiers in the city. But his description of the *gîte* begs the question: How exactly are the UN soldiers, like those David works with, living and lodging in Goma? Moreover, how might an understanding of peacekeepers' lives and living situations shed light on how people inhabit and make the city of Goma into a home, however temporary?

The *gîte* as a way of life for people who are not from Goma sets the frequency to which the rest of this book is tuned by introducing a critical problem space marked by questions of how the places city dwellers come from travel with them and become transposed, mediated, transformed, and generative of urban space. Emboldened by David's friend's comparison to UN soldiers, this book looks closely at the ways in which peacekeepers make their camps in Goma and how those processes of making relate to the urban world around them. I think about relation here on two levels. The first addresses the myriad empirical interstices, interactional spaces, and entanglements between peacekeeping camps and the city of Goma. Illustrating these relations offers a counternarrative of international interveners and their architecture as sealed off and completely separate from the urban environment and fabric in which they are situated (Duffield 2012; Autesserre 2014; Smirl 2015; Shoshan 2016; Büscher 2016; De Roulet 2022). The second considers the relational comparison made at the *gîte kindusien* and explores how ways of making camp might constitute a mode of making the city. I take this exchange at the *gîte* as an invitation to think about relation poetically (Glissant 1997). Approaching the urban from the peacekeeping camp—an elsewhere within here (Trinh 2011)—adopts a poetic commitment to nonhierarchical, comparative thought that does not sacrifice particularity but puts it to productive use (Glissant 1997; Jazeel 2019; Myers 2020). The men from Kindu agreed that there was explanatory value in relating their lived experience to that of the military contingents with whom they share the city. The aim of this book is to explore how. More precisely, it seeks to propose that in camping, people experience urbanity as a space of constant (re)arrangement between here and there, center and periphery, self and other, home and the world.

This book equally intervenes as a warm reply to a particularly pressing invitation in global urban studies. Jennifer Robinson's (2016, 2023) appeal to scholars to think cities through elsewhere is taken as an empirical and theoretical entry point in this book and provides the conceptual architecture for its contribution in three ways. First, developing an analytic heuristic from the peacekeeping camp represents a commitment to think about urban life from somewhere else—a type of camp that has been largely ignored by camp scholars working in the conflict-intervention nexus and a type of settlement that unsettles urban studies' rehearsed starting point of the city. I work toward a more global urban studies by putting the city into proverbial parentheses to begin my analysis elsewhere, in the peacekeeping camps of the UN mission in the Democratic Republic of Congo (DRC). Second, a foray into the lives and dwellings of foreign peacekeepers represents the productive crossing of a disciplinary threshold. The topical entry point of peacekeeping is an elsewhere for urban studies, typically reserved for peace, conflict, and security scholars but explored here in its sociality, spatiality, and materiality to generate novel empirics valuable to our concerns about modes of making and being together in human settlements. Lastly, I build on and expand Robinson's invitation by elaborating on the meaning and theoretical relevance of elsewhere. The analysis in this book leads me to offer up camping as a concept term to be added to our global vocabulary of urban practice in an effort to attune to the ways that people live cities as elsewheres. Reaching this role reversal of thinking cities as elsewheres in a world of "heres" and "theres" relies on stories that trace urbanity through human comings and goings and the ideas, ways of being, and ways of making that people carry with them. It relies on telling the story of the camp and the city together. It relies on telling the story of how people world the places they call home.

Writing Goma into the World

This book is as much about the places UN contingents come from and the camps they inhabit during their mission tenure as it is about Goma, a provincial capital city of over 1.2 million inhabitants located in the eastern DRC. Goma has largely garnered academic attention for its roles and positions within broader scholarly debates about war, state crises, weak governance, borderlands, and humanitarian emergencies. As such, understandings of urbanity in Goma are predominantly framed within the context of the city's relationship to violent conflict and explore the city's urbanization in the furtherance of understanding conflict urbanism (Verhoeve 2004; Pech, Büscher, and Lakes 2018; Büscher 2019; Hendriks and Büscher 2019; Verweijen 2019).[2] While peacekeeping camps equally find their genesis in the protracted conflict that continues to plague eastern DRC, the space and place of these camps and the military contingents that inhabit them have received little attention to date. The ensuing discussion and analysis of these places do not limit insights to a specific type of urbanity fueled or marked by conflict or multinational responses to it. Rather, understanding experiences of camping seeks to speak to different kinds of dwellings and dislocations that shape urban space more broadly.

In this sense, this book joins studies that look for more dilatable and relatable qualifiers to describe Goma's urban character. Goma has multiple personas as a city of opportunity, contestation, rebellion, refuge, and borderland (Büscher 2011). It is a youthful city experienced in love, chronic uncertainty, universities, driving motorcycle taxis, and waiting (Oldenburg 2015; 2016a; 2016b; 2018; 2019; 2020). Koen Vlassenroot and Karen Büscher (2009) offer several descriptions and paradigms of the city that could be said of other cities around the world, from an "autonomous space," "space of opportunity," and a zone of simultaneous "accumulation and contestation" to a city of "transborder mobility," "ambivalent refuge," and "rebellion." They carry forward the notion of the city as a "laboratory of change" and elaborate on urban experiments with identity primarily within the context and experience of the border or frontier zone. Yet while many of these descriptions imply the ongoing, processual nature of transformation in the city, we are left wondering about the human-driven centrifugal and centripetal forces shaping those transformations. How does the city as a specific "laboratory of change" connect to other experimental places beyond the city? Can the "ambivalent refuge" ever become a veritable home? The presence of approximately twenty UN military camps scattered across the city and in adjacent towns to the north and west between 2017 and 2019 both reinforces Goma's identity as a place of refuge, a home away from home protected by over four thousand armed peacekeepers, and adds new understandings of the city as a space in which people cast themselves out into the world.

Accounts of Goma as a paradigm of conflict urbanism have been joined by framings of the city as a case of humanitarian urbanism (Cooley and Ron 2002; Büscher and Vlassenroot 2013), reinforcing its image as an archetypical "Peaceland" or "Aidland": a series of enclaves inhabited by humanitarian workers living in a bubble that is disconnected from local worlds and realities (Mosse 2011; Autesserre 2014). At the heart of most accounts of such enclaves are descriptions of a multitude of contestations (political, military, social, economic, and spatial) often pitting the "local" against the "international" while the urban remains out of frame. The late Lisa Smirl (2015) alternatively highlights how humanitarians and development professionals from elsewhere experience the localities in which they work as "international" juxtaposed against their own home countries as a place of departure and return. However, these accounts of humanitarian spaces of practice rely on profiles of aid workers with identities rooted in Euro-American, predominantly white, "ex-pat" lifeworlds. The experiences of UN officers and soldiers from the Global South challenge predominant readings of this metaphorical Peaceland's reach, power dynamics, and negotiations of the local and international while also bringing back into focus the urban environment in which these play out.

Military personnel working within peacekeeping contingents trouble the geography of Peaceland both in the places they come from and the places they live in Goma. UN peacekeepers living in the city are not from just anywhere but reflect shifting geopolitical priorities since the end of the Cold War and a retreat of the West in UN peacekeeping missions that has led to an overwhelming reliance on soldiers from the Global South to fill the ranks (Cunliffe 2013). For the UN, contingent troops from these countries offer the advantages of cost-effectiveness, lessened political costs of interventions (due to troop-contributing countries being less powerful states), and legitimation of large deployments that might otherwise look too analogous to neocolonial occupation (121). While Cunliffe understands the geopolitics of peacekeeping through the southern geography of troop-contributing countries, spatial approaches that meet these particular peacekeepers in the mission spaces and fields to which they are deployed are lacking in the peacekeeping literature.

This book presents an urban ethnography of peacekeeping camps in Goma between 2017 and 2019—a period that, considering recent escalations of conflict and the resurgence of different armed groups, was relatively peaceful in the city and during which attitudes were more ambivalent about the presence of the UN mission. These peacekeeping camps accommodated contingents from Senegal, South Africa, Malawi, Tanzania, Guatemala, Uruguay, India, and Bangladesh and were situated within and across Goma, and in the peri-urban towns of Munigi and Mubambiro.[3] By breaking military contingents out of the Peaceland bubble (and its limited geographies of Western civilians living in more central and wealthier parts of town), this book expands the geographies and cultures of intervention that can be considered "international" and, in doing so, emphasizes "the embeddedness in multiple elsewheres of which the [African] continent actually speaks" (Mbembe and Nuttall 2004, 348). Studying the city through the UN peacekeeping camp thus broadens the scope of elsewheres with which we might write Goma into the world.

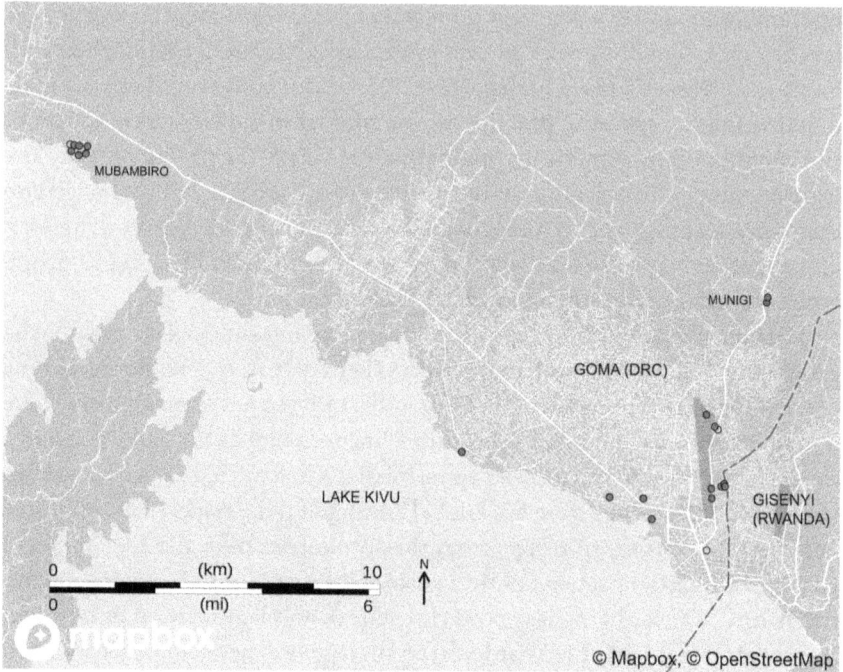

Map of peacekeeping camps as they appeared in Goma, Mubambiro, and Munigi between 2017 and 2019, including a detachment on Mount Goma and a transit camp. Bases dismantled during the same period are indicated in lighter colored dots. (©Mapbox; ©OpenStreetMap; data by author)

Peacekeeping Camps in a World of Camps

The peacekeeping camp as a spatial form open to scholarly reflection has only very recently been pioneered by Malkit Shoshan's (2016) exhibition *BLUE: Architecture of UN Peacekeeping Missions* at the 15th Venice Architecture Biennale. I share with Shoshan the desire to understand and argue UN peacekeeping missions as an urban phenomenon (6) but understand the nature and meanings of that phenomenon and its relevance differently. Shoshan's analysis of peacekeeping camp space focuses on the supercamp Gao—part of the United Nations Multidimensional Integrated Stabilization Mission in Mali (MINUSMA). She understands peacekeeping camps as "islands" and the supercamp as an "archipelago," arguing their separating and fragmenting effects

on the surrounding urban areas (13). Her "Design for Legacy" recommendations seek to promote more shared space between the UN bases and the local
community during and after the mission (40). Several findings presented in this
book challenge a vocabulary of islands and shed light on some of the fragmenting and connecting effects working on the camps themselves and on the surrounding city. Shoshan's work on peacekeeping camps since her exhibition has
focused on the environmental impacts of these bases and increasing their sustainability (Maertens and Shoshan 2018), a topic that also defines the limits of
how the UN itself currently seeks to understand and problematize the spaces of
its peacekeeping camps (UNEP and Totalförsvarets Forskningsinstitut 2012).

To explicitly study the peacekeeping camp as an architectural and sociocultural space has necessitated a review of the vast literature on peacekeeping as
a political project and a selective process of careful narrowing and closer reading. Unlike the agenda of much of this research, my study of UN peacekeeping
camps does not contend to contribute to an understanding of the challenges
and effectiveness of multinational peacekeeping; scholars of UN peacekeeping
missions in Africa already have much to say on what military personnel do, how
they do it, how effective they are, and what strategies can help improve their
effectiveness (Doyle and Sambanis 2000; Wills 2009; Bellamy, Williams, and
Griffin 2010; Adebajo 2011; Edström and Gyllensporre 2013; Mampilly 2014;
Tardy and Wyss 2015; Karim and Beardsley 2017). Rather, my inquiry emphasizes how they live and inhabit the city to which they deployed in an effort to
contribute to the interdiscipline of urban studies. Homing in on the literature
on peacekeeping in African contexts, I am nonetheless particularly inspired
by two relatively emergent themes therein and hope this study can be of use
to this scholarship.

The first is broadly conceived as studies concerned with the identities of
military peacekeepers. This set of literature regroups scholarship that foregrounds the geopolitics of reliance on troops from the Global South (Cunliffe
2013; Guyer 2013); the impact of diversity on effectiveness (Bove and Ruggeri 2016); considerations of peacekeepers' psychology and well-being (Britt
and Adler 2003; Loscalzo et al. 2018); and gendered identities in peacekeeping
(Whitworth 2004; Jennings 2008; Duncanson 2009; Kronsell 2012; Dharmapuri 2013; Karim and Beardsley 2017; Alchin, Gouws, and Heinecken 2018;
Jennings 2019), among other themes. While these considerations surely come
into play in the life of the camp and the city that hosts them, the present study
emphasizes peacekeepers' roles as social actors and urban dwellers who make
their camps and the city in both predictable and unexpected ways. This study

builds off more grounded investigations, for instance, of peacekeepers interactions and engagements with the peacekept population (Franke 2006; Pouligny 2006; Kahn 2010; Jennings 2015; Hellmüller 2018).

The second theme in the vast peacekeeping literature that resonates with this project includes studies that take seriously the space, place, and culture of UN missions. Ethnography has much to offer scholarly considerations of these aspects, though "relatively little sociologically or anthropologically informed qualitative fieldwork has been conducted in mission sites" (Higate and Henry 2009, 4).[4] The exceptions, however, tend to target institutional and bureaucratic cultures, retaining the international order and UN peacekeeping effectiveness as objects of analysis (Ghosh 1994; Rubinstein 2008; Ruffa 2018). Little remains known about the everyday lives of peacekeepers—an academic void that a focus on peacekeeping economies has helped fill (Henry 2015; Jennings 2015). Taking up the mundanities of life on mission, Paul Higate and Marsha Henry's influential book *Insecure Spaces* (2009) adopts a comparative approach to three peacekeeping operations to analyze perceptions and performances of security that shape the mission sites. Notably missing from this account, however, are the perceptions of peacekeepers themselves and explicit acknowledgment of the bases in which they live as coconstitutive of mission spaces. While peacekeeping camps are surely places where the culture and everyday lives of peacekeepers happen (and where several scholars have certainly ventured), they are rarely registered.[5] Cities are also places where peacekeeping happens. A more recent and emergent "urban" literature on peacekeeping emphasizes the materiality of peacebuilding (through infrastructure, for instance) (Bachmann and Schouten 2018; Danielak 2022) and the spatiality of peace and conflict (Smirl 2015; Björkdahl and Buckley-Zistel 2016; Büscher 2016; Danielsson 2020).

While navigating and engaging with this literature have enriched this monograph, I want to reiterate that the objective of my study of peacekeeping camps is not to say something about peacekeeping itself. Rather, my objective in centering these sociospatial formations as they appear in Goma is geared toward contributing to the study of encampment and urbanity. As such, my analysis of peacekeepers camping in Goma situates itself within rich literatures in not only urban studies but also the emerging subdiscipline of camp studies, located at the disciplinary intersections of anthropology, geography, and architecture. Just as this book contributes to writing Goma into a world of cities in the pursuit of a more global urban studies (Robinson 2005, 2006, 2016), it also seeks to write peacekeeping camps into a world of camps.[6]

Peacekeeping bases as camp spaces do not fit neatly into the theoretical typologies emerging in camp studies that have been built to possibly include them. For instance, Charlie Hailey's authoritative 2009 book, *Camps: A Guide to 21st-Century Space*, discusses camps under three conceptual headings—autonomy, control, and necessity—that reflect factors shaping the formation and function of camps, such as choice, power, and safety or assistance, respectively. Several of Hailey's 104 variations on the theme of the camp speak to many of the observed spatial grammars and social worlds of the peacekeeping camp but fail to grapple with their complexity and the very specific position they carve out between descriptions of other camps that he explores, such as "Planned Camp," "Urban Camp," and "Overseas Military Facility." Despite his warning that these categories are not exclusive and that they provide a starting point to "rethink these contemporary built environments," the nature of the peacekeeping camp renders these categories less useful (15). Thinking of camps through other themes and lenses creates a space for peacekeeping camps to enter the conversation on camps and for an analytic of camping to engage more directly with the city. Nonetheless, themes addressed in the studies of other types of camps, notably the refugee camp, are engaged here to investigate peacekeeping camp space.

The power of the camp as an analytical device with which to rethink our built environment has been particularly pronounced in studies that center the refugee camp. Anthropologist Michel Agier (2002) has been one of the most powerful figures of this literature and sums up the global purchase of rethinking the modern built environment with refugee camps thus: "The camps are both the emblem of the social condition created by the coupling of war with humanitarian action, the site where it is constructed in the most elaborate manner, as a life kept at a distance from the ordinary social and political world, and the experimentation of the large-scale segregations that are being established on a planetary scale" (320). Agier's particular interest in the refugee camp is its role in a wider apparatus of humanitarian governance and power. While I am not investigating peacekeeping camps for what they can reveal about the political project of multinational peacekeeping, Agier's notions about the subjectification of refugees that counteracts their framing as the "voiceless humanitarian victim" (Agier 2008, 64) opens up a space in which to consider the agency of those who live in camp settings. Agier's point particularly calls into question the dominant reading of camps as spaces lived in "bare life" (Agamben 1998).

Though Giorgio Agamben (1998, 123) was speaking about concentration camps, his conceptualization of the camp as a "pure, absolute, and impassable biopolitical space" arising from the imposition of the "state of exception" has achieved wide purchase and wide critique in scholars' descriptions and understandings of the refugee camp. Scholars have particularly taken issue with the singular sovereignty assumed by Agamben's exceptionalism, urging us to look instead at competing, multiple, and hybrid sovereignties in refugee camp space (S. Turner 2009; Ramadan 2013). Catherine-Lune Grayson's *Children of the Camp* (2017) joins this growing compendium, arguing that refugee camps "cannot be reduced to places where all exits are hermetically sealed and where the disciplinary mechanism is so precise that refugees are crushed, reduced to their biological functions" (6). Furthermore, while bare life is lived in confinement, Grayson lays important foundations for discussing camps as home spaces (of sorts) that are highly connected to the world. This line of argument is taken up most acutely in chapters 3 and 4.

Diana Martin finds a different limitation of Agamben's theory, arguing that the space of exception exceeds the Shatila refugee camp in Lebanon and has become entangled with the camp's surrounding informal settlements. This leads her to define the new spatial model of the "campscape." At the same time, she argues that the lens of laws and rights limits our understandings of the way biopolitics are shaped and produced in the camp (Martin 2015). The situation of Palestinian camps throughout the Middle East, particularly in their duration and urbanization, have been a fruitful analytical space through which to challenge Agamben and other readings of camp spaces that fail to acknowledge the agency of its inhabitants (Hassan 2010; Abourahme and Hilal 2012; Ramadan 2013; Sanyal 2014; Feldman 2015). This book joins this literature in seeking to illustrate alternative possibilities and processes at work in the making of the camp beyond the biopower of the sovereign.

Scholarly literature on refugee camps also emphasizes a concern for the temporal tensions of camp spaces. Transitions between temporality and permanence and entangled logics of both are often a defining feature of camps and become central to their inhabitants' experiences of space (Agier 2008; Hailey 2009; Ramadan 2013; Herz and ETH Studio Basel 2013; Feldman 2015; Hilal and Petti 2018). The camp foregrounds time as tension. The increased permanence of refugee camps, for instance, has been analyzed as an endless, extended, and immediate present established by the emergency regime in a way that excludes the future and the past (Agier 2011, 78). The temporality of the tent in the Sahrawi camps of the Western Sahara alternatively challenges this endless present, as it signifies a politics and future of return (Herz 2013, 376). Tracing the evolution of peacekeeping camps in Goma, considering how peacekeepers make the camp into a home in the world between their temporal deployment and an enduring mission, and an attention to camping as a process allows for an analysis of time and space together, as is insisted on by geographer Doreen Massey (2005, 18).

The identification of two particular conversations being held within this rich literature on camps is particularly useful to make space for peacekeeping camps to engage with the literature of camp studies and take it in new directions. These two related trends have emerged in interdisciplinary scholarship on humanitarianism, development studies, and refugee studies, bringing the city and the camp, as conceptual entities, into closer dialogue. The first trend corresponds with an increasing consideration of spatiality in social science research and the more specific "modest 'urban turn' in refugee studies" (Jansen 2016). This literature tends to examine the ways in which camps exhibit urbanity or relate to wider processes of urbanization. The second trend is an attempt to reconcile "developmental and humanitarian modes of power" (De Waal 2002; Minca 2015) and the agency and practices of those on the receiving end of this humanitarian power, notably refugees (Malkki 1995; Agier 2002; S. Turner 2009; Herz and ETH Studio Basel 2013; Ramadan 2013). Literature reviewed in this strand homes in on the latter concern, as scholars delve into ways of living in refugee camps that resonate with aspects of urban life.

The sociospatial form of the refugee camp is quick to be equated with notions of the urban in scholarship and public media alike. Michel Agier's term *city-camps* has been influential in drawing a parallel between the two sociospatial forms. The "unlikely city" or "accidental city" of Kakuma refugee camp (Oka 2011; Jansen 2019), the "city of thorns" that is the Dabaab refugee camp (Rawlence 2017), and the "Camp Cities" of Palestinian refugees (Hassan 2010) follow this trend. According to Agier (2002), the refugee camp is a global space emerging from the coupling of war and humanitarianism with the characteristics of agglomeration, durability, heterogeneity, service provision, and opportunities for encounter and exchange that we have come to associate with cities. "Everyone who has observed the refugee camps," he writes, "can see there a kind of town, not just in terms of size, but by the forms of life that seem to seek new expression" (Agier 2008, 57). The relationship between the city and the camp is one that is not just debated in academic circles but also capitalized on by journalists. Popular media is keen to intervene and report on camps' relationship to the urban in newsworthy moments in which long-term refugee camps are said to transform into "real cities."[7]

Just as refugee camps emerge from the coupling of war and a humanitarian response to it, so too are peacekeeping camps produced in the space between war and military intervention and express new ways of living within and beyond that nexus. Both exhibit urbanity but remain camps nonetheless. Bram Jansen's notion of the "accidental city" is influential as it foregrounds the agency of camp dwelling refugees to participate in the place-making of the camp as part and parcel of a "humanitarian urbanism." However, Jansen is cautious in his weaving of camp and city. He writes, "The urban reference, then, is mostly used as a metaphor to capture the socio-economic processes that occur within the camp setting, such as emerging camp economies, or processes of social change, set against the material and service structures that organize and regulate life and space, such as food aid, healthcare and education" (2019, 9). He admits that the urban as a metaphor falls apart when one considers the political and governmental dynamics of refugee camp space while pointing out that the urban reference is not meant to put the camp and any surrounding or adjacent city into any sort of theoretical correspondence. In this study, the urban reference operates as both a metaphor and an acknowledgment of the correspondences and ruptures between peacekeeping camps and the city of Goma.

Even within this urban turn in contemporary camp literature, scholars remain overwhelmingly concerned with relationships of structure and agency in the context of refugee camp space, often examining either the institutional objects of humanitarianism or its refugee subjects. In addition to exploring the formation of urbanity, much of the latter work has focused on human agency and identity formation in camps and camplike settings. The role of urbanity and its ability to forge, transform, or harden identities among the displaced is one that has been central to the early years of African urban anthropology and continues to be well documented in several African contexts (Moore 1993; Malkki 1995). In her work, Liisa Malkki has compared the environment of the city and the camp in the identity formation and transformation processes of Burundian refugees. Her main argument asserts that camps harden identities that were important in refugees' place of origin but that urban contexts offer opportunities to refugees and displaced persons to transform their identity. Peacekeeping camps located within the city of Goma afford both of these processes of identity formation to occur in ways similar to what Smirl (2015) calls liminal subjectivity. While Malkki's work foregrounds refugee agency, it persists in adopting a comparative direction of the city toward the camp, meaning that notions of the city are utilized to understand or problematize spatial and social forms of life in camp contexts. Camps are foregrounded as the object of analysis and are constantly mimicking cities (Sanyal 2014). Agamben and those who mobilize his concept of exception are some of the few to counter this trend (Martin 2015; Lancione and Simone 2020). Based on his understanding of the political life of man in the modern era, Agamben (1998, 174) argues, "If the essence of the camp consists in the materialization of the state of exception and in the subsequent creation of a space in which bare life and the juridical rule enter into a threshold of indistinction, then we must admit that we find ourselves virtually in the presence of a camp every time such a structure is created." This book simultaneously joins scholars like Agier in their concern for the urbanity of the camp as well as Agamben's ambition to theorize the essence of the camp and its transcendence from that particular place. In my approach to the particularities of peacekeeping camps embedded in the city, I seek to make space for the study of camps and camping in urban studies beyond a unidirectional comparison of camps to urban spaces. Foregrounding instead the camp and the city as the bifocal objects of analysis, I explore the relationship between the two in a double analytical direction, not only thinking the camp through the city but also thinking the city through the camp. This approach is mirrored by my spatial practice of staying in and moving through peacekeeping camps and my positions navigating the lifeworlds of these spaces and those of the city at large, elaborated on later in this introduction.

Although the academic literature on refugee camps has provided rich insights into the transformative, ambiguous quality of camp space, peacekeeping camps are not refugee camps but a type of military camp. This is an obvious yet important distinction. My contribution to the literature on the camp as a sociospatial form of human (un)settlement by no means seeks to be totalizing or to speak to human experiences of forced displacement and exile and their attendant, affective dimensions. However, refugee camps and peacekeeping camps share important theoretical terrain and a shared emergence within the nexus of violent conflict and interventionism. At the same time, approaches to military urbanism that consider the city as "battlespace" (Graham 2009) or "barracks" (Hoffman 2007) stand in contrast to the geographic realities of the conflict in the eastern DRC at the time of this study and an understanding of Goma as a "safe haven" (Büscher 2020) or (contentious) "refuge" (Vlassenroot and Büscher 2009; Trefon and Kabuyaya 2018). Camp space features prominently in military urbanism as military aesthetic and practice is collapsed with the notion of urban warfare. In this case, however, war and peace operations were occurring largely in the region's hinterland with the peacekeeping camps of Goma acting as an indirect grafting of rural conflict onto the cityscape. This has not prevented Goma from being exposed to war or for the planning considerations of the peacekeeping mission and city itself to be organized around logics of defense in ways that echo military operations as urban planning (Misselwitz and Weizman 2003). While peacekeeping camps are certainly military in nature, they differ substantially from the ways that military urbanism has been conceived through the technosocial lens of warfare. Rather than looking at the ways that military urbanism extends military ideas into the everyday life of cities from above, or from the position of the sovereign (Graham 2011), this book is more concerned with practices that constitute militarization through peacefare and how they become socially coproduced from various directions.

Here, There, and Goma

As Charlie Hailey (2008) writes in his first book on camps, while "camping, we reconsider time as duration and we reread place through our own itinerancy . . . we negotiate these paradoxes of time and place to understand home amidst contemporary itinerancies" (1). Those itinerancies, that errantry, or that journeying joins dwelling in a dialectic that produces a camping practice and necessarily alters the experience of dwelling through duration. In place-based terms, journeying is a practice of movement between a here and a there. It is this movement that allows the notion of an elsewhere to emerge. Robinson's (2016, 5) understanding of elsewhere, on the other hand, refers to "another case, a wider context, existing theoretical imaginations derived from other contexts, connections to other places." When combining these notions of itinerancy and elsewhere by looking closely at the derivations or connections of peacekeeping camps to other places made through journeying, it may be worth asking: What if elsewhere *as* theoretical imagination is enough?

Literary theorists have been particularly prolific in their efforts to understand the meaning and theoretical relevance of elsewhere. Their work on the effects of displacement emphasizes two important aspects of elsewhere that are important for developing my understanding of camping. The first is elsewhere's relationship to home in our sense of place. The second builds on the first to address how elsewhere affects our sense of self. While it may be semantically tempting to juxtapose home and elsewhere as discrete entities, scholars have seen such a provocation as fertile ground on which to conceptualize elsewhere as correlative (Newton 2005), within (Trinh 2011), and constitutive of home (Tuan 2012). Writing between literary criticism and philosophy, Adam Zachary Newton (2005, xii) writes, "Very possibly 'home and elsewhere' stand for properties of person maybe even more than they do of place, and that those whom we approach or who recede from us define the real coordinates of belonging at either a near distance or far." Tabish Khair (2009, 71) equally acknowledges the connection elsewhere forges between place and personhood: "for the relationship of 'elsewhere' to 'home' is also the relationship of the 'Other' to the

'Self.'" Imagining the city as elsewhere brings the personal and place-based understandings of home and the world into a tighter correspondence.

Like camping, elsewhere is in the conceptual business of breaking out of binary categories of understanding physical places and social spaces here or there. Reading elsewhere through analyses of written tales and spoken stories, Trinh T. Minh-ha's (2011, 27) articulation of elsewhere expresses its more triadic nature. "The traveling self is here both the self that moves physically from one place to another, following 'public routes and beaten tracks' within a mapped movement; and, the self that embarks on an undetermined journeying practice, having constantly to negotiate between home and abroad, native culture and adopted culture, or more creatively speaking, between a here, a there, *and* an elsewhere." This negotiated space is necessarily subjective, questioning and endlessly reconciling boundaries in the correspondence of here and there, this and that. As a subjective notion, elsewhere allows for multiple and infinite possibilities within and between dualistic spatial categories of proximity and distance as well as social constructs of belonging and difference. Prita Meier's (2016, 3) "architectures of elsewhere" on the Swahili coast succinctly captures the power of the built environment to express societal tensions between "the need for mobility and mixing on one hand and fixity and rootedness on the other hand." Similarly, as this book illustrates, dwelling and journeying constantly creates and re-creates the peacekeeping camps in and around Goma and, therefore, the *gîte* where David used to live and, possibly, the city itself. To think of a city like Goma as an elsewhere is to thus attune to the urban as a becoming, unfinished space in which negotiations of place and personhood are constantly (re)making it.

In this sense, the conceptual strength of elsewhere to contribute to an urban theory of camping lies in its ability to operate in a sociospatial sense that troubles the assumed divisions that separate physical places and social categories. Camping, then, might be understood as the process and outcome of reconciling disparate objects—generating elsewheres within here (Trinh 2011), spurring understandings of home as a place that can travel and as people (Jackson 1995), and giving us the ability to see others within ourselves. Exploring storytelling not from literary criticism but from the disciplinary lens of anthropology, Michael Jackson (2002, 22) argues that the very notions of selfhood and subjectivity (both vital to expressions of elsewhere) "are themselves creations of a *social* relation between self and other, and do not exist 'outside of, or prior to' the narrative process." Equally expressing the coconstitution of the self and other in selfhood, Newton (2005, xii) adds, "For is it not others who unseat us from what we thought was home, sending us elsewhere, and who also, we hope, redeem us from our homelessness, securing our only true and genuine place?" The sociospatial processes of dislodging, reconciling, and redeeming that are illustrated throughout shape my understanding of the urbanity created between the camp and the city as an elsewhere.

Thinking about camping as an urban practice instead of the camp as an urban formation, I focus my scholarly attention on the people who make these spaces by dwelling within them, although never at the expense of ignoring those who merely pass through them or exploring the circumstances that propel the form to emerge. The ways that different people move in, out, and through the camp are critical to understanding how they are made into social, cultural, and architectural spaces. Yet when we study people on the move, we must ask ourselves, as Mary Des Chene (1997, 71) does, "What makes the place where one happens to catch up with them in itself revelatory of that mobility and its meanings?" Des Chene found the site she had chosen to study Gurkha soldiery and life courses (a large village with high rates of recruitment) as an insufficient field from which to glean answers to her initial question, since "the object of study radiated in so many directions beyond it" (73). It is precisely this radiation in different directions *as* the object of study that peacekeeping camps in Goma empirically and theoretically capture. To answer Des Chene's initial question then, "catching up" with deployed peacekeepers in the city of Goma and their respective camps within that city revealed new understandings of how mobility reconfigures the conceptual relationship between the camp and the city in ways that allow camping to be understood for its city-making, homemaking, and world-making potential.

Catching up with peacekeepers was, in and of itself, a way of moving through fieldwork. As Barbara Heer (2019, 278) points out in her comparative ethnography of Johannesburg and Maputo, the intellectual endeavor of thinking cities through elsewhere is also a practical endeavor for the ethnographer of "experiencing cities through elsewhere." Beyond the suggestion that the mind and body of the ethnographer are engaged in constant comparison, we are left wondering how to hold two or more places together in this process. How do we hold on to elsewheres while conducting fieldwork in a single site at any given moment? I think of this mental, social, and spatial plane of the ethnographer thinking and doing through elsewhere as "tenacious research," and mobilize it as methodological resource to inform my attendant vocabulary and theory building of what it means to be camping.

Tenacious Research

Carrying out tenacious research is not about being determined and persever-
ing, though these attributes can certainly be helpful to the research endeavor.
Rather, the sense of tenacity I am interested in exploring here draws on geographical philosopher Edward Casey's (2001, 688) understanding of tenacity
as one of the ways in which place comes into the body or, for my purposes,
becomes an indelible part of the ethnographic self: "Places come into us lastingly; once having been in a particular place for any considerable time—or
even briefly, if our experience there has been intense—we are forever marked
by that place, which lingers in us indefinitely and in a thousand ways, many
too subtle for us to name."[8] He refers to this lingering and enduring nature of
place as the impressionism of place—how we feel a place's presence. As such,
tenacious research more closely engages a topographical approach that attunes
to the reciprocal relationship between the researcher's perception of place and
how that alters the place she studies (Hastrup 2010); it pays attention to the
spatial constitution of intersubjectivity. A more geographic way of understanding researcher positionality and reflexivity, then, is a matter of acknowledging
how "being there"—to use a popular way anthropologists understand the value
of fieldwork (see Geertz 1988; Hannerz 2003)—is always affected by having
been elsewhere.

Casey's notion of tenacity draws on Pierre Bourdieu's concept of habitus,
which he considers as a mediator between place and self, to describe the enacting of habitus in the "place-world" as "habitation." Casey (2001, 687) insists
that the meaning of the term is not limited to "settled dwelling" but should
be taken at its Latin root, *habère*, meaning to have or to hold: "This is how the
durability of habitus is expressed: by my tenacious holding onto a place so as
to prolong what I experience beyond the present moment. In this way, place
and self actively collude." Understanding that to inhabit is to hold opens up a
much-needed conversation about spatial practices of movement during fieldwork. Despite the relatively short distances—and, at times, collapse of distance—between the camps and the city understudy, I understand this research
project very much through the lens of multisited ethnography. To embrace
the multisitedness of this study is to already acknowledge and foreshadow the
variability in the socially constructed meanings of the different places that are
featured here. Many of the sites discussed are not places that I inhabited in the
sense of dwelling in a settled manner. I was able to make several multiday and

overnight visits to peacekeeping camps but ultimately understand myself as having temporarily inhabited the city. To insist that this research is multisited, however, is to foreground my movements and journeys before, during, and after fieldwork in a methodologically productive way.

Attention to the spatiality, mobility, and geographical emplacement of the self in multisited fieldwork is still lacking by the scholars who have championed this anthropological way of working (Marcus 1995; Hannerz 2003). The most extensively reflected on spatial practice of fieldwork remains "intensive dwell- ing" (Clifford 1997, 190). While George E. Marcus (1995) gives ethnographers several strategies by which to track their multisited object ("follow the people," "follow the thing") we are left unsure of what following entails and how to be reflexive about it. Travel, however, is deeply important to the anthropological project and construction of our located fields (Gupta and Ferguson 1997; Cole- man and Collins 2006). "Fieldwork thus 'takes place' in worldly, contingent relations of travel, not in controlled sites of research" (Clifford 1997, 198). It is our *tenacity* that is required when traveling to hold disparate places together in empirically, methodologically, and theoretically generative ways. My tenacious holding of different places became particularly relevant to how I accessed and understood different sites and encounters.

I moved to Goma ten years after having moved to Senegal, where I spent a year of my undergraduate studies at the Université Gaston Berger in Saint Louis. Senegal came into me lastingly at an impressionable time in my life, lingering in me through language, gestures, and familiarity with different cus- toms, cuisines, and traditions. It was this experience (and its recognition by others) through which I understand my initial invitation to spend time in the Senegalese peacekeeping camp. Over repeated visits, I got to know officers in this camp who attended Gaston Berger at the same time or trained at nearby facilities in Saint Louis. These connections led to relationships that allowed me into the camp for holiday celebrations, a few rounds of *ataaya*, a workout at the gym, or a round of billiards.

Other camps were accessed through a sort of snowballing technique (Flick 2009). The impetus for this process began at my apartment in Goma with the man from whom I rented a room during one research stay—a former Uru- guayan soldier then working for the mission in a civilian capacity. He put me in touch with an officer at the URUBATT camp. A few weeks later, I sat down with the commander for an initial interview. He invited me back the following weekend to have lunch with the officers—a tradition that continued and grew as I met more of the men and women in the camp. It was through an event at

URUBATT that I met officers from the Guatemalan Special Forces (GUAS-FOR) and the Indian-run Central Sector Brigade. It was through officers at the brigade that I met peacekeepers from the Indian Rapidly Deployable Battalions (INDRDBs), Bangladeshi Military Police (BANMP) camps, the South African Aviation camp, and the force headquarters. Gaining access, in these ways, relied on having lived in Senegal as well as having rented a room in the apartment of a former Uruguayan soldier in Goma.

My ability to enter peacekeeping camps was ultimately dependent on the willingness and openness of the individual military commanders responsible for each camp, whom I would approach through the social contacts I first made at the kinds of gatherings mentioned. This often involved the production of different concept notes explaining my research focus on the everyday life of the camp and initial interviews with the commander before I could enter the more participant-observation phases of the research. I made the choice early on in this research to purposefully abstain from conducting research on the operations conducted by each contingent. I stand by this choice, as it proved to be a very helpful trust-building measure and way of ensuring an amicable relationship with my interlocutors and repeated invitations to events in the camp. I equally chose to refrain from reaching out to contingents who were members of the Force Intervention Brigade (South Africa, Malawi, and Tanzania), as they were the most involved in operations. The sole exception was the South African Aviation unit, where I had many social contacts and made camp visits in my capacity as a friend of the neighboring contingent rather than any formal interviews or camp tours. It follows, of course, that the making of the peacekeeping camp can only limitedly be analyzed in relation to the operations soldiers conduct beyond it.

As my presence and research focus became more familiar and clear to different commanding officers, however, I was invited to join various operational patrols (in Goma, Masisi Territory, and Rutshuru Territory) as well as a standing combat deployment (SCD). In the rapidly changing security situation that marks the conflict space of eastern Congo, however, my interlocutors and I decided against me joining the SCD. In an effort to strengthen an understanding of what might distinguish the camps in Goma from camps in more rural surroundings, I also visited three different camps outside of the city. An Indian Battalion (INDBATT) camp in the rural town of Kiwanja (Rutshuru Territory, North Kivu) was the subject of an overnight visit. I also toured and spent the day at two camps in Kavumu (Kalehe Territory, South Kivu)—those of the Uruguayan Aviation Unit and the Uruguayan Airfield Support Unit.

As my research progressed in the direction of these camps, I sought to uphold transparency by meeting with and discussing my research with MONUSCO's head of office in Goma, who subsequently provided written confirmation that I was free to talk to any and all mission staff who were willing to participate in the study. This study has been conducted free from interference from the MONUSCO mission or UN organization; rather, I conducted it through cooperative working relationships. The findings and analysis shared herein in no way represent or seek to represent the views of these institutions.

My growing involvement in the social lives of contingent officers led to a rhythm of engagement whereby, by my second trip to Goma, I was spending time with peacekeepers in or out of camp daily based on shared will and camaraderie. In line with the theme of this work, I tend to understand the ability to gain quick social proximity to our shared sense of dislocation, among other factors described in the following passages. The anthropologist and the military professional are both deployed in a sense. We voluntarily join institutions where our deployment becomes both a command and a responsibility. Despite several axes of difference between myself and the peacekeepers in Goma, African, Asian, and Latin American soldiers and I shared an identity of being from elsewhere and participating in other jobs relative to the Congolese and international community of interveners, which made much of this research possible and made my social relations with peacekeepers thicker. At the same time, however, my identity as a white, civilian, American woman shaped my positionality in ways that detached me from the men and women I was working with and allowed me to additionally become part (to varying degrees) of Congolese social scenes and foreign interveners' circles with an ease that was not shared by military personnel.

At various presentations of this research in the Global North, I have detected gendered and racialized assumptions that a white woman such as myself would face greater challenges in the militarized environments of army barracks and postconflict areas populated by soldiers from the Global South. My own experience of research, however, strongly resonates with Maria Eriksson Baaz's (2019) work with the Congolese army (FARDC) and realization that much of the fear and precaution about perceived (sexualized) risks for women researchers around military men has been misguided. If my female identity has come to the fore in any of my interactions with peacekeepers, it largely resulted in a greater sense of protection, courtesy, and performative chivalry on the part of my interlocutors. Many of my interlocutors agreed that being a woman likely gave me an advantage over male researchers, whose participation and observation of foreign militaries would be perceived as a greater threat. It also made access more difficult in some instances. In all-male contingent camps, there were very few places deemed appropriate for a woman to be other than the officers' mess, ultimately limiting my ability to interact freely with male troops below the level of officers. As such, this ethnography foregrounds the lifeworlds and discourses of a diverse officer class (mostly ranging from captains to colonels) living in contingent camps. Their insights are nevertheless supplemented throughout by observations of and more structured encounters with noncommissioned officers and rank soldiers. Officers had variable responsibilities for the governance of the camp but were mostly subjected to the orders and governing structures laid out by their own commanders. This required, for instance, officers to seek different permissions to exit the camp or to invite me to enter, something that rank-and-file soldiers were not at liberty to request. Moreover, officers and myself were the closest in age and had similar educational backgrounds, having attended university. These comparable backgrounds had given us similar life experiences and shared social habits over which we could discuss things openly and in a relaxed manner. As a white woman who had come to Goma alone, however, I was someone whom officers felt they needed to both look after and, for some, look out for.

"There is an indirect mistrust of the US when it comes to the military," Major Baba once told me as my anxieties about how I was being perceived mounted.[9] My identity as a foreign national to the armies present in and around Goma, and particularly a foreign national from the United States, did not go unnoticed by certain interlocutors in a way that created some initial distrust. The US government has a sordid history and reputation of snooping on its friends and allies. In one instance of combatting this perception, the Indian officers with whom I became closest and who negotiated my continued presence in their camps with their superiors evoked my position as a doctoral student in a Swiss university and place meanings attached to Switzerland (particularly in terms of its military neutrality) to assuage fears of foreign espionage. Working in Switzerland prior to coming to the DRC altered my positionality and access to the people and places I wanted to study—illustrating once again how having been elsewhere shapes the fieldwork experience of "being there." That my being there in the peacekeeping camp was thus permissible is rooted in the tenacity of place and the way we carry the places we have been, as well as how others perceive and position us within those places. As Kirstin Hastrup (2010, 203) has put it, "Intersubjectivity is not simply a matter of relationships between persons but involves relations between people and places and ideas about places."

To collect data on people, places, and ideas about places in Goma, I overwhelmingly relied on anthropological methods of participant-observation, complemented by semistructured interviews and focus group discussions, all of which formed a large compendium of field notes from which my empirics and analysis are drawn.[10] Paul Rabinow (2011) discusses the productive tension of participation and observation as a dialectical spiral that defines the space of anthropology. This spiral imitates social life more broadly, which, according to Norbert Elias (1956), is a continuum between involvement and detachment. Such a dialectical dance pushes the anthropologist to adopt a narrative voice that is constantly shifting between "we" and "they" in describing her research subject(s).[11] This method runs throughout the book as an incongruent writing style that selectively places me inside or outside what is happening, attempting to say something about the social lives of peacekeepers and the residents of Goma as well as the social life of the ethnographer along the way. Tenacious research, then, is about recognizing our emplaced selves in our research settings in ways that enhance our empirical findings and theoretical positions, adding a spatial dimension to the ways in which we think about intersubjectivity. Recognizing the ways in which we carry places with us, no matter where or in what city we may choose to conduct research, can greatly enhance the scope of what we are able to find out about both the cities we study and the places that shape who we are as people and who we become as urban scholars.

Plan of the Book

Worlding Home explores peacekeeping camps for their camp-making, city-making, home-making, and world-making potential and practice. This book constitutes the first time that the specific iteration of the peacekeeping camp has been described and analyzed in a way that attunes to the disciplinary concerns of urban studies and anthropology. Uncovering the social lives of officers and soldiers, I describe the impetuses, evolutions, rules, routines, freedoms, amenities, performances, architectures, social lives, and cultural spaces shaping everyday life in these camps. I theorize the peacekeeping camp as emerging between the camp and the city, between the extraordinary and the ordinary, between home and the world. I theorize camping as an embodied practice of worlding home. The organization of the empirical chapters of the book (2–5) echo these tensions and progress through the rubric of city, camp, home, and world.

First, however, chapter 1 introduces the reader to Goma by telling the story of the city through a rich history of the camps that have shaped its urban development. From precolonial settlement patterns for defense; to Belgian, German,

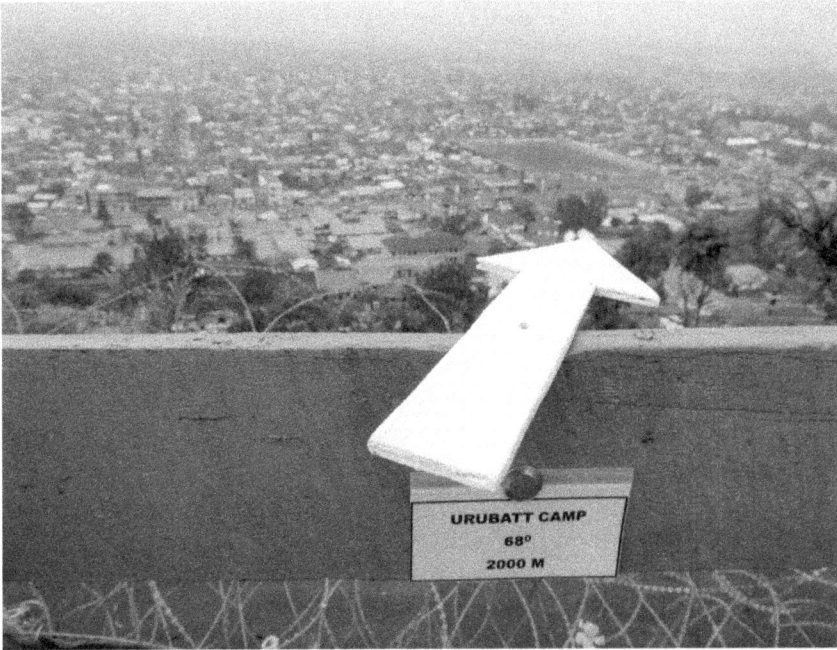

Northeastern view from UN post atop Mount Goma. (Photo by author)

and British military camps; through to camps for Rwandan refugees, Goma has a long history of playing host to diverse types of camps and camplike settlements. This chapter empirically connects contemporary urban areas and camps to this broader history of various camp typologies as they have emerged in Goma over the past century. In doing so, the chapter demonstrates that making camp has long been part and parcel of making the city. Discussing the refugee camps that emerged in Goma in the late 1990s, in particular, allows me to discuss the history of conflict within which the current MONUSCO mission finds its genesis. The contemporary camps of the mission are discussed in terms of their diversity of form, location, and taskings and in relation to other UN civilian architectures.

Chapter 2 brings peacekeeping camps into focus by discussing the ways that peacekeepers and Congolese civilians move in, out, through, and around their camps and the city. Vignettes home in on the base features and peacekeeper practices that act as edges, interstices, and interactional spaces between inside and outside. I follow peacekeepers out into the city and Congolese people into the camp to discover how such processes shape and co-construct a particular brand of urbanity between these two places.

A day in the life of a blue helmet is a mundane yet structured experience charged with specific biopolitical considerations. Chapter 3 steps into the interior spaces of the peacekeeping camp to explore how its routines, amenities, and daily activities express entangled logics of care for and control of the individual soldier within the confines of the camp perimeter. I discuss measures of control particularly as they are constructed around the object of the sexualized, male, soldiering body and analyze the role that women play in shaping the camp as an (extra)ordinary space. I discuss internal in-group and out-group dynamics in the camp and the ways that certain camp features reinforce and reflect military unit hierarchies, regimental identities, and rank relations, while others dissolve them to appeal to a sense of unity and family living.

Chapter 4 carries this idea of the camp as a domestic space further to discuss the ways peacekeepers make themselves at home in the camp. I explore how the camp blends aesthetics, flavors, and temporalities from their countries of origin and from Goma to enhance their sense of comfort and security. Chapter 5 details how peacekeepers inscribe these home spaces into multiple notions of "the world" through performances of national and multinational identities. Peacekeepers take hosting responsibilities very seriously, activating their camps as spaces of spectacle, distinction, and connection. Peacekeeping camps play a significant role in shaping how peacekeepers develop a sense of their own cosmopolitanism, of their belonging to the world. The concluding chapter takes the novel empirics as they have emerged in the camp-city nexus and puts them to productive use in revising camp and urban theory as they currently exist. From these empirics emerges an important revision to the notion of worlding for urban theory as well as a vocabulary of camping that urges urban scholars to attune to the elsewheres that co-constitute urban places and urban ways of life.

1

Urbanization and Encampment

A Century in the City

The city and the camp. The city against the camp. The city as the camp. These tend to be the relationalities—conjunctional, oppositional, analogical—with which we try to make sense of the stubborn shadow the camp casts on modern urban life. For all the differences between these formulations, symptomatically they all point to the same thing: city and camp in contemporary urban and political thought seem hopelessly entangled.

—Nasser Abourahme, "The Camp," 35

The settlement typology of the camp has emerged as a feature of an expansive range of phenomena unfolding on Congolese territory. Camps have long accommodated the laborers of extractive industries like mining and logging, acted as refuges for populations displaced internally and across international borders, provided both basic and glamourous respite for the weary tourist, and acted as barracks for both local and foreign military powers. Beyond merely accommodating these diverse populations, policies of encampment have long accompanied and furthered colonial exploitation, racialized labor politics, movements of transnational capital, experiential and ecological travel, and spatial governance (De Meulder 1996; T. Hendriks 2015; Rubbers 2019; T. Hendriks 2022).

"The camp" then, as an abstraction, offers the possibility to account for a diverse combination of global forces and phenomenon as they quite literally hit the ground, activating various sites, built environments, and dwelling practices (Hailey 2009). The camp resists easy definition, acting instead as "an epistemological ground 'opened' for debate" (Hailey 2008b, 27). It is through this quality of resisting clear definition that "the camp" becomes a heuristic, storytelling device in this chapter—a way to empirically and narratively apply Jennifer Robinson's (2016) theoretical proposition to think cities through elsewhere by reading and writing parts of Goma's development trajectory through the elsewhere (or elsewhat) of "the camp." While straying from the theoretical intention of Robinson's comparative gesture, this exercise maintains an attention to opening up alternative starting points from which we can grasp insights into urban life and the continuity of certain urban forms. Thinking through such a "fluid field of meaning" as the camp also allows for the inclusion of camplike spaces, particularly those that share the camp's discursive framing as somehow anti- or proto-urban (Hailey 2008b, 27).

What follows is a partial tracing of the hopeless entanglement of the city and the camp by looking at the history and spatiality of various encampments in and around Goma from the early twentieth century to the present. This nonexhaustive history illustrates how colonialism, economic transformation, and conflict have been spatiotemporally registered within and beyond the city, shaping Goma's expansion, urban form, and fabric as well as the emplacement of contemporary peacekeeping camps. The importance of tracing the way different kinds of camps have left their mark on Goma is manifold. First, such a detour acknowledges that Goma has had multiple and variable relationships with different kinds of camps that predate the emergence of the peacekeeping camps at the heart of this book. This historical review insists that the appearance of a peacekeeping campscape in Goma is not novel in and of itself but emerges in ways that often correspond with earlier camp geographies in and around the city. As such, the dynamics of these contemporary camps in the city should be seen as continuations of (or ruptures with) earlier processes and spatial forms of control, settlement, occupation, fortification, and refuge.

Second, and methodologically, it provides a spatiotemporal analysis of urban space that seeks to overcome the trend toward ahistoricity in ethnographic discourse (Des Chene 1997). A brief foray into available archives and a review of secondary historical sources complements the story that can be told based on fieldwork alone and expands it beyond the period of my being there. To curtail the tendency of ethnographies to overessentialize the present, this chapter emphasizes instead connections between historical camp settlements and Goma's story of urbanization. It is through an understanding of encampments past that I introduce and situate the city's geography of peacekeeping camps in the late 2010s.

Third, taking stock of camps as they have appeared in Goma across time reemphasizes the oft-overlooked *urban* geographies of camps in the Democratic Republic of the Congo (DRC). Despite its strong associations with rurality, frontiers, removal, and respite from the city in popular imagination, camping is also a phenomenon that takes place in and shapes urban areas. For instance, Filip De Boeck and Sammy Baloji (2016) take note of the importance of camps and camplike settlements in the precolonial and colonial topographies of power that shape Kinshasa, while others have acknowledged the appearance of internally displaced person (IDP) camps and military barracks in contemporary Goma as symptomatic of the displacement and militarization driving intraurban growth and development (Pech, Büscher, and Lakes 2018). Echoing these examples, this chapter provides important context for examining and discussing camps for their entanglements with and consequences for the city of Goma and for theorizing the urban at large.

Recounting the urban growth and development of Goma by telling the story of the camps that have appeared in and around the city over time offers an opportunity to approach seemingly disparate (and often separately treated) historical phenomena together. To weave these together, this chapter is structured chronologically around three different histories and functions of encampment, all of which have left their mark on Goma's urban fabric and spatial form. Such a structure echoes Charlie Hailey's tripartite categorization of camps from his guidebook, *Camps: A Guide to 21st-Century Space* (2009), but changes his categories of "response" to fit Goma's particular circumstances.[1] The first camps I look at are camps of defense, which allude to the colonial military camps erected in the early 1900s to defend territorial gains and that worked to inscribe Goma into Belgian colonial space and put Goma on the map of empire. Second, I turn to the camps emerging between 1930 and 1960 that sought to control and govern laborers and local populations. This includes Goma's own *cité indigène*, a settlement that was frequently mobilized by colonial powers on the African continent to accommodate and separate the local population from the colonially administered *ville*, or city. Lastly, this chapter considers Goma's making through and with the refugee camps that appeared in the 1990s in the wake of the Rwandan genocide. This last period in particular allows for a brief introduction to conflict dynamics that not only generated camps to accommodate millions of refugees but subsequently impelled the installation of camps to accommodate UN peacekeepers intervening in an effort to end the violence that ensued in Congo. Picking up from the aftermath of the Rwandan genocide as it played out in eastern DRC, a brief discussion of the inauguration of the peacekeeping mission provides important institutional context for the installation and eventually expansion of camp space in the city of Goma. While the first half of the chapter takes the analytical position of reading the city of Goma through multiple iterations of the camp, the latter half introduces the reader to contemporary peacekeeping camps by looking at their proliferation and different instantiations throughout the city during the period under study (2017–19). I home in on three areas of encampment—north, west, and lakeshore—situating different peacekeeping camps and compounds within broader mission geographies as well as more immediate urban settlement patterns, plans, and politics.

Camps of Defense

The northern shore of Lake Kivu, where Goma sits today, did not appear to be inhabited in any permanent way prior to colonial incursions. Nor was territorial governmentality and cultural identity ever stable (Mathys 2021). The mountainous topography north of present-day Goma acted as a rough geographical boundary and driver of trade and connection between societies who lived in the forest interiors of Congo and those who lived nearer the Great Lakes in the early nineteenth century (Newbury 1980). While the Hunde and Nyanga people are credited with facilitating this early trade along the northern shore of Lake Kivu, the identity groups living in the area of the lake were multiple and also included Banyarwanda pastoralists (Newbury 1991; Büscher 2011). Due to the high mobility of an activity like animal husbandry, settlements in this region were known to use natural, ephemeral materials, leaving little architectural evidence to suggest more permanent inhabitation (Blier 2011).

The proximity of the Nyiragongo volcano and its continued ability to transform the terrain north of the lake also shapes the impermanence of settlement patterns in the area. Early accounts of the area by colonial officials from the first decade of the 1900s describe large swaths of terrain covered by hardened lava sheets from Mount Nyiragongo to the lake, devoid of water, rarely vegetated, and difficult to traverse (Wangermée 1909; Darwin et al. 1913; Jack 1913). For a society largely dependent on agriculture and livestock grazing, such ground with little vegetation was less attractive for permanent habitation. At the shoreline itself, however, former vice-governor general of the Congo Free State Émile Wangermée (1909) found fertile hills inhabited by shepherds with flocks of large sheep and goats upon his arrival in 1904. With the exception of the shepherds on these scrubby, lacustrine hillsides, most Indigenous settlements were reportedly two to three hours away from the lake by foot (Jack 1913).

The arrival of colonial encampments, established to secure the boundaries of colonies decided at the Berlin Conference, would indelibly shift the geopolitical center of gravity of the region from the volcanic hills north of the lake to the lakefront itself. In the early twentieth century, the small lakeside outpost established by the Belgians was located at the nexus of overlapping territorial claims between King Leopold II's Congo State and German East Africa, with slight involvement from the British Protectorate of Uganda. The complexities of these claims were reticulated in an extensive international military campscape. The border scuffles that ensued would place the site of present-day Goma at its epicenter.

Despite the establishment of the Congo Free State in 1885 (five years before the Germans and the British had completed divvying up their believed shares of eastern Africa), it wasn't until 1894 that the first European would arrive on the shores of Lake Kivu (Louis 1963).[2] A German contingent sent to survey the Kivus arrived on the lake's northern shores eight years later and established a temporary post in modern-day Gisenyi in 1905 (Büscher and Mathys 2013; Louis 1963).[3] A Belgian post and military camp in Goma appeared in 1906 as a response to the Germans (Büscher 2011) and was strategically located on Mount Goma, an ancient sublacustrine volcano jutting out into the lake. This position maintained its strategic importance until the time of this study, hosting a small detachment of UN peacekeepers on its summit.

One year later, in 1907, the German post at Gisenyi transformed into a permanent post (Louis 1963). The northern shore of Lake Kivu would witness several quarrels between the Belgians and the Germans due to conflicting borderlines attached to different agreements to which both parties were signatories. Until the precise border could be delimited, the area around Goma remained contested, and therefore, various posts and temporary camps became significant yet shifting features of the landscape. In 1909, German soldiers likely occupied the Belgian post in Goma. J. M. Coote (1956), who led the Kivu Expedition for the British, reported arriving near Lake Kivu in late June 1909 only to find German soldiers occupying the shore who claimed to have pushed the Belgians all the way to the western shore of the lake.[4] In November of that same year, a certain Captain Ireland reported that the camp at Mount Goma belonged again to the Belgians, housing one European and twenty-four *askaris* (Rutanga 2011).

The Kivu Expedition was a final push by Great Britain to secure a piece of the region north of Lake Kivu, which they referred to as Mufumbiro after the Baganda (Darwin et al. 1913). This region corresponds to the chain of active and dormant volcanoes in the Albertine Rift Valley that stretches from Mount Muhabura to Mount Nyiragongo, just twenty kilometers north of Goma. They had several reasons to be interested in this area and to attempt to set up a post south of Mufumbiro on the northern shores of Lake Kivu where present-day Goma sits. First, the British were looking to establish a corridor through which the future Cape–Cairo route could pass. In line with the vision of the Cape–Cairo plan to enhance trade communication and connect British-controlled territories on the continent, many administrators saw obtaining access to the northern shore of the lake as one of the final pieces of the puzzle that would connect them to Lake Tanganyika via the Ruzizi River. Second, the British had adopted the "finders, keepers" adage, justifying their right to the territory based on the fact that British explorer John Hanning Speke had first seen and described the mountainous area (Louis 1963). Lastly, several records speak to the beauty of the landscape. One official reportedly went so far as to pin the hopes of acquiring Mufumbiro on the dream of an African counterpart to the British-Indian getaway of Shimla (Coote 1956). The farthest post that the British were able to establish on the Kivu Expedition, however, was located at Kibumba, approximately twenty-eight kilometers north of Goma (War Office 1909; Coote 1956).[5] This position dominated the only passage from the Mufumbiro Mountains to the lake, was adequately proximate yet distant from the Belgian stronghold at Rutshuru, and was nearest the last foreseeable water supply before the lake (War Office 1909; Louis 1963).

Nearly a century later, Kibumba's location between Rutshuru and Goma continues to be of strategic importance for military and humanitarian actors. It has been alternately a site where violent clashes between armed groups and Congolese forces play out and the host of a variety of refugee and displaced persons camps. The town hosted a tented camp for tourists visiting Virunga National Park at the time of this study. In late 2023, the March 23 Movement (M23) took the town of Kibumba, before advancing toward Goma in the armed group's latest resurgence.

Much of the controversy over the borders between these colonial holdings stemmed from Belgian and German territorial claims based on two different boundaries: one based on the Congolese-German Convention of November 1884 (German claim) and one based on the Declaration of Neutrality of 1885 (Belgian claim). Goma represented a central geography in these overlapping claims. The British sided with the German's idea of controlling the majority of the northeastern shoreline in hopes of recovering some of Mufumbiro and possibly lake access. The German's physical occupation of the island of Idjwi in the middle of the lake in 1899 and the continued presence of German missionaries on the island would not make conceding any part of the northern lakeshore to the Belgians any easier (Louis 1963).[6] The Belgians were largely unshakeable on their stance about the northern shore of Lake Kivu, however, since they

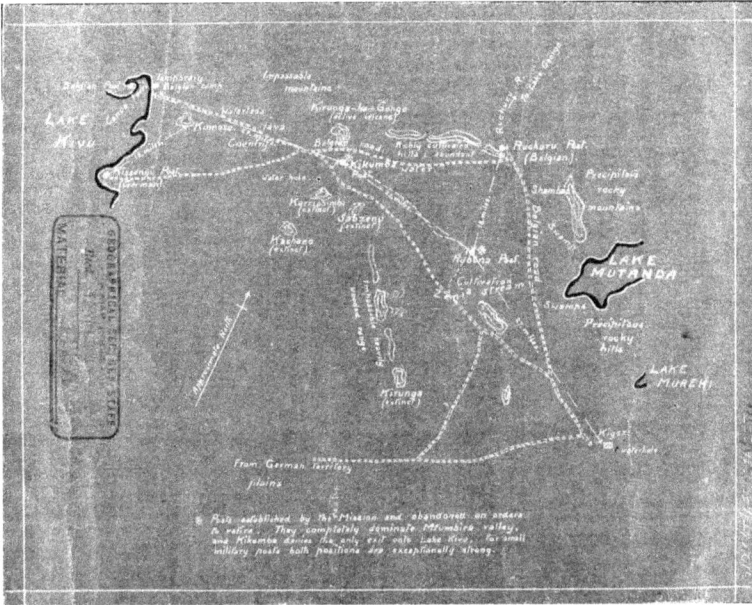

Map of routes between Lakes Kivu and Mutanda showing the location of the
British post at Kibumba ("Kikumba"). (Source: War Office 1909, WOMAT/
AFR/BEA/207/1)

had already begun constructing a road to connect their ferry port on the lake
to Rutshuru (Rutanga 2011).

The Kivu-Mufumbiro Conference of 1910 experienced a series of deadlocked
negotiations until Germany finally conceded Goma and Idjwi to Belgium, establishing the present-day border between the DRC and Rwanda at what was
then the halfway point between Goma and Gisenyi (Louis 1963).[7] Despite intense fighting along the border during World War I and the Germans' destruc-
tion and brief occupation of Goma in 1915, the border has largely remained
unchanged (Büscher 2011). Today, thousands cross this border daily as Congolese and Rwandan traders and distributors leverage and exploit it to generate opportunity in between and across Goma and Gisenyi (Vlassenroot and
Büscher 2009; Doevenspeck 2011; Lamarque 2013; Vlassenroot and Büscher
2013; Rokhideh 2019). The spatial positioning, holding, and defending of camps
was essential in laying the early groundwork on which subsequent political, societal, and cultural dynamics would shape this emergent transboundary space
and the city yet to come.

Camps of Control

The colonial project in eastern Congo not only gave rise to outposts and military camps to defend claims to territory but also later relied on camplike settlements in an effort to exert control over local populations and distance them from Belgian-held parts of the city. In the city and countryside alike, encampment became an essential instrument for colonial economic development and territorializing a politics of racial segregation that defined the early layout of the city.[8]

One of the earliest maps of Goma that the provincial urbanism office had on hand in 2017 was a 1931 parcel map produced by the Commerce-Industrie et Mines (CIM) company that showed the situation of a *cité indigène* in the northeastern periphery of Goma. The *cité indigène* was a housing innovation central to urban (or rather, antiurban) policies of colonial Central Africa—the result of what Bruno De Meulder (2005, 141) calls a "brutally imposed modernization." This particular spatial logic of racial segregation followed a widespread planning approach used by French and Belgian administrators in African cities across the continent (Beeckmans 2010). In Goma, the *cité*'s significantly smaller lot sizes, self-contained grid layout, density, and distance from city's residential and administrative neighborhoods bear visually striking resemblances to the design and planning practices associated with camps. Moreover, the *cité indigène* shares several discursive framings with camps—from direct scholarly analogies with labor camps (Biaya 1994) to their creation by colonial powers in opposition, apart, dependent on, yet separate from, the city. Charlotte Grabli's (2019) work on the *cité indigène* of Leopoldville (modern-day Kinshasa) illustrates how the antiurban nature of these spaces is countered through such practices as listening to the radio in ways that resonate with scholarship of how camp dwellers manage to create new encounters, connections, and claims to urbanity despite imposed distances.

In Goma, the urban antipode of the *cité indigène* was centered along the lakefront, which was exploited for trade and small commerce among Europeans and was thus populated by large villas and smaller industrial operations. Large plots along the lake were allotted to Xavier Dierckx—one of the first colonist-coffee plantation owners in Kivu (De Maere d'Aertrycke 2011; Van Melkebeke 2020)—and to Georges Papazoglakis, a Greek businessman with an import-export company (Antippas 2016). The lakefront's economic importance to the Belgian administration enhanced the perceived necessity of planning the *cité indigène* at the northeastern edge of the nascent town, adjacent to the Rwandan border, in the name of health and sanitation. While the "white hospital" (*hôpital blancs*) was located on the lakeshore nearest the large, European-oc-cupied villas, the "black hospital" (*hôpital noirs*) was located at the other end of town, across the street from the *cité*. Today, Goma's lakefront continues to be a space occupied and frequented by foreigners. The former site of the white hospital and Dierckx's landholdings, for instance, was occupied by some of the main offices of the Mission de l'Organisation des Nations Unies en République Démocratique du Congo (MONUSCO).

Conversely, it is in the approximate area of the *cité indigène* that one finds the popular neighborhood of Birere, the contemporary heart of urban commerce and trade in Goma. Birere is simultaneously home to some of the city's poorest residents, who suffer from multiple and overlapping service and infrastructure deficiencies.[9] This area's economic importance today is largely a function of its proximity to the border. Regulatory and economic asymmetry between the DRC and Rwanda has engendered intense cross-border mobility and trade, at the heart of which are Birere's numerous markets, shops, and warehouses. Boutique toponymy throughout Goma nod to the neighborhood's economic influence with the phrase "bei ya Birere" (Birere prices) sometimes attached to the names of shops in attempts to attract customers. Illicit activities and criminality also flourish in this neighborhood-cum-borderland (Büscher and Mathys 2013) that is spatially characterized by a dense and unplanned settle-ment pattern. Given the relatively early planning of the area by the Belgians and the presence of the *cité indigène*, infrastructure dating back to the colonial era has been overwhelmed by demographic growth, while colonial brick build-ings still stand in various states of dilapidation. Its long-standing inhabitation and spontaneous development also render the ex-post-facto process of land administration and planning extremely difficult in Birere. What several of-ficials refer to as "anarchic constructions" (*constructions arachiques*) continue unremittingly in this area among those who seek to leverage this distinct so-cioeconomic space of opportunity. Birere is shaped by not only spaces on the other side of the border but also Congolese elsewheres and the inter-Congolese migration dynamics that, for instance, gave rise to David's *gîte kindusien* in this part of the city (see introduction to this volume).

Not only did camplike settlements like the *cité indigène* shape settlement patterns that would have a lasting effect on Goma's urban development, but the city must also be situated within regional dynamics related to colonial governance of Indigenous mobility and the settlement politics of plantation-based labor supply and demand. The growth of coffee plantations in the Kivu region between the 1920s and 1950s in particular necessitated large labor forces in often remote and underpopulated parts of the territory. Labor requirements

C.I.M. map of Goma (1931) with circle overlay to indicate the
location of the *cité indigène*. (Photo by author)

for coffee in the Kivu province were predominantly temporary and were regulated by colonial recruitment policies that privileged more proximate laborers.
A colonial decree in 1922 obliged estate owners to provide room and board for
laborers traveling more than five kilometers, though defiance of this decree was
the norm rather than the exception and even laborers from within that radius
would often settle temporarily on or near the plantation (Van Melkebeke 2016).
Sven Van Melkebeke's (2016, 2020) evidence of laborers equating the plantation
to a prison, along with the settlement patterns that resulted from the biopower
exercised on coffee estates, highlights the ways in which the camping practices
of laborers either squatting on concessions or finding accommodation in labor
camps were crucial to sustaining plantation economies, which in turn shaped
urban patterns of colonial settlement and commerce.

Roadworks connecting Goma to Masisi and Rutshuru, completed in 1929
and 1939 (respectively), coincided with a period of expanding agricultural
production and, thus, higher demand for agricultural laborers in the Kivus
(Northrup 1988). Around mid-century, emerging industries in cities like Goma
and Bukavu provided new competition for the plantations in terms of labor
markets. The 1950s were a period of accelerated urbanization in Goma, which
saw substantial growth in its agro-industrial, banking, commercial, transport,
social services, and security sectors, provoking demographic growth as well

as spatial expansion (Büscher 2011). New security structures for the rapidly growing city feature largely in the 1954 General Development Plan drawn up by the Comité National du Kivu. An imposing military camp was planned at the (then) northwestern frontier of the city, near Mount Goma and the existing port and next to the planned radio tower, hospital, prison, and police camp. Its location and general form have endured since then. Today, this military camp—Camp Katindo—hosts elements of the national armed forces (Force Armée de la Republique Démocratique du Congo, FARDC) and their families. However, it is regarded by Goma residents as more of an unsafe *bidonville* than a military barracks. In recent years, it has been the subject of frequent operations to seize weapons and ammunitions held by civilians living illegally in the borderless camp space (Radio Okapi 2018). The densification of this camp between 2005 and 2014 attests to the militarization of space as a persistent pattern of Goma's urbanization into the new millennium (Pech, Büscher, and Lakes 2018).

Camps of Refuge

Goma added another type of camp to its repertoire and garnered global attention during the Rwandan genocide of 1994 as thousands of Rwandans as well as *génocidaires* (perpetrators of the genocide) fled across the border to (then) Zaire. The genocide and its consequences deeply destabilized regional security. Its aftermath is largely viewed by area scholars as the genesis of the conflict that continues to plague eastern DRC today.[10] This protracted conflict has engendered waves of displacement—first of Rwandan refugees and second of IDPs from more rural areas in eastern DRC—that have fueled rapid urbanization in Goma as people from elsewhere make new homes in the relative sanctuary of the city.

In the summer of 1994, an estimated 1.2 million Rwandans crossed the then Zairian border into Goma and surrounding towns up to twenty kilometers north (UNHCR 2000). Their arrival was precipitated and oriented by the advances of the Rwandan Patriotic Front (RPF). Fearing violent retaliations by the RPF and heading toward the last remaining Rwandan Armed Forces stronghold in the northwest (rather than the "Turquoise Zone" delimited by the French military in the southwest), the first refugees arrived in Goma on the morning of July 14, 1994 (Médecins sans Frontières 2013). Described as a "river," "tidal wave," and "flood," refugees were first channeled into a stadium in Goma with UN agencies seemingly unprepared for the deluge (France 2 1994; Médecins sans Frontières 2013). Eventually six main refugee camps emerged and operated between 1994 and 1996: Kituku, Mugunga, and Lac Vert on the western axis road out of Goma and Kibumba, Katale, and Kahindo on the northern axis road toward Rutshuru (Bradol and Le Pape 2017).[11] The scale of the crisis in and around Goma in the immediate aftermath of the genocide was unprecedented.

Emergent camps constituted insecure spaces from the points of view of health, access to food and water, and threat of physical violence. Within one week of the first refugee arrivals in Goma, Médecins sans Frontières (MSF) was reporting eight hundred cholera deaths in the "Goma camps," as this group of camps were called. By the following week, that number skyrocketed to fourteen thousand and included those dying of dysentery, thirst, and malnutrition. The distance of many camps from the lake caused complications for humanitarians in delivering water, while budgets frequently compromised the availability and distribution of food, water, and other materials (only a small minority of refugees in the camps were living in proper tents). In the city itself, tensions were high. The Goma airport was bombed, approximately a third of Goma residents fled the city, and Zairean soldiers had resorted to indiscriminate looting (including among refugees). The camps offered little reprieve from the general insecurity in Goma, acting as breeding grounds for the regrouping of perpetrators of the genocide and important recruitment centers for the defeated Rwandan Armed Forces and Hutu militias (including Interahamwe). Many former members of these armed forces took up leadership roles in the camp, patrolled them, or eventually took control of them through armed incursions.[12] By August 1994, a separate military headquarter camp had emerged close to the refugee camps west of Goma, from which these *génocidaires* reportedly commandeered 40 to 60 percent of humanitarian aid destined for the one hundred thousand refugees in Mugunga, a trend that continued across several camps for more than a year. By the end of September, an armed militia claimed control of the Katale camp (Médecins sans Frontières 2013).

As a humanitarian emergency, the Rwandan refugee crisis also opened the floodgates to what would become an enduring presence of international humanitarian organizations in Goma, though the situation in 1994 raised several moral and ethical dilemmas to the groups on the ground at the time. Approximately one hundred NGOs showed up to assist refugees in Goma in 1994, many prompted by the sheer scale of the situation (covered extensively by the media) and the devastation wreaked by the cholera outbreak (Stockton 1998). Among them were various sections of MSF, who had several internal debates about their continued assistance in the camps given the presence and activities of the *génocidaires*. The situation in the camps prompted MSF France to withdraw from camps in eastern Congo in November 1994, while MSF Belgium and MSF Holland stayed on in Goma. These latter sections believed that their presence in the camps would strengthen their strategy of "humanitarian resistance" and ability to bear witness in order to pressure the UN and international community to act (Médecins sans Frontières 2013).

As highly militarized spaces controlled by the exiled Rwandan Armed Forces through militias, violence pervaded the camps. Regrouped armed forces unleashed assaults against refugees, particularly those accused of being Tutsi or agents of the RPF and those considering return. Intimidation and murders halted the United Nations High Commissioner for Refugees' (UNHCR) early efforts to organize repatriation and worked to consolidate the former military regime's authority over the refugee population. Their exile equally provided the means to continue to train for and wage war, launching several attacks into Rwanda from their positions in eastern Congo (Prunier 2010). In the span of one year (1994–95), it was reported that four thousand people were killed in the camps in and around Goma at the hands of Zairean and (former) Rwandan armed forces, militias, and other refugees (Borton 1996; Stearns 2011).

Understood as "Rwanda outside Rwanda" (Prunier 2010) forged through camps seen as "miniature states" (Médecins sans Frontières 2013), the defeated army restructured and rearmed itself in the political and military sanctuary afforded by the alliance of Mobutu and Habyarimana.[13] Camps like the *bananerie* near the camps of Mugunga and Lac Vert acted as the administrative headquarters of the exiled and regrouping Rwandan Armed Forces (Prunier 2010). Zairean authorities not only permitted the military restructuring of the former regime to occur on its territory but often facilitated their armament and movement of equipment (Adelman and Rao 2004). Their control of refugee camps and ability to operate from their own administrative camps worked to meet their political objectives, creating a networked camp space that operated as a sort of exiled Rwandan state, calling for a return to Rwanda (and to power) by force. Camps of refuge in this context, then, refers to not only settlements that accommodate refugees but also spaces that allow armed elements to shelter while sustaining violence, create new strongholds, and reconsolidate power.

The prolonged presence of the genocidal regime on Zairean territory added to existing ethnic tensions, ultimately leading to the First Congo War. The regrouped armed elements previously mentioned turned their murderous attention toward ethnic Tutsis in the surrounding territories of eastern Congo, while the camps around Goma became the sites of targeted attacks by the Alliance des Forces Démocratiques pour la Libération du Congo-Zaïre (AFDL), a rebel group backed by forces from Rwanda, Uganda, and Burundi.[14] The second-largest camp, in Kibumba (about 200,000 refugees), was the first to be attacked in late June 1996 and the first to fall to the rebels in late October. Attacks continued on the Katale and Kahindo camps, forcing refugees to flee to the camps west of Goma. By mid-November, the AFDL took Goma and eventually surrounded and attacked the Mugunga camp. They killed around 200 refugees attempting to flee the camp and forced the repatriation of between 350,000 and 500,000 people back to Rwanda (OHCHR 2010).

The site of the Mugunga refugee camp in particular would continue to host waves of people displaced by violence. From the First Congo War (1996–97) to the protracted fighting that continues in the Kivus today, Mugunga has become nearly synonymous with displaced populations and insecurity. The single Mugunga refugee camp of 1994–96 transformed into multiple IDP camps with the proliferation and acceleration of armed conflict in the Kivus after the Second Congo War (1998–2003). Mugunga 3, the largest and most enduring of these camps, was established in 2007 to accommodate people internally displaced by protracted conflict following the end of the Second Congo War between a proliferating number of national and foreign armed groups and the Congolese army (M. Hendriks and Büscher 2019; Nguya 2019). In 2008, it welcomed IDPs transferred from the sites of Kibati 1 and Kibati 2, a period that saw several confrontations between the Congrès National pour la Défense du Peuple (CNDP) and the Congolese army in the territories of Masisi and Walikale (Mwenyemali 2017; M. Hendriks and Büscher 2019).[15] In 2009, Mugunga 3 continued to act as a camp of consolidation with the closure of Mugunga 1 and 2 and accommodated a small number of displaced persons who could not return home due to physical handicaps, chronic illnesses, or old age (Mwenyemali 2017). The population of the camp would grow again in 2012–13 with the advances of another rebel movement, M23, throughout North Kivu and their eventual arrival in Goma on November 20, 2012 (Berwouts 2017).

Toward the end of one of Mugunga 3's lifecycles in 2017, urban space and camp space tended to blur and overlap. The camp had an urbanizing effect on its immediate surroundings, creating new markets and generating different economic enterprises (including illicit activities such as charcoal harvesting from the nearby Virunga National Park). More urban livelihoods were practiced in the camp; NGOs trained and organized displaced persons (who had generally practiced agriculture in their villages of origin) in soap production, brick production, and bread making. Small carpentry shops also opened up, providing livelihood opportunities for locals and IDPs alike. Both groups also ended up benefiting from the health center and school that had been established in the camp. Given the freedom of movement between the camp, the Mugunga neighborhood, and other parts of the city, many of the camp's residents worked in Goma—spontaneously leaving the camp to reinstall themselves in other urban neighborhoods.[16]

In 2017, the National Commission for Refugees (CNR), whose mandate includes the management of IDPs, closed twelve camps, among them Mugunga 3, which was dismantled that summer. According to the commission's closure report, "The site presented the image of a veritable desert before the official ceremony to return the land to its owners" (Mwenyemali 2017). Many of the former residents had dismantled their shelters, taking the building materials (including sticks) with them. One month after the official closure, all that remained on the site was a Vodocom boutique (moved to the parcel of the landowner wishing to claim it), low, volcanic rock walls delimiting the plots to be returned, two water points, and a smattering of trees. Across the access road from the camp, small wooden buildings previously hosting the NGOs responsible for camp management were quickly occupied by Congolese security forces.

The decision to close the camp was based on a variety of factors, including reestablished security in the zones from which the camp population was originally displaced, reduced humanitarian assistance in the camp sites, continued consolidation of sites, the spontaneous departure of displaced persons, and national policy (Mwenyemali 2017). The broader closure strategy of the government, for instance, dates back to 2015 and favors sustainable shelter solutions for the displaced, such as local integration and return.[17] The governor of North Kivu supported this national policy and saw the camps as tarnishing the province's image, inhibiting foreign investment due to real and perceived levels of criminality emanating from IDP camps (IRIN 2014). Some members of the international humanitarian community, however, saw the durable solutions approach as lending itself to the manipulation of initiatives by political groups and a shrinking "humanitarian space" (Brauman 1993; CCCM DR Congo 2016). They have been reticent to contribute financially or materially to resource kits (*kit d'accompagnement*) according to the CNR head of office in Goma. These kits consist of food aid, tarpaulin sheets, and seeds and grains to begin agricultural activities in an effort to assist returnees in their transition to their places of origin or integration. According to figures obtained from UNHCR (2017), nearly half of the 3,746 IDPs still living in Mugunga 3 at the time of closure intended to settle in and around Goma. Since the conclusion of this study, a displaced persons camp has reopened in Mugunga. In May 2024, it was the target of a violent attack that Congolese and US officials attributed to M23 and the Rwandan army.

Camps of *Casques Bleus*

The Rwandan genocide set in motion a cycle of violence and splintering of armed groups that continues to plague eastern DRC today. Such conflicts, when paired with interventionism, can give rise to camps for those who are forcibly displaced by violent warfare and, as the remainder of this chapter addresses, those who are deployed for peacefare. In 1999, the beginnings of the protracted conflict that would emerge in the genocide's aftermath provoked the involvement of the United Nations, which deployed the multinational peacekeeping mission MONUC to the country.[18] MONUC would be followed by the MONUSCO mission—the military encampments and lifeworlds of which form the object of the present study.

In April 1999, the United Nations Security Council began to consider its involvement in implementing a ceasefire agreement to end the Second Congo War (UNSC 1999).[19] The Second Congo War began in 1998 with the fallout between Laurent Desiré Kabila and the Rwandan and Ugandan allies who had helped bring him into power.[20] This souring of relations pitted Rwanda and Uganda against Kabila's regime (backed politically and militarily by Angola, Namibia, and Zimbabwe), spurring violent conflict fought among at least twenty-nine armed groups (including national armies, rebel forces, and various militias) (OHCHR 2010; Stearns 2011). Goma gained importance during this period as the headquarters of the Rassemblement Congolais pour la Démocratie–Goma (RCD–Goma), a Rwandan-backed political and military movement that took over the city in August 1998. The countries and armed groups party to the conflict signed the Lusaka Ceasefire Agreement on July 10, 1999, in the presence of the Organization of African Unity (OAU), UN, and Southern African Development Community (SADC).[21] The constitution, facilitation, and deployment of a peacekeeping force by the UN in collaboration with the OAU was stipulated in the agreement itself (Article III), including a joint military commission charged with monitoring the ceasefire until UN military observers (MILOBs) could be deployed.[22]

By the first few months of the new millennium, seventy-nine of the ninety intended military liaison officers had been deployed and the Security Council had sought authorization for the deployment of five hundred MILOBs in addition to approximately fifty-five hundred contingent troops (UNSC 2000a;

Edström and Gyllensporre 2013). This envisioned troop strength translated into four battalions to be located in Mbandaka, Kisangani, Mbuji Mayi, and Kindu (Edström and Gyllensporre 2013). The tasking of this planned deployment would go beyond monitoring the ceasefire to include ensuring the withdrawal of foreign forces and disarmament, demobilization, repatriation, and resettlement of armed combatants—the first expansions in what would be an ever-expanding and evolving mandate.[23] It was not until after the assassination of Kabila on January 16, 2001, by one of his bodyguards that significant deployments actually began. By October of that year, there were nearly twenty-five hundred military personnel in the DRC, including soldiers from Morocco, Senegal, Tunisia, and Uruguay—countries that would continue to contribute troops to the mission (MacQueen 2002, 95). With the arrival of infantry troops to fill the battalions foreseen during this period, MONUC's contingent strength became operational.

By the time troops began to be deployed, the Lusaka Ceasefire Agreement had all but disintegrated. Attempts at another ceasefire, the Sun City Agreement signed in 2002, proved equally futile at ending armed conflict but ushered in a period of political transition that would last until democratic elections could be held.[24] This period was marked by significant international influence and intervener presence that emphasized elections and security sector reform, and privileged the repatriation of combatants over mechanisms for local conflict resolution (Autesserre 2010). Joseph Kabila, who succeeded his father, Laurent, upon his assassination, defeated Jean-Pierre Bemba in the 2006 general elections, ushering in a period that would shift MONUC's center of gravity toward Goma.

Laurent Nkunda had already launched a rebellion in 2004, aimed at protecting Congolese Tutsis against armed aggression and maintaining the influence of the RCD (Stearns 2011). Within days of Kabila announcing victory in the elections in November 2006, Nkunda marched on Goma, only to be pushed back by MONUC troops based in Saké (Büscher 2011). From his stronghold in Masisi, Nkunda's area of influence in North Kivu province shifted eastward between mid-2006 and mid-2008 (Stearns 2012), heightening the threat of an attack on Goma from the north. Reacting to these developments, a Uruguayan battalion moved to its current position near the airport and near the northern outskirts of the city for the purpose of tactical defense. Within this same timeframe, Goma welcomed an Indian field hospital, a Malawian combat support company, and an additional Indian battalion. These contingents joined an already-existing Indian brigade headquarters, Indian battalion, two aviation squadrons, and South African engineering company in the city (Department of

Peacekeeping Operations 2006; Department of Field Support 2008; Center on International Cooperation 2017). Renamed MONUSCO in 2010, various mission offices and civilian personnel followed the military shift eastward in 2013, as the UN condemned increased armed group activities in the province and expressed deep concern regarding the presence of M23 in the vicinity of Goma (UNSC 2013). Force leadership shifted their headquarters to Goma beginning with the police commissioner in late 2013 and followed shortly thereafter by the force commander in early 2014 (UNSC 2014).

By 2019, the twentieth year of the mission, the urban agglomeration of Goma-Saké-Munigi boasted the highest number of UN peacekeeping camps in the country. Based on estimates gathered across individual contingents, camps in Goma accommodated between 2,300 and 2,400 contingent troops and officers with an additional 380 based in the village of Munigi to the north and over 1,300 in Mubambiro, a small village west of Goma on the eastern outskirts of Saké. During the period under consideration here, Goma hosted nine contingents across eleven different camps or officially company operating bases (COBs), including a military hospital.[25] In addition to these bases, the city also hosted a small camp on the top of Mount Goma manned by a single detachment and a transit camp accommodating troops that were inducted through Goma but were deploying farther afield. Mubambiro hosted six contingents in seven bases colocated in a combined garrison, while the village of Munigi (north of Goma) hosted two adjacent bases.[26]

The location of peacekeeping bases and compounds in the city follow numerous logics with shifting temporalities, including fluctuations in contingent strengths, the changing spatiality and intensity of conflict, budget changes, and land availability. The mission's procurement section manages the leasing of land for COBs in the city from both the Congolese state and private landowners. Private lands occupied by past and present camps in Goma and its urban periphery have been owned by a coffee estate, aspiring politicians, traditional authorities, private business elites, and various religious organizations. Private leases, however, are becoming increasingly rare. Many of the most recent shifts in the mission geography in the city are directly related to cost-saving measures forced by budget cuts to the mission. Considered a high-priority cost-saving measure, camps and compounds such as the former Senegalese Formed Police Unit (SEN-FPU) camp, the former Level III hospital, and one of two INDRDB camps in Mubambiro had been dismantled and the land transferred back to private owners by the end of 2019.[27] All three contingents moved to new bases on public lands, which are rent-free for the mission.

In the case of the Level III hospital in town, occupying a former hotel, rents had reportedly reached USD 35,000 per month for a mission that was looking to cut USD 2 million in leases over the course of 2018.[28] The Level III hospital thus became part of MONUSCO's logistics base, located on ten hectares of land owned by the national Regie des Voies Aériennes (RVA). The site's vacant land was formerly being farmed by a group of Congolese women while various *auto écoles* used the gravel frontage along the arterial rode to train novice drivers. With the acquisition of the site by the mission in 2016, the land was cleared to accommodate the new hospital, as well as administrative offices, warehouses, and workshops for mission sections such as Engineering, Logistics, Supply Chain, and the UN Mine Action Service (UNMAS). The new rations warehouse, inaugurated in 2019, consolidated the former ration unit, which had been located within the airfield of the Goma International Airport. This move allowed the SEN-FPU to move from Camp Jambaar,[29] which was being leased to the mission by a coffee estate, to the former ration warehouse site in the airfield to cut costs.

In a context of rapid and dense urbanization as experienced in Goma, urban land held by the public authority responsible for air transportation is highly amenable for the installation of military bases. Not only are many RVA-owned sites concentrated at or around the airport, facilitating the logistics of troop movements, but landholdings like airfields and associated parcels have the advantage for the mission of being large and undeveloped. While bases on these RVA-owned sites enjoy larger spaces over which to extend camp infrastructures, the land is otherwise undevelopable due to its dangerous proximity to the airport runway—a safety and security concern that is not lost on the peacekeepers inhabiting these otherwise uninhabitable spaces.

Given the operational responsibilities of the military contingents accommodated in peacekeeping camps in and around Goma, tasking orders also play a crucial role in determining the locations of different bases. Not all peacekeepers stationed in Goma have the same job or are even under the same hierarchy of command. Goma's peacekeeping campscape regroups military contingents of armed forces, special forces, FPUs, military police, and reserves carrying out mandates across varying scales and in different geographies. As the remainder of this chapter attests, the operational significance of different peacekeeping camp locations in the city collide with site planning challenges, the dynamics of urbanization, and colonial geographies of occupation. The following sections look at three specific sites in the city occupied by MONUSCO's peacekeeping camps: the city's airport in the north, the rapidly urbanizing western flank, and the lakefront near the city center. These sites are illustrative of the strategic positioning and diverse politics of international interveners "making camp" in different areas around and across the city.

Camping at the Airport

The South African Air Force (SAAF) occupies the northernmost peacekeeping camp within the administrative boundaries of the city of Goma. This Composite Helicopter Unit (CHU) is directly adjacent to the helipad at the Goma International Airport for operational efficiency.[30] Like many of the peacekeeping camps in Goma, the SAAF took over the base in early 2009 in the wake of a period of heavy fighting between Laurent Nkunda's CNDP and the FARDC.

The particular aviation unit inhabiting this camp in the late 2010s began its service to MONUC in Kamina after the closure of the UN peacekeeping mission in Burundi in 2006. Unit aviators stayed there for about two years before moving to Goma, replacing the Indian aviation contingent that had built up the CHU camp site since 2003 (Indian Air Force 2019). The SAAF unit arrived in Goma with two helicopters (each with a crew of three people) along with support personnel in logistics, operations, and intelligence, totaling approximately twenty-five people. Ground that had been leveled in the northeastern corner of the airport to make space for the helicopter hangars formed the man-made hill atop which unit personnel were accommodated. By 2010, the headcount in the camp had already jumped to forty-five.

"Then the camp exploded," Arno added before taking a swig of his coffee. I sat with Arno at the café of the force headquarters, where he ordered his coffee "big and hot." His large build and unabashed dance moves made him an unmissable character in UN social circles and his cheesy potatoes were in high demand at weekend *braais*. Arno and I had run into each other two days prior to our coffee at one such braai. Upon hearing some of his memories of Goma over the years and learning of his experience in various missions, I asked if I could stop by his office to hear more. Arno had been coming and going from the CHU camp since February 2006 before pivoting into a role at headquarters and had some long-winded and opinionated recollections about its growth over the years. The "explosion" that Arno mentioned referred to the additional air assets and personnel that accompanied South Africa's increased peacekeeping contribution around 2013—a result of the establishment of the Force Intervention Brigade (FIB) (UNSC 2013). As part of the expanded mandate and increased troop contribution from South Africa, the CHU camp added three Oryx helicopters to the existing two and deployed two of three Rooivalk attack helicopters sent by South Africa to the mission (Helfrich 2013), bringing the crew strength alone to nineteen people. As the camp began to welcome additional support staff for the new helicopters, as well as technicians and the medical sick bay team, the camp on top of the small mound could no longer accommodate the entire unit. To expand the camp, new accommodations for NCOs were erected at the foot of the hill, closer to the hangars, while officers remained in the oldest part of the camp on the top of the hill. In early 2020, the entire camp boasted a population of approximately 160 people.

Following the capture of the airport by M23 in 2012 and an attack on the airport in 2015, the CHU camp began to seriously ramp up its own protection. As Arno recalled the events of 2012, mortars were falling on the airport from a landmark known to the mission as "triple towers"—three communication towers positioned on hilltops in Kibati. Without adequate defenses at the camp, he says, the unit's only options were to evacuate the air assets and "grab two bottles of whiskey." The helicopters were immediately flown out to Kavumu Airport outside of Bukavu and to Mushake, in nearby Masisi Territory. Arno didn't specify where he and his whiskey ended up.

Regarding the 2015 attack, government officials inculpated Mai Mai militias who were presumably targeting Congolese air force assets (Stearns 2015), though Arno believes that the true details of that attack remain unclear.[31] In the aftermath of this attack (which damaged three UN aircrafts), the unit requested assistance from MONUSCO's Engineering Section to install bomb shelters and construct sentinel towers inside the camp. Arno and his unit sought to recycle mission materials and attempted to order decommissioned shipping containers to prepare defenses, but the mission sent them brand-new containers instead. The unit proceeded nonetheless to cut the containers to make protection shells before receiving a massive bill from the mission. Arno reacted in his retelling with some choice expletives directed at MONUSCO.

Arno's account of his unit's experience in Goma was peppered throughout with four-letter words, sarcastic banter, and brazen critiques of the mission, many of which revolved around the theme of site planning. The location of the CHU camp, with or without physical fortifications, imposed serious space constraints on the base by Arno's assessment. "Goma Airport is too crammed and our camp up there is the only camp that's not properly closed," he lamented. Cramped living quarters, however, are rather familiar to air force personnel as flight crews are already accustomed to sharing close quarters. In the SAAF, aircrews of three sleep together to facilitate command and control but also to keep crewmembers accountable to one another. Even with these tighter internal configurations, the camp simply feels too small and too exposed for Arno's liking. Compounding his anxieties around the spatiality of the camp, Arno mentioned that the UN had recently installed a petrol plant in proximity to the CHU base. Arno admitted he was baffled by this site decision and brought it up to his buddy, the UN chief of fuel, who tried to reassure him that the plant didn't pose a risk to the base as the petrol wasn't flammable. Arno looked at me with wide eyes, expecting to incite a reaction: "A fucking petrol plant!"

Arno's issues with the UN's site selection for military installations date back to his tour in Burundi. As that mission had begun as a SADC initiative, the South African airmen and airwomen stationed at Bujumbura Airport had the liberty to construct their camp according to their own needs and standards. He recalls that when the UN got involved, they moved his team to "an utter swamp." This memory resonated with his experience in Beni (DRC), where Arno lamented the poor partition of an ablutions unit in one camp and the lack of a functioning kitchen in another, taking the initiative himself to request and build up new infrastructures. Regarding the locations and conditions of military bases in the MONUSCO mission, Arno sums up the role of the UN as "putting national forces in shit."

The CHU camp is one of about half a dozen camps located in and around the airport in northeast Goma, and while the unit is left to cope with cramped living quarters, a lack of a more fortified perimeter, and proximity to hazards associated with aviation, it is hard to imagine a better site, particularly for an air force, than an airport. Even for land service branches, the military appeal of proximity to this critical infrastructure is operationally and tactically informed. Securing the airport is vital to counterinsurgency tactics as it represents a port of entry to the country and an important economic gateway for import/export businesses and domestic trade. Public demonstrations and protests have often sought to disturb traffic along roadways leading to and from the airport as a matter of claim-making, leading to the mission's placement of the SEN-FPU on the Airport Road itself to ensure that they are able to deploy and conduct crowd control operations.[32] Furthermore, the poor road conditions in the country increase mission staff's and contingents' reliance on air transport to fulfill their operational mandates in other parts of the province and country.

Not only do the peacekeeping camps concentrated near the airport benefit from the operational efficiency of being able to rapidly transport troops by air, but the terrain features of this area also hold great defensive importance, shaping settlement patterns both historically and today. Byahi, for instance, is often recognized as one of the earliest-known permanent settlements nearest to modern Goma and is located just northeast of the airport. Byahi's position, set back from the lake on more elevated terrain, gave its inhabitants a strategic vantage point from which they could foresee potential attacks from the south by the Bahavu (Birhahwa 1974 cited in Büscher 2011). Continuing north from Byahi one comes to Munigi, where the occupation of "Eastern Hill," as the Indian force calls it, is a determining landmark in Goma's contemporary security landscape. Major Ravish, whose peacekeeping contingent lives at the foot of the hill, attributes the criticality of this feature to its role in previous military offensives. Deployment to Eastern Hill is seen by him and his fellow officers as crucial to avoiding a repeat of 2012, during which M23 occupied the hill and fired mortars on the airport, opening the floodgates to the invasion of Goma. "You can dominate this RN2 axis from this hill," Major Ravish points out, suggesting that whoever controls Eastern Hill ultimately controls movement in and out of the city.[33] Ravish is referring to Route Nationale, or National Road 2, a trunk highway running north–south along the Rwandan and Ugandan borders of North Kivu, connecting Goma to Beni in the north and to Mbuji Mayi in the southwest. Dominating the hill and highway relies on an operating base between the foot of the hill and the road in addition to a permanent detachment of between fourteen and twenty peacekeepers camped on the middle of the hillside. From this smattering of weather havens encircled by razor wire, individual soldiers are deployed to man lookout posts offering panoramic views akin to those that made Byahi and its surrounds such an invaluable and defensive position to occupy.

Camping Out West

Several recent developments in western Goma are shifting different centers of gravity in the city westward, increasing the strategic significance of peacekeeping camps located in this part of the city. This continued urban expansion builds on dynamics already set in motion in the early 1990s. During this time, parcel plans were made for the western neighborhoods of Himbi and Keyshero as they welcomed new waves of migrants from South Kivu. These early planning efforts, however, could not keep up with the demographic explosion that accompanied the escalation of violent conflict and the choice among many refugees from the genocide to stay. Neighborhoods like Ndosho and Mugunga, which became administrative districts of the city in 1996, grew to accommodate these populations and welcome new businesses, schools, and churches following the 2002 volcanic eruption. Between 1993 and 2003, Goma added approximately four hundred thousand people to its population and twenty-five square kilometers to its area, with most of this growth concentrated in the west (Verhoeve 2004).

In these westernmost neighborhoods, planning and construction projects are underway for a new university campus, international stadium, provincial assembly office, police headquarters, and cathedral. Mock-ups for the new University of Goma campus, spread out over two concessions in the Lac Vert neighborhood, were unveiled at a fundraising ceremony in May 2017. The plans feature residences for professors, an amphitheater, a swimming pool, a language center, a mining research center, a digital competences center, and cooperative production units for milk, potatoes, fruits, and vegetables. The features of the new campus, according to the rector, would be crucial to achieving his visions of the university as a temple of knowledge, factory of human capital, the province's strategic center, and the nation's nerve center of modernity (with explicit reference to the Kabilist revolution of modernity).[34] The rector's discourse suggested that none of these centers and visions were possible from the university's current location, nor were they achievable within the confines of the current buildings rented by the university.

Equally frustrated by being mere renters of buildings in downtown Goma, the provincial assembly plans to move to the neighborhood of Lac Vert. Lacking space at their current office complex in Himbi, this legislative body rents space at the Banque de Développement des Etats des Grands Lacs building in downtown Goma for its plenary sessions. Francis, an assembly member's brother and regular at my neighbor's bar, viewed the shift as capable of shaping public perceptions of the city. According to Francis, the new provincial assembly offices could encourage the population to reshape their conception of Goma to include the totality of the city's neighborhoods and provide a new growth pole to attract new residences and businesses. Moving such an institution out west could also help ensure security in places where households would not be willing or able to provide it, increasing the attractiveness of this part of town. Commenting on the speed of such an expansion of the city, Francis adds, "We could not imagine that Mugunga would be part of the city one day."[35]

Predating the plans of the university and the provincial government to move onto sites in the west of the city, the Catholic Church has both followed and led the city's expansion pattern in recent decades. Keyshero is home to numerous large religious institutions, such as the Université de la Sapentia and the large Pallottine complex. In the words of a *chef d'avenue* from the neighborhood, "les prêtres prévoit"—priests plan or predict—in the double sense that such religious institutions seem to anticipate and direct the city's growth trajectories based on the locations where they establish themselves. The Catholic Church's landholdings in this part of town involve much more than a simple savvy for predicting growth trends however. In preparing for the one hundredth anniversary of the Catholic Mission in the DRC, Raymond, an aspiring politician and member of a prominent Goma family, began researching the ways that the spread of Catholicism and his family history intertwined. He explained that many of the church's large landholdings near the lake emerged out of an alliance with the Belgian administration built on education, combined with the religious zeal to compete with the Protestant Mission farther north in Lubero Territory. As such, "the Catholic Church always has the best land in DRC," Raymond concluded. Be it due to incredible forecasting or historical circumstances, the newest development by the Catholic Diocese—the Mama Wa Amani Cathedral—is being built on a two-hectare plot near Kituku market, the economic heart of the Keyshero neighborhood.[36] It is poised to be the third-largest cathedral on the continent (Babunga 2018), though building progress has experienced fits and starts. Construction was initially planned to commence in 2014 and the cathedral remained under construction as of 2022. Many Goma residents and government officials see the new cathedral as another landmark institution that can attract new residents to Keyshero, usher in a wider socioeconomic shift in the city, and perhaps change how residents perceive their own city's limits.

It is in these dynamic, western neighborhoods that one also finds a base of the elite INDRDB, whose tasking involves operational responsibility for the city of Goma itself. Since these troops are responsible for fulfilling the mission mandate "in place," the airport is less crucial for their operations (though they do deploy a platoon-sized detachment at the airport, mainly to protect UN assets). Their camp is located about twenty minutes from the city center in the Sotraki quarter, named for the enterprise that owns a coffee processing plant in the area. Given the strong religious character of this part of the city, it should come as no surprise that the base rents its land from the monks of Mokoto, a Trappist order under the Diocese of Goma.[37] Despite their physical distance from downtown, camp leadership understand their base as a highly connected "island of cooperation" in the city.

Because of their distance from the northeasternmost neighborhoods of Goma, the INDRDB base, referred to by the brigade as Himbi, also looks after the Rusayo *groupement* in Nyiragongo Territory (inhabited by several people formerly living in the Mugunga 3 camp).[38] In exchange, the INDRDB base in Munigi is responsible for the Goma neighborhood of Bujovu. The positioning of this camp in the west of Goma needs to be understood in the context of previous configurations of the INDRDB in the city. Earlier, when the security situation in Goma provoked the mission to deploy a stronger operational troop presence, Himbi COB and Munigi COB shared their tasking in Goma with two other operational bases in the city: one at a former tea factory and one at the airport. These four COBs were able to divide Goma (their area of responsibility) into smaller quadrants until funding reductions forced the battalions' spatial consolidation as recently as 2017. Despite abandoning the centrally located base known simply as Tea Factory (now used as a transit camp during troop rotations), the battalion maintains an operational presence in town with a permanent detachment on Mount Goma.

"This is my city, *yaar!*" Lieutenant Colonel Dev exclaims at one of our many meetings. Dev is confident and clean-cut; even his frequent grin is orderly. With the peacekeeping mission having divided the country into different areas of responsibility, he is right, from an operational perspective. Goma is "his" city. "I'm handling a city of 1.1 million souls with 120 guys," he said. Dev's "handling" of the city ranges from ensuring the protection of civilians to securing UN assets. To fulfill such a mandate, his contingent's tasks include the deployment of quick reaction forces (QRFs) to respond to events as well as regular patrols of the city to prevent threats from materializing. In relation to previous eras (when the city had multiple companies tasked with fulfilling the MONUSCO mandate in Goma), Dev feels that his contingent has had to show its presence that much more. Despite the relative lack of armed group conflict unfolding in Goma itself, Dev emphasizes that "showing the presence of blue helmets is still important in this city." He benefits from the colocation of the battalion headquarters and his contingent because more manpower translates into fewer guard duties for troops stationed at Himbi, meaning that there are more troops available to move out if necessary.

Regarding his contingent's location in the city, Dev insists that "being at a limb doesn't affect operations because of the concept of prepositioning of QRFs." QRFs were especially active in the city in the run-up to the general election of 2018. One QRF was stationed within one of the lakeside compounds of MONUSCO to prepare for any violence that might break out in either the anticipation or aftermath of election day. Military leadership had even mapped out (down to the neighborhood level) multiple scenarios, indicating which areas of Goma could flare up if either Martin Fayulu, Félix Tshisekedi, or Emannuel Ramazani Shadary were to win. Exchanging texts during the election period and debating the possible outcomes, Dev wrote, "As I said, it's a dynamic city, and that's why they have a dynamic officer here."

The Himbi base is simultaneously at a limb of the city and at the heart of a wider operational geography for MONUSCO. The camp not only accommodates one of the four companies of the INDRDB but also serves as the battalion headquarters. Previously located in the Mubambiro complex, the battalion headquarters coordinates the operations of several peacekeeping camps in Walikale and Masisi Territories. In the summer of 2017, however, three bases in Walikale Territory and two in Masisi Territory were closed, all of which had been occupied by Indian battalions.[39] Those troops who had not been repatriated began to concentrate in Mubambiro alongside other contingents whose combined garrison plays an important role in securing the western entry and exit point of the city. Here, the battalion adopted a "protection through projection" approach through which it selectively deploys standing combat contingents to territories farther west. This new, mission-specific operational concept was adopted by the INDRDB in light of a climate of increasing base closures but also justifies and strengthens the strategic location of the new headquarters at the Himbi base, situated at a midpoint location between the brigade and mission headquarters in Goma and the INDRDB companies in Mubambiro.

Camping on the Lake

While the MONUSCO compounds on the lakeshore in downtown Goma do not accommodate military contingents overnight like peacekeeping camps do, events like elections can prompt the mission to deploy soldiers to camp within one or more of these compounds. Between 2017 and 2019, Goma's lakefront hosted four distinct mission compounds, referred to in peacekeeper parlance as Regional, TMK, Lava Site, and, its eastern adjacent, Bravo Site.[40] In addition to the Indian QRF, a Senegalese QRF camped within Lava Site between the casting of ballots in late 2018 and the announcement of election results in early 2019. The team of six had been camping in a sort of shed designated as a gathering point in case of an emergency. On one particular visit, I joined the team for an after-lunch dessert, prepared by Amina, the only woman in the group. She had prepared an improvised *soow* (sour milk) combining individual pots of yogurt, bananas, and Cyprina juice from their UN ration stores. Immediately after serving dessert, she started on the fish for dinner. Meanwhile, the men were sitting and lying around on wood pallet benches and cot beds, preparing and circulating *ataaya* (sweet mint tea served in three or more rounds). I helped Amina clear some of the dishes from the lunch, dropping them off in a small room used to store their temporary camping supplies like cookware and extra mattresses. Such QRF deployments, by their presence and practices, are capable of turning even the most administrative of UN compounds into campsites.

Barring the exceptional circumstances that brought Amina and others to camp out at the Lava Site compound, these facilities are used by the UN as office complexes. They accommodate civilian staff from various mission sections and serve as administrative offices for such units as mission support, the central sector brigade, and the force commander. Lava Site abuts one of the city center's radial boulevards and is the largest of the lakeside compounds, containing

a wastewater treatment plant, Level I hospital, and a helipad. The adjoining
Bravo Site has its own branch of the Congolese Trust Merchant Bank as well
as a branch office of Satguru Travel, a popular travel company used by mission staff looking for a place to spend their next paid leave.[41] Three of the four
compounds also have their own restaurants, operated by contractors who also
run some of the most popular restaurants among international interveners and
wealthier Congolese in town. The Lava Site café, run by a member of an elite
local family of hoteliers and restauranteurs, was particularly popular on Friday
evenings for its happy hour, bringing together military and civilian mission
personnel for two-for-one Castell beers and snacks. Contracts for managing
the other two restaurants passed hands in 2019 from a local Belgo-Congolese
family to an Indian businessman, whose success in Bunia led him to open a bar
and restaurant on the main boulevard for nightlife in downtown Goma. Across
the street from the MONUSCO compounds, two new restaurants, also run by
Indian businessmen, have sprung up. One is owned by a long-standing member
of Goma's Indian community who also owns a popular grocery store in town;
the other is run by a pair of young entrepreneurs who began their African business activities in the beverage industry.

As mentioned earlier, the TMK, Bravo Site, and Lava Site compounds occupy land that, during colonial times, hosted the white hospital and an agricultural concession, with large Belgian villas occupying the lots across the
street. In addition to hosting these MONUSCO compounds, this neighborhood appears constantly under construction, with large multistory residences
proliferating that cater to mission staff. Some of these residences are occupied
by military staff officers and MILOBs and organized as "national houses" (e.g.,
Senegal House, Malawi House, etc.). Some of these national houses are organized like hotels to accommodate people passing through, with weekly menus
posted in the kitchen or room tariffs and house rules posted in the living area.
Residents of national houses adorn their windows and balcony railings with
their national flags as if they were embassies or consulates. While this part
of town is well-known for hosting the accommodations and offices of Euro-
American interveners (and researchers like myself), most of the flags flying
outside of multifamily residences represent countries in the Global South.

The significance of this particular part of the lakeshore, built on legacies of
colonial trade regimes and settlement patterns, is socially constructed in both
economic and political terms today. Given the civilian and military headquarters located within MONUSCO's lakeside parcels, Congolese citizens have
frequently mobilized space on the abutting road and at the gates of these compounds to protest and raise claims against the mission. In July 2018, individual

contractors (ICs) hired by the mission staged what would become a five-month long sit-in outside of the Lava Site compound. The ICs were bringing forth compensation claims having to do with issues related to the subcontracting of the United Nations Office of Project Services (UNOPS) to manage their work contracts. Former ICs had begun lodging complaints about missing work certificates in 2015, one year after the outsourcing of subcontracting from MONUSCO to UNOPS, but it was only in the summer of 2018 that those demands fueled the establishment of a protest camp right next to the compound gate.

On October 29, the 105th day of the ICs' sit-in, tensions flared between the mission and former contractors. I was in the TMK compound in the early afternoon when Indian officers working there received a text alert that told all MONUSCO personnel to close their offices and leave. Earlier that day, protestors camping outside of Lava Site down the road had entered the compound along with scores of schoolchildren, sitting and singing inside the gate all day. The protestors had also brought a tarp inside as it had started raining, stirring anxieties within the mission that the protest camp outside had effectively leaked inside.

Major Baba was on his way back to camp when he texted to tell me that the situation had apparently escalated. I walked back down to the lake to find a massive crowd blocking the road outside the compound, the SEN-FPU in full riot gear securing the Bravo Site gate, and an abandoned UN vehicle with its hazard lights flashing after having crashed into multiple parked cars. A few Congolese police officers had gathered around the empty Land Cruiser and were passing around a joint. Major Baba would later tell me that the driver had to be treated at the Level III hospital for the beating he had received by the mob (as Major Baba called it), which included a broken jaw. Protestors I spoke to made no comment about such violence, saying that they were merely trying to tell the driver to slow down before he swerved and crashed.

Many at the site interpreted my presence as a journalistic endeavor and, despite my corrections, approached me to express their grievances. The first man that approached me started quoting lyrics from the Tiken Jah Fakoly song "Plus rien m'étonnes" while another called the Senegalese (charged with crowd control in these types of situations) "dogs." Other insults levied at the Senegalese included that their colonization by the French was to blame for their "complexe" and that they were thieves. One man alleged that they had stolen the phone and money that fell out of his pocket during the scuffle of exiting the compound. People were ushering others who had been in the altercation over to show me their injuries, including a man with an open gash on the back of his head. Another man approached to recount his version of events, asking that I record them. I pulled out my phone and obliged: "Ehh. Enregistrez, enregistrez. Ehh. Monsieur [name redacted] ali sema hivi: Vous les IC, je vous ordonne de quitter à l'extèriur, si vous le voulez pas, je donne l'ordre qu'on tire sur vous. Une, deux, trois, feu!"[42] Another man's voice joined him on *feu*, adding that this announcement was made with a megaphone. I was surprised that the men recognized the voice; this was clearly not their first encounter with MONUSCO security. They highlighted the women and children who were injured in the skirmish, repeating that nineteen people had been sent to the hospital.

I had been there maybe thirty minutes, the time it takes for early dusk to turn to darkness in Goma, when a Congolese police officer came out of the compound among several civilian personnel from the Department of Safety and Security, drawing the crowd's attention. The men I had been speaking to reported back to me. "Kesho. Huit heure. Bata régler situation. Situation ita maliza. Tuna fungolo jia."[43] They broke off as everyone cleared to either side of the street. As I was putting away my notebook, I asked two men nearby what they did when they worked as contractors for MONUSCO. "The Indian camp at Saké . . . we built it," they replied.

One of the people within MONUSCO who had negotiated with the contractors that next morning later explained the logic of the IC sit-in to me as one run by "manipulators" promising participants a share of any financial compensation they might obtain through their confrontation with the mission. While there is likely some truth to that assessment, it is also true that many of the men joining the protest were in fact responsible for building and maintaining the peacekeeping camps and compounds in and around the city. Camps were at the heart of many of their claims for compensation and at the heart of their claim-making practice as both the architecture of the sit-in and site at which they staged their protest. As the IC sit-in and many of the camps reviewed in this chapter attest, encampment in and around Goma tends to beget further encampment as different groups of people struggle for recognition, protection, power, and peace. Days after the sit-in was disbanded, razor wire was installed around the perimeter of the Lava Site compound.

It is worth mentioning that the IC sit-in of 2018 raised specific claims against the mission about working conditions and compensation for Congolese contractors that cannot easily be compared to the more large-scale protests and deadly encounters of recent years between Congolese civilians and the mission.[44] As Sam Kniknie (2022) has illustrated, increasing resentment of the peacekeeping mission in the early 2020s, which has manifested in explicitly anti-MONUSCO citywide protests, have to be seen in light of the resurgence of the M23 armed group. While Congolese perceptions of the force's

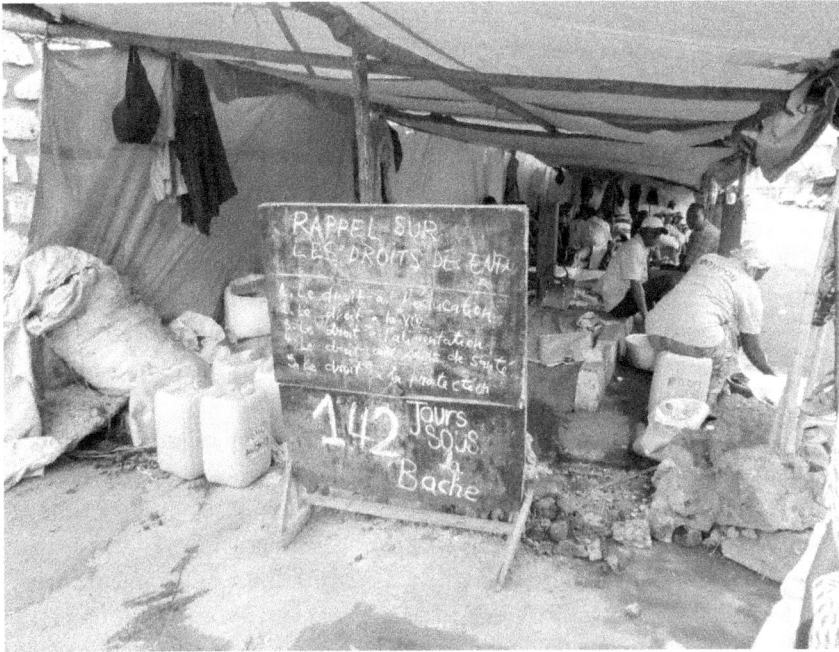

IC sit-in outside of the MONUSCO compound known as Lava Site. (Photo by author)

ineffectiveness were already rather widespread in Goma, they were not acted on between 2017 and 2019 in the same ways and types of confrontations that we've seen more recently. Considerations of the mission as "a white occupying force in the same way that the colonial regime once was" are amended and partially upheld in intricate ways in encounters with nonwhite military men and women (Kniknie 2023). For instance in the IC encounter with Senegalese police, the latter's colonization by the French is acknowledged in the interpretation of their actions. Moreover, as illustrated in subsequent chapters, many peacekeepers serving the mission share Congolese civilians' critiques of MONUSCO.

Conclusion: One Hundred Years of Camping in Goma

This chapter has sought to introduce the reader to the city of Goma through the aperture of the camp as a means of situating the present peacekeeping campscape within a longer history of encampment and more recent urbanization dynamics. Such an entry point has illuminated the various ways in which historical and contemporary iterations of encampment have followed, accompanied, shaped, worked against, and at times driven Goma's urbanization since the early twentieth century. Despite the temporality associated with these spaces, camps have left lasting traces on Goma's urban form and fabric. Histories of encampment figure into the city's security apparatuses, economic development, and social relations in both subtle and decided ways—ways that have proven themselves continuously prone to change. Their appearance (and disappearance) has shaped urban spaces, patterns, and practices, impacting the types of settlements, plot sizes, occupants, built environments, and spatial configurations that were observable in their place and across the cityscape in the late 2010s. Legacies of previous camps endure as historical campscapes are reactivated. Along the city's downtown lakeshore for instance, the geography of MONUSCO compounds and residences inhabited by mission staff follow colonial settlement patterns visible in the city over eighty years prior. Lakefront topographies of power are reactivated by the mission in troops' (re)occupation of colonial military outposts like Mount Goma and military and civilian staff's use of former sites critical to the colonial administration and economy. Given the nature of the facilities and population that work within them, the UN compounds along Lake Kivu both reflect earlier geographies of colonial planning and create new urban configurations by drawing new businesses and residential construction to this part of town that cater to foreign interveners (beyond Euro-Americans). Recognition of the growing service industry catering to MONUSCO staff near the lake, for instance, brings the growth and expansion of the city's entrepreneurial Indian diaspora and their business footprint to the fore.

Colonial settlement patterns are both imitated and contrasted by the contemporary urban geography of MONUSCO. While the mission's administrative headquarters and civilian offices reify the restricted, enclave-esque geography and materiality of Peaceland and its fortified aid compounds (Duffield 2012; Autesserre 2014), situating and contextualizing the location of peacekeeping camps in and around the city expands this geography to parts of the city not normally dwelt on when thinking about the spatiality of international intervention. Peacekeeping camps are located where they are today for several reasons including strategic considerations, operational viability, economic efficiency, and political convenience. It is critical to recognize the responsibilities and functions of different peacekeeping camps and compounds to understand the logic of their physical location in the city. Concentrations of camps on the northern and western axis roads are important to dominate these and other critical infrastructures, such as the airport, and to facilitate temporary deployments to active conflict zones further afield. In contrast to the politics of military occupation, the geographies of peacekeeping camps are not the result of the brute force of MONUSCO's military component. Rather, their territorialization can be seen as the result of exchanges between multiple actors across various times and scales. Given the duration of the mission and its preparations for an eventual withdrawal, budget constraints and available land began playing an increasingly important role in the situation of various bases around the city (and their dismantling).

As in any military base, shifting conflict dynamics and operational responses by armed forces shape the spatial and material environments of peacekeepers living in camps in and around the city. The spatial evolution of conflict and of the peacekeeping mission itself has been a determining factor in the progressive shift of personnel and equipment to Goma over the past decade and the proliferation of COBs in and around the city. As troop presence has increased, many bases like the South African CHU camp have had limited opportunities for growth and expansion, forcing contingents to rely on their own resources, initiatives, and creativity to solve issues related to space constraints.

Camps are key to the architecture of peacekeeping's efforts to end violent conflict and, for Goma, the origins of it. The aftermath of the Rwandan genocide as it played out around Goma highlights how encampment played an incredibly geopolitical role in the escalation of violence that would finally elicit a response from the international community. Making camp can articulate broader claims of legitimacy and territory and of controlling elsewheres beyond the confines of the camp itself. The exploitation by *génocidaires* of the protection and assistance that refugee camps north and west of Goma provided allowed them to regroup and sustain armed elements, rearm for a reprisal of armed conflict, and reconsolidate power through their authority over the camps. In ways similar to other iterations of camps of exile (cf. Herz and ETH Studio Basel 2013), Goma's refugee camps became a political instrument for the former Rwandan regime. Control of elsewhere for the *génocidaires* was as much about exercising their authority in Goma as it was about claiming political legitimacy in Rwanda. This historical example is just one of the many ways that actors occupy and operationalize camp space to make claims at broader scales and reveals the nature of insights that can be gleaned by looking at the protracted conflict in the eastern DRC through the lens of the camp.

This influential camp moment in Goma's history equally elucidates the fluid characteristic of camps. The liquid metaphors used to describe the Rwandan refugees' arrival in Goma (e.g., river, wave, and flood) are an important reminder of the "unsettled" nature of camp settlements, their fundamental connections to human mobility, and the theoretical relevance of a liquidity that attunes one to the flows and journeys that underpin the camp. Unlike Zygmunt Bauman's (2000, 2) understanding of the liquid metaphor however, camps in Goma do not emphasize the flow of time in lieu of the significance of their spatial dimensions. They seep into the place of the city as much as they spill over in time. The enduring real and symbolic power of camps in Mugunga, for instance, attest to the way that land holds on to its experience of camp, regenerating new iterations in the same places. Camp space in Goma is not constructed on land that is tabula rasa but rather continues and transforms earlier forms of camping that have shaped how the city has grown and what it continues to become. The camps described here can therefore be said to have a fluid nature in their ability to seep into the land, altering citywide growth and urbanization dynamics for decades to come while retaining a level of unsettledness and ephemerality. Subsequent chapters maintain an attention to the contradictions of camps highlighted here—settled and unsettled, spatially bound and liquid, enduring and ephemeral—to unpack what camping in Goma means today and the impacts it continues to have in the making of the city.

In introducing the reader to the city of Goma as read through its camp spaces and practices, it becomes clear that "making camp" is intimately intertwined with the making of the city. In some respects, camps have literally and figuratively put Goma on the map—from the first Belgian outpost in the small village of Ngoma, to labor encampments that helped fuel the economy of Goma during the Interwar period, to the international media attention around the Rwandan refugee experience in the Zairean camps. While peacekeeping camps remain "off the map" in terms of their academic consideration as a feature and factor in Goma's urban landscape today, this chapter has sought to situate them within the story of the city's urbanization, the evolution of peacekeeping in eastern Congo, and the conflict dynamics to which the mission continues to respond. Such a site-specific genealogy has allowed for an account of the historical interplay and co-construction between "the camp" and "the city"—a dynamic, I argue, that persists today in forging Goma's urban character.

2

Through the Gates

For there to be an interior and an exterior one must go in and come out, rather than crossing from side to side. The spaces of dwelling are not already given, in the layout of the building, but are created in movement.

—Timothy Ingold, *Making*, 85

Having reviewed the historical campscape and more contemporary geography of peacekeeping camps in Goma, this chapter turns to approach the gates of peacekeeping camps. As architecturally solid yet penetrable, the gates of the peacekeeping camp represent a productive tension that complicates clear distinctions between the dwelling spaces of foreign peacekeepers and residents of Goma. Beginning at the threshold where these two spaces are most visibly united offers a literal and notional threshold space through which to explore contemporary formations of urbanity between the city of Goma and the peacekeeping camps it hosts. Camp gates are points of porousness that form a boundary between city and barracks, acknowledging that "a boundary is not that at which something stops but, as the Greeks recognized, the boundary is that from which something *begins its presencing*" (Heidegger 1971, 154; emphasis in original, cited in Casey 2001). Neither the dwelling space of the camp nor the city stops at the gates of a given base. Rather, as this chapter illustrates, they leak into one another through the movements of city dwellers and soldiers in and out.

Thinking through the gates allows me to trace the ways that movement in and out of the camp shape the social landscape of which they are a part. I use a vocabulary of landscape to understand a process of forming social and subjective identities—one that is constantly becoming (Mitchell 2012; Biehl and Locke 2017). John Urry's (2005) words highlight the relevance of adopting a language of "-scapes" within which to discuss places created, in part, by a mobile, deployed group like peacekeepers. He writes: "The language of landscape is thus a language of mobility, of abstract characteristics. It is not just that such mobility is necessary if one is to develop the capacity to be reflexive about landscape. It is also that landscape talk is itself an expression of the lifeworld of mobile groups" (81). Talk of a common social landscape also allows for attunement to the flows and leaks between various elements emanating from but not remaining strictly within any spatially bounded notion of the city or the camp (Appadurai 1996; Martin 2015).

As Paul Rabinow's (2011, xi) field notes remind us, field data are the "constructs of the process by which we acquire them." Travel through the gates was one of the primary ways in which I "discursively mapped and corporeally practiced" the space of my field—one that I chose to locate between the camp and the city as analytical objects (Clifford 1997, 186). They also came to constitute an important field site in and of themselves. As we shall see in this chapter, the camp as an interactional space and peacekeepers' disposition to interacting with Goma's inhabitants are constructed through both experiences of nearness and encounter, as well as distanciation and separation. The operational activities of peacekeepers remain important to the analysis, but only insofar as peacekeepers' lives become visible (or invisible) in Goma as a city rather than as a zone of intervention. This shift in perspective allows us to explore multiple modes of existence among peacekeepers, to multiply the lifeworlds they dwell and journey in, and to foreground the social correspondences between encamped peacekeepers and Goma's urbanites.

In the pages that follow, I follow people through the gates in both directions, exploring multiple interactions and perceptions that shape understandings and experiences of peacekeepers' presence in the city. I start at the gates themselves, where we meet polyglot children, shop for new gym clothes, and begin to question existing understandings of the nexus between international intervention and the urban environment. I then accompany Major Baba to an English classroom where he is confronted with some of the negative perspectives and sentiments of the local population from a youth perspective, which provide some context against which to trace "winning hearts and minds" (WHAM) activities that peacekeeping contingents carry out in Goma and in their camps to counter these attitudes. Attending an Urafiki Meeting that brings Congolese civilians and contingent leadership together in a base offers a glimpse into the ambivalence created by certain encounters.[1] We leave the camp again to follow peacekeepers as they conduct activities related to their operational mandate. I discuss the politics of knowledge and the (mis)understandings that shape how contingents intervene (or not) in different security scenarios in Goma and how their views of the city are shaped more generally. Lastly, this chapter accompanies David and Pierre, two Congolese language assistants (LAs) back to the camp to discuss the roles played by different Congolese civilians to military contingents. Language work and community liaising constitute an important part of peacekeeping, one that inevitably creates unlikely and predictable entanglements between the city and its peacekeeping camps.

Instead of merely reinforcing the notion that foreign interveners live in a bubble in Goma and other urban contexts like it (Bittner, Hackenbroich, and Vöckler 2010; Autesserre 2014; Smirl 2015; Büscher 2016), I explore some of the cultural concepts underpinning how peacekeepers work to burst certain bubbles and how they themselves understand the necessity of maintaining others. In both encounters with the local population and avoidance of certain situations, peacekeepers are constantly coproducing understandings of place across and between their camps and the city. To focus on how peacekeepers understand the conflict in relation to their mandate and how that understanding shapes their spatial practices in Goma is to realize that peacekeeping camps— through peacekeepers and others' movements in and out—are anything but self-contained bubbles or isolated islands.

At the Gates of the Camp

In northeastern Goma, where camps are concentrated in and around the airport, neighborhood youth turn peacekeeping camp gates into gathering spaces. The older ones, in their early teens, chit-chat with the soldiers stationed in the sentinel towers or sitting inside the doorway. Younger children play with bottlecaps and other trash littered around the camp perimeters, waiting for a chance to chase after vehicles moving in and out of the camps and sometimes even catching a short ride down the road. Water trucks offer particularly good opportunities for one or more of the children to latch on before being shooed off as they enter the base.

Young cliques can often be seen outside of the shared Tanzanian and Bangladeshi base keeping the local police officer company while waiting for peacekeepers to pass. Peacekeepers' movements to and from the base provide the children with a window within which they often entreat the troops for cookies (*biscuits*), with occasional success. On one particular visit, the perimeter of the neighboring Ukrainian camp was covered in meal ready-to-eat packaging,

Children at the gate of the former Camp Jambaar. (Photo by author)

signs of successful ration negotiations on the part of the youngsters. Through their assembly at these sites, they transform infrastructures of entry and exit into key hangout spots and spaces of opportunity, even if those opportunities are limited to a packet of cookies or two.

MONUSCO officially forbids contingents from sharing rations with local civilians, though several, if not most contingents have broken this rule at one point or another. Colonel Martín admitted that his battalion shares rations and uses medical stockpiles to treat local civilians outside of formal medical campaigns when no one is looking, practices that are met with harsh reprimands by the UN. He justified his actions and rebuked the UN leadership who created these regulations saying, "They are not seeing them [Congolese children] grabbing the concertina wire, looking at [us] saying, 'I'm hungry.'"

Farther up airport road, before Camp Jambaar was closed, the Senegalese camp gate was a recreational one—complete with a small billiard table to amuse the children between demands for food. The Senegalese, however, were a bit more cautious with their leftovers. There had been an incident in 2016 or

2017 that caused a bit of a stir in the neighborhood and prompted the *chef du quartier* of Bujovu to confront the Senegalese about their selective sharing of rations. Senegalese enjoy mutton in their cuisine but generally do not eat the sheep's intestines. The Congolese, on the other hand, do. As such, the Senegalese had a habit of giving the entrails of the sheep they had killed in their camp to their "girlfriends," creating some tensions in the neighborhood between the "haves" and the "have nots." According to the chef himself, he approached the colonel of the camp directly and the practice ceased.

Across from the former Camp Jambaar is the Indian Brigade camp. Up until early 2018, barbed wire fencing backed up by corrugated galvanized iron sheets delimited the boundaries of the camp. To strengthen the camp's security in the run-up to the 2018 election, the brigade transformed its fence into a permanent, walled perimeter. The solidification of this separating feature has not stopped small exchanges from happening on the camp's edges. The wall has since been painted with Primus beer advertisements, and kids mill about exchanging greetings with officers and *jawans* in Hindi, including requests for chapati.[2] While all camps have their own small groups of children who gather near the gates, no gate is more popular or interactive than that of the Uruguayan battalion (URUBATT). With their long-standing presence in Goma, Uruguayans are particularly popular among young teens. And if the group of teenagers who loiter around peacekeeping camp gates had a ringleader, it would certainly be Fidel.

Fidel has grown up in Bujovu near Kwa Bisimwa, the main square of the neighborhood. He and his friends tread paths through the town's first and largest cemetery to get to Airport Road's stretch of peacekeeping camps almost daily. On any given day, Fidel can be spotted insulting and exchanging jokes with soldiers through the metal cutout of the Uruguayan camp gate, tagging along with Bangladeshi soldiers on their trips to small pop-up markets next to their camps, or standing across from the Senegalese camp gate waiting for someone to buy him a stick of meat. He has managed to get all sorts of things out of almost every contingent in his neighborhood, but the Uruguayan camp is his primary turf.

Fidel's privileged relationship and familiarity with URUBATT has much to do with the duration of the Uruguayan army's presence in Goma and the small size of their military. URUBATT has existed in Goma since the CNDP era (2006–8), when Fidel was just a toddler. Uruguay's small army and UN troop contributing reputation makes it easy for soldiers to make repeated tours in Goma. For one of the officers at the URUBATT camp in 2018—one who did not get along well with Fidel—this was his sixth tour in Congo and second in Goma. Such repeated exposure to the mission environment is a common refrain from Uruguayans when asked to substantiate the closeness many of them feel to the local population. Bringing more "mature soldiers," as one commander put it, may breed complacency but also has its advantages. In 2018, a soldier guarding the perimeter of the base recognized one of the young men milling around their gate as someone who was smuggling narcotics onto the base three years prior and was therefore able to prevent a repeated incident.

Given these unique characteristics of the Uruguayan army in Goma, Fidel, along with many other children from Bujovu, have grown up with the soldiers of URUBATT. One of the effects of this sustained encounter is Fidel and his friends' ability to speak fluent Spanish. Most of the neighborhood gate kids have adopted Spanish names and, with each rotation, quickly learn the names, ranks, and roles of at least every officer in the camp. Fidel recognizes the rich social capital his gate practice has gotten him and sees himself going to work for the Uruguayans as an LA or community liaison assistant (CLA) when he is older. David, the current Congolese LA for URUBATT (whom we meet in the introduction and meet again later in this chapter), sees Fidel's strategy a little differently. He points out that most of the children at the gates cut school to earn whatever little money they can get out of the different soldiers, adding, "If they don't want to study, they will stay like that."[3]

Fidel is of course not alone in his truancy and mendicancy. Children around camp gates converse with peacekeepers in Spanish, Wolof, Hindi, and Russian, with varying degrees of fluency, as a means of improving their chances of getting something from the soldiers. Multilingual kids like Fidel and others at different camp gates reveal the multisensorial way that the camp leaks into the city around it. The specific languages that are leaking additionally work to challenge existing ideas about language in the intervention nexus and the dialectical relationship between the city and the camp in shaping a worlded form of urbanity. Gates and other physical interstices between Goma and the camps provide some of the most visible markers of how camps create a break with the city, as well as some of the most audible indicators of connection.

The few discussions that exist on language in peacekeeping generally focus on the linguistic ability of troops. Their ability or inability to speak the language of the mission environment is often analyzed in terms of consequences on their operational performance and relationships with communities (Heinecken and Ferreira 2012; Aning and Edu-Afful 2017). Maria Rose Garrido's (2017) analysis of multilingualism in humanitarianism more broadly discusses the cosmopolitan capital constructed by the iconization of French and English and the mobility of expatriate staff. The fluency of neighboring children in Spanish or Hindi reveals that the tactics of local residents to access the opportunities brought by this international presence need not rely solely on competences in English and French (the common working languages of many international organizations and nongovernmental organizations [NGOs]). Young people create their own cosmopolitan identities rooted in more anonymous languages and aspirations of mobility that transcend their current situation in Goma. Rather than acquiring standard and universal languages "from nowhere" to world themselves, they adopt the local languages of peacekeepers—languages "from somewhere" or, in this case, multiple elsewheres (Garrido 2017). The urbanity thus forged in gate spaces is worlded along new and numerous trajectories, rather than normative centers associated with English and French.

These youngsters' linguistic efforts to encounter peacekeepers also need to be seen within the context of the distance that language barriers create. With the exception of the francophone Senegalese and the swahiliphone Tanzanians, local language knowledge among peacekeeping officers is often limited to single-word cautions and greetings. Warning words my peacekeeper interlocutors knew in Swahili included "No," "Stop," "No food," and "I don't bring money." Many knew greetings for "Hello" and "How are you" as well as the word "friend" in both French and Swahili. The phrase made famous by Disney's *The Lion King*—"hakuna matata"—often represented the extent of their local language knowledge. To help the sentinels guarding the perimeters of the Bangladeshi Military Police's (BANMP) camp in Goma, a laminated script is kept at all lookout posts with the warning. "Umoja wa mataifa, simama, kama haiku vile nda kupiga masisi" (MONUSCO. Stop there. If you do not, I will shoot you). The script is translated into English, French, Swahili, and Lingala. Bangla transliterations accompany the latter three translations.

When peacekeepers descend from their sentinel towers and leave their camps, Fidel and other multilingual children follow, positioning themselves as liaisons within the camp-city interface at small pop-up markets that appear in the city around camp perimeters. The most popular of these is what peacekeepers refer to simply as Sunday Market. Sunday Market offers UN military personnel from across the city and its outskirts bargains on electronics, souvenirs, and secondhand sportswear. Sportswear is the most prevalent item at the market, reflecting Congolese vendors' keen understanding of the importance of physical training for their target customers. Despite the overwhelmingly gendered profile of contingent troops, used athletic wear for men, women, and children is available and purchased by peacekeepers for their families. Children poised to accompany troops through the market position themselves at the entrance and tag along with marketgoers, often looking out for specific soldiers who consider them to be their buddy pair or personal shopping assistant. Different kids approach different nationalities based on their language abilities. Only one of the older children speaks some Russian and therefore hops around between Ukrainian shoppers, helping them communicate with the vendors in hopes of a small kickback—some cash, a banana, or some fresh *frites* frying near the entrance. Uruguayans, who live just across the street from the market, are considered some of the most valuable customers.

In July 2019, when Goma registered its first Ebola case in the DRC's longest and largest outbreak to date, several contingents swiftly halted their outings to Sunday Market and other shops around town. On one Sunday that the Uruguayans were absent, Fidel hurled insults about them while vendors complained about the slow business. I offered up the optimistic observation that the Bangladeshis were still coming to the market, only for one vendor to rebut that Bangladesh was an "inchi ya maskini"—a country of poor people. Without the Ukrainians and Uruguayans coming to shop, the vendors described life in the market as "hauna holari." No dollars. As David, the URUBATT LA, confirmed, "Without the Uruguayans, they [the market vendors] don't have a life."[4] This distinction among peacekeepers highlights the heterogeneity of peacekeeping troops and Congolese perceptions of them. It also highlights a perception of whiteness as a marker of wealth that expands the geographies more commonly associated with such a racial category in international interventions and in African contexts (namely, the United States and Western Europe) (Pierre 2013; T. Hendriks 2017). Such differences are deemed substantial by the vendors though rarely accounted for in discussions of urban spaces of peacekeeping and the small peacekeeping economies that the market is a part of (Jennings 2015; Oldenburg 2015).

Focusing on the gates of peacekeeping camps adds an explicit place-based dimension to such frameworks. This allows for ensuing analyses and theorizations to transcend a focus on understanding this conflict nexus in favor of concentrating on an urban nexus that accounts for the ways in which the places peacekeepers come from shape peacekept places and practices. By reterritorializing the intervention nexus through peacekeeping camps and their urban, host environment, gates become illuminative spaces. Peacekeeping camp gates do not simply separate the camp from the city. They act as important spaces of encounter that shape different spatial, social, and peacekeeping practices in the city and those of the communities that live nearby. Communicative practices and new urban spaces like those of the markets that spring up around

Congolese youth translate and negotiate prices for military personnel as they shop at the Sunday Market held next to the ITIG football grounds. (Photo by author)

peacekeeping bases illustrate unexpected correspondences between these camps and the city that audibly and transactionally transcend the boundaries between them.

Winning Goma's Hearts and Minds

Camp-city encounters occur not only when residents approach the camp looking for opportunities big and small but also when peacekeepers go out looking for opportunities to leave a positive impression on the city. Beyond more leisurely Sunday Market excursions, peacekeepers engage in activities aimed at winning hearts and minds, activities more often described as WHAM in military lingo. The phrase as military doctrine traces its origins to French projects of colonial conquest and has received renewed attention as militaries involved in counterinsurgency operations have sought to adopt more population-centric approaches (González 2008; Egnell 2010; Porch 2010). My focus here on

WHAM seeks to understand how such practices take shape in the context of peacekeeping and are perceived in Goma, in turn shaping how Congolese civilians and foreign peacekeepers live together (and apart). Only one peacekeeping camp has an operational mandate to protect civilians in Goma but nearly all contingents based in the city organize activities that they qualify as WHAM. For many officers, winning the hearts and minds of Goma's residents is not only critical to the success of their mission but also one of the most personally fulfilling parts of their tenure. In relation to military operations in their home countries, many see peacekeeping operations and the room accorded to civil-military coordination (CIMIC) as allowing them to show a more human side of themselves. Officers in Goma emphasize the importance of the trust-building measures and goodwill gestures involved in WHAM in terms of relying on the population for information and enhancing the safety of troops in the mission area. Other contingent commanders see winning hearts and minds not as a means, but as an end, framing the importance of different activities for their impacts on the local population. Resigned to the impossibility of achieving the mission mandate, Lieutenant Colonel Dev once put it thus: "If you can't stop armed groups, focus on WHAM."

To understand how peacekeeping contingents approach these activities, it is worth briefly discussing the baseline status of the community's hearts and minds that peacekeepers so eagerly work to win. Several reports conclude that the Congolese population in general had a low opinion of MONUC/MONUSCO during the years under study here (Vinck, Pham, and Makoond 2017; Novosseloff et al. 2019). A series of surveys led by the Harvard Humanitarian Initiative in Goma between 2013 and 2017 have highlighted that people's confidence in MONUSCO to ensure security fluctuates but hit new lows in early 2017. The majority of respondents in Goma had an average or bad opinion of MONUSCO but, compared to several other regions across eastern Congo, had the lowest percent of respondents reporting a very bad opinion (1%) (Vinck, Pham, and Makoond 2017). However, attitudes toward the mission seem to have worsened since this study's completion, culminating in the violent protests that erupted in July 2022 that left thirty-six people dead (including four peacekeepers). Tensions in Goma never reached such a tenor between 2017 and 2020, though protests like the IC sit-in (detailed in the previous chapter) and several individual encounters illustrated a mix of animosity and indifference.

These mixed feelings (and some of their origins) are perhaps best exemplified in a series of exchanges with students at one of Goma's many English clubs. On one of my visits, I was asked to present some of my preliminary research findings and concluded my presentation by asking attendees about their own encounters with and ideas about MONUSCO personnel. Club members' attitudes ranged from seeing peacekeepers as self-interested do-nothings to accusing them of conducting illegal activities. Grace, a woman in her late twenties, proclaimed that "there is something going wrong" with MONUSCO soldiers, earlier claiming that peacekeepers were collecting resources and "stealing" from Congo. The Congolese students were highly critical of the fact that peacekeepers come from countries in the Global South. They called the Indians "weird" and commented on their perceived lack of education. Furaha, who fled Congo with her family during the First Congo War and lived in a camp in Kenya before resettling in Scandinavia, expressed that, "when I see them, I feel weird. I see a person looking for his own interest. They just want to win money—like *mayibobos* in their country."[5] One student went so far as to say that if the international community wanted to finish insecurity, they could do it, though not perhaps with the current profile of peacekeepers: "Europe and America can decide and finish it."

Peacekeepers from the Global South are perceived as having some power, however, as one student thought that their presence alone was pushing Congolese people further into poverty through a combination of rising prices in town and limited job opportunities that MONUSCO and other NGOs provide to the local population. As our time ran up, the discussion took a particularly reflexive turn, with English Club members questioning their own attitudes, wondering if their perspectives were shaped by having higher expectations of peacekeepers than what their mandate requires. Someone suggested that peacekeepers "ask us what we expect from them." This led another person to chime in, "Maybe we want MONUSCO to leave because we don't know what they do. They should tell people about their mission." I knew the perfect person to comply with the students' request.

Major Baba was initially hesitant about visiting and presenting at the English Club. On the one hand, he saw the benefits that such an exchange could offer in raising awareness about the mission among Goma residents. He was keenly aware that "perception management" was part of his mandate as a peacekeeper. On the other hand, however, such activities were the job of the public information part of the mission, and he was unsure if his military superiors would approve of such an activity. He eventually obliged, justifying his participation as informal and voluntary. The students were not the "shark tank" that Major Baba was anticipating but were as courteous as always, greeting him as they filed in. After briefly introducing himself, students' hands started flying up. The first exchange set the tone, "What exactly is the mission?" Gédeon, a club regular, asked. Major Baba smiled and replied, "I ask myself this question."

Nearly one-third of Goma residents did not know what MONUSCO's role was in 2017 (Vinck, Pham, and Makoond 2017).

The students continued bringing forth personal testimonies of peacekeeping inaction and asking the major's opinion about various mission dynamics. Several of the students' questions were framed by the notion that, as Gédéon put it, "According to Congolese people, MONUSCO is a part of the conflict in DRC." Major Baba fielded the questions and brought facts to bear on some of the rumors that attendees had heard about the mission, particularly in relation to the government's authorization for peacekeepers to be there, the government going into debt by paying peacekeepers, MONUSCO's involvement in the natural resources trades, and their impunity in sexual exploitation and abuse (SEA) cases. He made sure that the English students knew that MONUSCO and the DRC had a contract and that if anyone violates that contract, "the government can send us back." He was also particularly keen to correct one student's perception around the last point, pointing out different accountability mechanisms in place and the general decrease in SEA cases over time in the mission. He asserted that the Indian army, for instance, has not had an SEA case brought against them in MONUSCO in several years.

One student testified that he witnessed people being killed in front of a MONUSCO base in Beni, asking Major Baba if he saw this as a failure of peacekeeping. Major Baba took his time before responding, "I see it as a failure," qualifying that it is often the speed and intensity of attacks that leave peacekeepers little time to react, even when the violence is happening just outside the gates. "If we know about it, we can prevent the attack from happening." For Major Baba, knowing about and assessing the likelihood of violence depends in large part on the Congolese civilian assistants working with the mission, as they constitute a primary link to the population and "the filter through which all information is flowing." When another student asked how they could contact peacekeepers with problems, Major Baba circulated the telephone number that forms part of MONUSCO's Community Alert Network, of which none of the students were previously aware. He clarified that as military personnel, it is not their job to interact directly with the population, later admitting several exceptions, including playing games with locals to create goodwill.

I debriefed with Major Baba over pizza and beers. After the English Club encounter, he had a renewed sense of the importance of WHAM and its ability to provide a better image of peacekeepers than those that currently circulate in many of the hearts and minds of Goma. WHAM creates the space for encounters with the population, a space that can also strategically shrink through rules and regulations dealing with peacekeepers' conduct in the mission area (as we see later in this chapter). Two related activities—quick impact projects (QIPs) and those that peacekeepers refer to as CIMIC activities—are key ways in which contingents in Goma practice community engagement in the name of WHAM. While QIPs occur out in the city and involve brick-and-mortar projects, CIMIC activities can take place within contingent camps themselves, building bridges with the community not by going out to meet it but by inviting it in. Despite different conceptual origins, doctrines, and military definitions of CIMIC (Franke 2006; DPKO and DFS 2014), peacekeepers in Goma use CIMIC and WHAM nearly interchangeably to describe organized, community engagement activities. Often, individual national contingents mobilize their own resources to conduct activities that establish a relationship with the people in the immediate vicinity of their bases. These efforts, which go well beyond mission requirements for conducting CIMIC activities or QIPs, seek to project a positive image not only of the United Nations peacekeeper but particularly of the national soldier and his country of origin. These activities, impelled by obligation, benevolence, or soft diplomacy, constitute some of, if not *the* primary bridge between peacekeeping camps and the city.

Engaging the Community in the City and the Camp

UN peacekeeping sees QIPs as confidence building measures that reinforce the mission's idea that infrastructure can help create the social conditions for peace.[6] Longer-term projects, like the rehabilitation of the prison in Goma (Musenze) and various roadwork improvements are often cited as QIPs because of the material permanence these projects carry although they have much larger budgets than the quick-impact maximum of USD 50,000 and are spearheaded by different actors (namely, different UN agencies). These larger projects, particularly roadwork, were exclusively cited by former mayor Roger Rachid Tumbula when asked about the mission's presence and impact relative to urban development. Military and civilian personnel equally cite these projects as the most visible impacts that the peacekeeping presence has on the built environment of Goma. Projects funded through QIPs and completed in Goma in the late 2010s include the development of a solid waste dumping site, improvement of garbage collection (through new garbage collection trucks gifted to the municipality), and a tree planting initiative (conceived of for the reintegration of ex-combatants through the DDRRR program). The head of office admits, however, that many of the small assets that the mission has helped procure for the City of Goma through these projects having fallen into disrepair.

Paul, a middle-aged Congolese MONUSCO staffer who manages these projects, calls QIPs the civilian equivalent to the military's WHAM, acknowledging that it was in fact the military practice of winning hearts and minds that inspired quick-impact projects to be spearheaded by civilian sections. While the military remains more strictly focused on reaching the hearts and minds of Goma's residents through community engagement, the mission as a whole increasingly fuses a hearts-and-minds approach with a literally concrete approach, one that privileges using infrastructure as a tool for peace (Bachmann and Schouten 2018; Danielak 2022). Paul describes QIPs as emerging in the space between people's lack of awareness about what MONUSCO does and the state's inability to fulfill its role in different sectors. According to him, QIPs seek to follow a formal process that begins with the needs expressed by the community and to "accompany things that work already so that they work better." The benefits for peace to be gained by QIPs are thus not only articulated in terms of the infrastructural output but also the processes that such projects engender. MONUSCO favors projects that bring people together with more frequency and makes them work together. As Paul put it, stakeholders begin to understand that it is only through their cooperation that project funding can be unlocked or won.

Paul recounts that QIPs were originally meant to build up the capacity and legitimacy of the state in line with the mission-wide stabilization strategy. As a result, government offices built by the mission sprang up across the region. In Goma, MONUSCO helped rehabilitate the Governor's Office and police motorcycles brandished with the MONUSCO logo still circulate in parts of Ndosho, reflecting the quick-impact strategy before the mission shifted toward more general capacity building and larger infrastructure projects. These projects are, however, overwhelmingly implemented by different civilian sections in the mission, with only about 20 percent of project funding being allocated to military contingents.[7] Contingents' share of QIPs decreased largely as a result of their greater visibility (in relation to civilian staff) and of the WHAM activities they were already undertaking on their own. Rather than creating connections between different communities, encamped contingents in Goma are more concerned with forging connections between themselves and local communities and sharing these achievements with their communities back home. Civil-military coordination is key to making these connections.

Many of the efforts of contingents to win Goma's hearts and minds have foregone the brick-and-mortar emphasis illustrated in quick-impact projects and instead have been focused on organizing sporting events, English language classes, and skills development courses. The BANMP contingent has a

Bangladesh Military Police organize a football match in Goma between ITIG and Don Bosco Academy. (Photo by author)

particularly strong interest in enhancing friendly relationships with the community due to the type of work they do in the city. One of the key tasks of BANMP is to promote the safety of MONUSCO military personnel in the city and investigate any incidents or accidents that involve these actors. This includes traffic accidents, which are common in Goma's busy streets and are quick to create a point of tension between the mission and Goma residents. As such, Lieutenant Colonel Janeeb cites a lack of cooperation among local civilians and the Congolese National Police (PNC) as a particular challenge to their operations in Goma. CIMIC activities are one of the main ways through which BANMP attempts to create conditions that foster trust between their contingent and the local community. It was in this vein that one rotation of BANMP organized a friendly football match for teams from two schools situated next their base. The contingent donated some of their funds to the participating organizations and provided "Bangladesh"-branded football uniforms in red and green to the players. Winners received a trophy and goodie bag that contained notebooks adorned with the Bangladeshi flag and a map of "Beautiful Bangladesh" along with packets of oral rehydration salts.[8]

Sports fields are a popular place to create friendly encounters between the MONUSCO force and the community in Goma, as are peacekeeping camps themselves. In addition to going out to engage communities through sports matches, Lieutenant Colonel Dev equally developed and implemented English language lessons and skills development courses that brought Goma residents into his camp. Noncommissioned officers (NCOs) ran the English courses in the camp's lecture hall (supervised by a junior commissioned officer), while *jawans* from the battalion's engineering unit ran the skills development courses, which covered basic computer skills, carpentry, mechanics, welding, vehicle maintenance, and firefighting. The contingent recruited thirty students at a time (all from a single neighborhood) through its LAs and CLAs, ensuring that only one person per household participated for the widest impact. Courses ran for six weeks before students were recruited from another neighborhood. Dev hoped to get through all eighteen neighborhoods before he left. He calls both the English and skills development courses offered in his base "peacekeeping by empowerment," something he relates to activities conducted in field areas in India. The language and vocational trainings offered by the battalion are seen as giving participants a wide range of skills to better help them enter the job market. In Lieutenant Colonel Dev's own words: "I started skill development courses for civilians here because the society here wanted a sort of a vocational training. And maybe out of 120 odd locals trained till now, only 20 would have got employment. But I see it as transforming 20 families not 20 individuals. And all these small ingredients of peacekeeping is what will make the city self-sustaining without in the end a requirement of an IPF [international peacekeeping force]. Empower people for themselves so much that joining an armed group isn't an option. That would be my end game." Even contingents like Uruguay's, which does not have a direct operational mandate in Goma, carry out projects in the city outside of any codified obligation to conduct WHAM or CIMIC. These activities consist mainly of charitable giving through food and clothing donations as well as beautification projects. Regarding donations, Major Alonso recounted being surprised when, one day, the mission asked his battalion about the value of the donations coming from Uruguay. It had never occurred to him that the UN would consider the significance of these donations in financial terms and that Uruguay's contribution to peacekeeping could be offset through such altruistic actions. This was never, in his mind, the intent behind the battalion's charitable giving.

Combining benevolence and aesthetics, Uruguayan artist Walter Blanco flies in with incoming contingents to the DRC, painting murals in different orphanages by day and working on paintings on the sides of the CORIMEC prefabs in URUBATT by night, before flying back with the outgoing contingent. The battalion's community engagement lasts well beyond when Walter leaves, as NCOs organize different food donations, psychological services, and recreational activities in these same orphanages.[9] Colonel Martín asserted that the Uruguayan army had been doing WHAM activities in peacekeeping areas before the UN had truly embraced it as a concept. He spoke of URUBATT III's experience in Angola, whereby every soldier in the battalion used to look after one or two children who lived nearby. They wrote letters back home to Uruguay to let the incoming troops know what size clothing to bring before handing over responsibility for the child to the new rotation, informing the newcomer of the child's treatment history at the infirmary, for instance. URUBATT III was also giving their leftovers to the local population until the line of people waiting became so long that the cooks were making extra food to be able to feed everyone. The battalion in Goma (URUBATT IV) obeys the UN regulations forbidding ration spending on local civilians. Most of the time.

Examples of charitable giving, capacity-building programs, or sporting events illustrate the ways in which peacekeepers present in Goma engage with the communities that they camp among in ways that far surpass UN-mandated coordination activities (for better or worse). For contingents operationally responsible for the city, however, the UN mandates one specific type of community engagement activity conceptualized in the direct service of enhancing civilian protection—Urafiki Meetings.

Urafiki Meetings constitute a key engagement strategy between peacekeepers and the populations that they are mandated to protect. They also constitute another rare occasion in Goma during which urban actors (represented by local governments, religious organizations, NGOs, and security forces) are invited inside of the camp. Peacekeeping camps that have operational responsibilities for Goma and its peripheral communities hold monthly Urafiki Meetings to communicate with the population about their security concerns and receive community feedback about different activities conducted by the contingent. On the morning of his first Urafiki of the year, Lieutenant Colonel Ranbir was running around the officers' administrative quarters wrapping up his daily checklist, situation report, and fuel transaction form. He would wait until everyone had arrived at the camp to make his entrance to the meeting. Meanwhile, a group of *jawans* were busy setting up tables for serving chai and biscuits next to the gazebo labeled *nukta za mkutano*, or "meeting point" in Swahili. Guests filed in slowly, delaying teatime and the meeting. Back in the administrative quarters of the camp, Lieutenant Colonel Ranbir let me know that they were expecting a representative from the Force Armée de la Republique Démocratique du Congo (FARDC) at this meeting and that this could create tensions with the civilians present. "They will fight. You will see."

We walked together with the CLA, who would translate the meeting, to the gazebo where seventeen different chiefs (of villages and *groupements*), Local Protection Committee members, NGO representatives, and a captain from the FARDC were waiting. We took our seats on one side of the gazebo behind a small glass coffee table. Lieutenant Colonel Ranbir congratulated the Congolese for their peaceful elections, quickly reported on some of his contingent's recent operations, and elicited inputs on suspected armed group activity in the area and places that may need heavier patrolling. The first participant to speak complained about FARDC soldiers drinking and shooting their guns in the night; another of an FARDC soldier firing on a civilian. One area was facing a crisis of legitimacy between two chiefs, or *mwamis*, with meeting participants blaming MONUSCO for not communicating with the government to install who they believed was the rightful heir to authority. The CLA-cum-translator took liberties responding directly to participants rather than translating dialogue to and from Lieutenant Colonel Ranbir. He reminded them that MONUSCO maintains political neutrality in such matters. People in the group also brought up issues with unidentified armed bandits, large groups of them with vehicles and weapons going around, looting households, kidnapping women and children, and stealing goats. Often while drunk. With regards to the increased insecurity, one man intervened to make "one recommendation for MONUSCO." He claimed that the contingent had conducted very few activities in the area and asked that they multiply their efforts in the coming year. The disparate grievances compelled Lieutenant Colonel Ranbir to respond, "Just tell us security-related situations."

The fight between the FARDC captain and community never materialized beyond some scowls and pointed remarks, a fact that Lieutenant Colonel Ranbir attributed to my presence at the meeting. Lieutenant Colonel Ranbir's insistence to discuss matters only within his mandate illustrates how such Urafiki Meetings are organized within a logic that views encounter as an asset for peacekeepers to provide better security and protection of civilians. Yet, Urafiki Meetings as a platform for engagement in MONUSCO have been known to enhance the communicative interface between the force and population in some communities and deepen distrust in others (Kahn 2010). An Urafiki Meeting farther north in Rutshuru Territory illustrates the latter while giving us a better understanding of how encounter is paired with distanciation in a dialectic that informs peacekeepers' spatial and social practices with and among the communities in which they operate.

Keeping a Striking Distance

Lieutenant Colonel Ranbir's Urafiki Meeting was the first in three months. All civic engagement activities on the part of military contingents were put on hold during the 2018–19 election period because some Urafiki Meeting participants in and around Goma were *in* the elections, while others had very clear stakes in the outcome. Inviting these actors into MONUSCO peacekeeping bases during this time could have been seen as compromising peacekeepers' political neutrality. Peacekeepers also refrained from hosting CIMIC activities out in the city since different neighborhoods have different ethnic profiles—mapped out by MONUSCO and understood for their alignment with different political parties—which could equally jeopardize the mission's image if people understand the choice of where to conduct CIMIC as favoring one neighborhood over another (INDRDB 2019). Other extraordinary circumstances since the elections, like the Ebola outbreak and the COVID-19 pandemic, forced contingents to refrain from CIMIC and other WHAM activities as a matter of upholding troops' health and safety. Even when such community engagement activities are allowed or encouraged, frustrations with MONUSCO's perceived inaction create distance and tension within these encounters. Exchanges in Lieutenant Colonel Ranbir's Urafiki Meeting may have been relatively calm; Lieutenant Colonel Prem's, on the other hand, was not.

Lieutenant Colonel Prem sat at the front of his camp's Ops Room facing the Urafiki participants, including members of the mission's Joint Protection Team, who, Prem explained, could bring concerns raised in the meeting to the Force Headquarters in Goma. Prem kicked off the meeting with a modest, "Bonjour. Comment ça va?" before participants started jumping in with comments. "Banditisme ina sumbua sana," said one woman.[10] With the help of his LA, Lieutenant Colonel Prem responded immediately. Unlike Lieutenant Colonel Ranbir, Prem seemed less concerned with hearing the community's complaints about security than he was with evaluating his contingent's impact. "How much have we been able to address?" he asks to his LA for translation. "What about the people on the ground? Do they feel any change?" No participants volunteer a reply. Lieutenant Colonel Prem holds his hand out to the women's group in attendance. "Ladies first."

They continued their assessment of security, not of MONUSCO: "Kidnapping is picking up," they said.[11] So is rape. Bandits are terrorizing farmers. No one is looking after the demobilized child soldiers in the area. A conflict between the Hutu and Twa community has reignited despite the intervention of Prem's contingent. FARDC soldiers are harassing the local population and are quick to *piga masasi*—shoot their guns. These community comments are strikingly similar to those gathered by Lieutenant Colonel Ranbir in Goma. Prem intervenes again, this time trying to orient the conversation away from generalized insecurity and toward a focus on ethnic tensions. "Does any community have a problem with another community?" "Are there any problems between Hutu and Nyanga?" The conversation quickly reverted to suspected collusion between bandits and national security forces. Participants suggested a rotation of local authorities and security forces in their territory, thinking this would bring about a new, small peace (*mpya kasalama kidogo*). Prem tried once more to bring the conversation back to the realm of MONUSCO's interventions and results while participants became visibly annoyed. One attendee said aloud what many were likely thinking: "We come but nothing changes."

Lieutenant Colonel Prem fired back a long-winded response reminiscent of a lecture. He suggested that attendees not focus on the negative parts of their lives but be more positive. He cited the saying that "when you point a finger at someone else there are three pointing back at you" in an attempt to inspire some personal responsibility. "This is not clarifying the role of MONUSCO," he said declaratively. "You're not ready to change your approach. . . . How well you use the platform is up to you. I facilitate." He insists that the "FARDC and PNC are Congolese. They are you," adding in the same breath, "We are bound by a certain mandate."

Lieutenant Colonel Prem's reactions and Lieutenant Colonel Ranbir's remarks to just "focus on security-related situations" seemed dissonant when juxtaposed against the many insecurities faced and shared by the Congolese meeting participants. However, insecurity as it is experienced by rural and urban populations in Congo and as it is understood by peacekeepers differs significantly. Even in such camp encounters as Urafiki Meetings between peacekeepers and the Congolese population, these different understandings of what constitutes a secure or an insecure environment or city create a marked social distance and tension between the two parties as expectations on both sides go unmet. What Lieutenant Colonel Prem and Lieutenant Colonel Ranbir alluded to in their Urafiki Meetings, Major Baba addressed outright back at the English Club. Baba was explaining night patrols as critical to keeping the peace in Goma when the club coordinator Simon asked, "Why is the patrol not done in the neighborhoods?" Simon pointed out that he only sees patrols happening on main roads, while his personal experiences in the city have made him the victim of attacks occurring on smaller, less well-lit neighborhood paths. Major Baba clarified that the nature of insecurity experienced in these places constituted "law-and-order problems" in the eyes of the mission—problems that his and other contingents do not have a directive to solve.

The types of security issues that plague Goma, Major Baba claimed, are the primary responsibility of the PNC as law enforcers. As came up in the Urafiki Meetings, looting, thievery, kidnapping, and other such crimes fall under the law-and-order category by military peacekeepers' interpretations. Evident frustration from the officers in their respective Urafiki Meetings reflects peacekeepers' understanding of and inability to intervene in law-and-order situations. Peacekeepers' ability to place general banditry in a category of insecurity beyond the purview of their mandate relies, in part, on how they understand and distinguish perpetrators. Lieutenant Colonel Ranbir hinted at this puzzle in his Urafiki Meeting, asking participants: "Everytime I get information . . . the people are 'unidentified.' Why?" When bandits cannot be identified by the population as being a part of an armed group, even though they may be carrying weapons, Ranbir and others consider these actors and their actions to be outside of their mandate of intervention. Unidentified bandits that are not dressed in military tenue create too much ambiguity for peacekeepers. Banditry in the context of conflict in eastern DRC blurs the lines between when someone stops being a "civilian" and starts being understood as a "combatant." This distinction is a crucial principle underpinning customary international humanitarian law (Henckaerts et al. 2005), which must be upheld by UN peacekeepers. Furthermore, Core Pre-Deployment Training Materials for military peacekeepers stipulate, "In case of doubt whether a person is a civilian, that person should be considered a civilian" (DPKO and DFS 2017). Military actors, therefore, carry out orders to protect civilians within the context of armed conflict insofar as parties to the conflict can be distinguished as combatants associated with armed groups.

Peacekeepers' explicit and primary mandate to "protect civilians under imminent threat of physical violence" (V. Holt, Taylor, and Kelly 2009) is simply referred to by most MONUSCO staff as POC—the protection of civilians. Military personnel in particular more commonly use POC to describe threats (or situations that could emerge from threats) rather than their own operational responses. One of the primary threats, or precursors for violence, that peacekeepers understand as a POC issue is ethnic tension (broadly conceived). Back at the English Club, Major Baba brought up ethnic violence as the context

Meeting point for Urafiki Meetings in a peacekeeping camp. (Photo by author)

in which he understood the justification for a multinational peacekeeping force, as a catalyst for intervention and as a deciding factor in selecting where contingents go. When asked by a student, "How do you choose the places you [peacekeepers] go?" Major Baba used tectonic metaphors to describe taking up geostrategic positions related to ethnic tensions within communities, elaborating that one of his brigade's companies was stationed on what the mission considered an ethnic fault line. He explained, "We place ourselves there to prevent an earthquake." In his Urafiki Meeting, Lieutenant Colonel Prem showed much greater interest in eliciting community inputs relative to ethnic tensions, as the presence of discord between ethnic groups creates one of the clearest paths for military cadres to identify a POC issue and intervene.

Séverine Autesserre (2014) has critiqued the reduction of complex conflicts into singular, dominant narratives by international interveners for the unintended consequences they engender. Montgomery McFate (2018) makes a similar argument specifically concerning militaries, whose understandings of complex conflicts rely on simplifications and conceptual orderings that may help them generate actionable strategies but all too often limit their perspectives. As such, peacekeepers' emphasis on ethnic fault lines may cause them to ignore other dimensions of conflict, whether or not they relate to their mandate or can intervene. More importantly for my argument, however, is the fact that the conceptual categories made by peacekeepers inevitably shapes the encounters peacekeepers have with civilians (in Urafiki Meetings, for instance) and the persistent perceptions among Congolese civilians that the mission is "doing nothing." From peacekeepers' own perspectives, they are "doing nothing" about certain security situations as a matter of following mission orders, which creates a shared jadedness between many of the humanitarian-hearted military peacekeepers and the residents of eastern Congo.

These conceptual categories of insecurity help create cartographic distinctions between rural and urban areas for peacekeepers as well. The distinction between law-and-order problems and POC issues helps peacekeepers and mission staff more generally distinguish Goma, defined by the former problems, from other, more rural parts of the country with more acute instances of the latter. High-ranking civilian staff in the mission consistently confirmed this divide, acknowledging the high level of criminality in Goma and explaining lessened cases of ethnic confrontation in the city due to the density and proximity of various ethnic communities. Even within Goma, however, the lines separating the two types of security dilemmas can become blurry for the peacekeepers operating there. With Dev's experience commanding quick reaction forces in Goma, he knows all too well the contradictions within the mandate as they manifest on the ground. He raises the example of how public order problems, like crimes committed during a large political demonstration, can turn into a POC issue in an instant, as civilians may require protection from their own security forces. On the one hand, MONUSCO is involved in security sector reform, which necessitates working with and building the capacity of the PNC and FARDC. Peacekeepers like Dev are not always present at different protests in Goma since the mission is "trying to project the strong face of local law enforcement," as he puts it. At the same time, PNC officers have been known to use excessive force to control larger demonstrations. If PNC agents were to begin firing on civilians, MONUSCO's military contingents would have the authorization to fire upon the Congolese security forces, since they would be fulfilling their POC mandate. As Lieutenant Colonel Dev once said off the cuff: "My armed groups are the PNC and FARDC."[12]

International norms and institutional mandates, with their ambiguities and contradictions, are just a few of the many ways peacekeepers justify Congolese perceptions that they are "doing nothing" about urban violence as it is experienced in Goma (see Verweijen 2019). While international humanitarian law and peacekeepers' interpretations of their mandate rely on distinctions between armed combatants and civilians, local communities do not distinguish their experiences of insecurity by perpetrator. Even in encounters, such as those my neighbor Didier and I experienced in the Les Volcans neighborhood with different armed men in partial military dress, Didier often struggled to confidently attach known aggressors to any particular armed group or national security force. What Congolese civilians experience as inaction to reduce insecurity in Goma on behalf of MONUSCO (leading to frustration and disillusionment with the mission), military personnel experience as a complex web of institutional constraints. This should not be read as an attempt to justify the actions, reactions, and inactions of international forces operating in MONUSCO. Rather, illustrating the perspectives and practices of peacekeepers themselves seeks to shed light on the ways that distance is constructed between military personnel and the population they are mandated to protect and to explain some of the factors that shape contingents' ways of encountering, being with, and knowing the people and places they meet when they leave their camps for operations or invite civilians in through the gates.

When asked about their extra-camp encounters with Congolese civilians living in Goma, peacekeepers are quick to cite MONUSCO's nonfraternization policy for military personnel. As a matter of upholding this policy, Indian peacekeepers, for instance, have been explicitly instructed not to engage verbally with the local community, especially in situations that appear heated or aggressive. Major Hari thought that this directive had already revealed its flaws in practice, leaving him to assess that his own force comes off as too submissive. He recalled an instance in which some members of his contingent were starting to be surrounded by a group of Congolese civilians, but because they followed the order not to communicate or negotiate with the local population, they resorted to dispersing the crowd by handing over a one-hundred-dollar bill (US currency). Lieutenant Colonel Ram understands the nonfraternization policy on the basis that "familiarity breeds contempt" and that the army should "bring a little bit of fear." According to him, fraternizing humanizes peacekeepers to the Congolese. Major Neel's sentiments follow this logic. "The military is not supposed to be human. It is supposed to be like a surgical knife." In their relationship with kids at the gate and with different people at Sunday Market, a group of Uruguayan officers echoed some of the Indian officers' feelings, pointing out a tension between having a good attitude and a sense of humor and showing strength as a member of the military. "We are not here to mingle," says Lieutenant Colonel Juan, moments before he stresses the closeness of his contingent to the local population.[13]

In addition to compliance with mission-wide mandates, distance between UN peacekeepers and the population of Goma is constructed through abidance to commands handed down from national brigade or battalion commanders, who set curfews, for instance. The enforcement of curfews and delimitation of "out-of-bounds" areas in the city work to confine peacekeepers to certain neighborhoods at certain times to avoid mingling and misconduct. I was out to dinner with a few Indian officers one night when Lieutenant Colonel Shoora started bemoaning the fact that they would have to leave soon to make it back to the camp. We were on the complete opposite side of Goma from their base, feasting on an assortment of spicy meats and *sabzi* at the newest Indian-owned bar-resto in town.[14] I checked my phone: 22:40. We hadn't been there more than an hour and a half, but 22:40 was the absolute latest that the crew of officers could leave to make it back to the base before their 23:00 curfew. They compared themselves to other Indian officers serving as military observers (MILOBs), who can stay out on the town until 01:00 on weeknights and 02:00 on weekends, calling themselves and other encamped officers the lowest on the proverbial food chain in terms of their freedoms. "It's like we're in a cage," Shoora said frustratedly as he stood up and walked briskly to the Mahindra Scorpio waiting for him outside. Lieutenant Colonel Shoora isn't the only one who laments the strict enforcement of curfews in the name of ensuring good conduct. Officers whose enjoyment of Goma's vibrant nightlife is curtailed by curfews and regulations that apply only to contingent troops frequently liken their camps to prisons and themselves to prisoners.

The UN curfew for contingent troops is 18:00, just before sunset. Only officers in certain camps can request permission from their commanding officer for a later curfew. For instance, when Indian officers *are* allowed to leave the camp in the evening, they still must obey a brigade-ordered 23:00 curfew, as Lieutenant Colonel Shoora had that night after dinner. Such restrictions on movement and curfews in Goma lead to a lot of cribbing among officers. Part of this complaining has to do with the tempo of nightlife in Goma, as people only really start pouring into the bars and clubs around 22:30 (at the earliest). Several humanitarian organizations follow the UN's lead on later curfews for civilians and restrict their staff from being out beyond 02:00.[15] Meanwhile, young Gomatracians can be found drinking and dancing into the early morning hours no matter the day of the week. As a result of these curfews, however, peacekeepers are restricted from knowing much about this side of Goma and must stay in their camps while a vibrant nightlife grips the city. If officers are allowed to go out in the evening for leisure, many operate on a "buddy system," particularly in Indian contingents; larger groups are often granted permission to go out and enjoy dinner or drinks in Goma more easily than single pairs. Exceptions can and have been made for individuals being invited out by civilian counterparts, as battalion leadership is increasingly recognizing the political importance of cultivating a certain level of sociality between military and civilian UN personnel. This regulation of after-work leisure beyond the camp in pairs and groups is the decision of the commanding officer of any particular contingent, creating variable frequencies of encounter between officers from different camps and residents of Goma. My own civilian-foreign national position, as well as that of various members of the Indian diaspora, managed to lead to instances of leniency about curfews for some Indian battalions (sometimes), as our language abilities and social proximities to both groups helped us occupy what some commanders could have seen as middle positions or mediating roles between foreign officers and Congolese civilians.

Several bars and clubs with an international clientele are acceptable venues for peacekeepers' occasional nightly outings (before curfew, of course), but many clubs with more local patrons are considered "out-of-bounds." Civilian and military personnel working for the mission are strictly forbidden from being in any of the specific places or entire neighborhoods that are listed by the mission as out-of-bounds areas. BANMP contributes to identifying these areas and submits them to the Conduct and Discipline Team (CDT) in the Goma Field Office. Locations that make the out-of-bounds list are often isolated (for instance, places where security actors are not nearby to intervene in case of an incident) or disconnected (in terms of transportation access for the peacekeeper to get out or for an intervener to get in). Parts of the administrative districts of Mikeno, Mapendo, and Kahembe that collectively form the neighborhood known as Birere, for instance, are designated as an out-of-bounds area (GIS MONUSCO 2013). This has not stopped different battalions from making roadside purchases on the edges of these neighborhoods however, as I have accompanied various officers to these neighborhoods in the daytime to negotiate deals for things like furniture or handwashing stations. Individual eating and drinking establishments can also be designated as out-of-bounds; as of 2013, there were thirteen such premises scattered throughout the city (ibid.).[16] Major Siddharth, a military liaison officer working at the Goma CDT Field Office, explained that past cases of sexual exploitation and abuse committed by peacekeepers is a strong logic in informing the list of bars, clubs, and hotels on the list, in addition to observed drug use, child labor, and aggressive prostitution. In this way, encounters, past or perceived, can provoke greater distancing measures.

Keeping peacekeepers out of trouble also informs individual contingents' policies about how, where, and when vehicles can move out from the base (and, as the next chapter elaborates, works to keep peacekeepers inside of their camps as much as possible). Foreign military peacekeepers living in company operating bases (COBs) predominantly experience the wider landscape of Goma from Land Cruisers, Mahindra Scorpios, Xenons, and Ford pickup trucks. Except for Sunday Market (since it is so close to several bases), peacekeepers travel out of the camp exclusively in vehicles with armed escorts or armed personnel inside, constituting another method by which they simultaneously create proximity and distance between themselves and the urban population.

Vehicular Movements

Back at the English Club, Simon, the club coordinator, and the students had the impression that peacekeepers in Goma spent a lot of time "killing gas"—a critique of how often they see military personnel in their vehicles doing little more, in their minds, than wasting fuel. Peacekeepers based in Goma primarily experience the city through their vehicles—traveling to and from different compounds, conducting patrols, or running individual and contingent errands. Peacekeepers' impressions of Goma, particularly among enlisted ranks, overwhelmingly rely on their experiences of traveling the city's streets in vehicles. A series of focus group discussions with troops from Uruguay, Senegal, and Guatemala reinforced the centrality of vehicles in their experience of the city, as many of their impressions of the urban landscape were rooted in observations of road and traffic conditions. Senegalese police, for instance describe the city as "anarchic" based on the city's traffic patterns. "On circule comme on veut." "Les motos passe à gauche à droite." The rules of the road, they summarized, are not normal.[17] Bangladeshis, who enforce road safety regulations among military mission personnel, also note the operational challenge of "reckless and extensive movements of local motorcycles" (BANMP 2018). Furthermore, Uruguayan troops, as well as some of the contingent's officers who have made several tours of Goma, are quick to point to the paving of roads and increases in traffic as indicators of the city's development progress over time.

Vehicle patrols are also one of the primary ways that peacekeepers think about how they show force and exert their presence in Goma, which is perceived as a means to their end of protecting civilians. In fact, any time a peacekeeper is moving or being driven in a vehicle, it is considered an operational patrol. These operational logics, as well as the paramount import of the peacekeepers' safety and protection of the vehicle itself as a UN asset, influence the way these vehicles look—with large black UN logos for easy identification, window protector cages, large radio antennas, speed limit alerts, and key card access systems. Peacekeepers are well aware of the way that these protective features assert a more aggressive face of the mission and vehicle movements are often cited by peacekeepers as a contrast to the friendlier relationships they curate with their neighbors through things like CIMIC and their attendance at the Sunday Market.

I was admittedly taken aback when Major Neel mentioned that his contingent counts all vehicle movements through town (including between the camp and office compound) as a patrol. To my mind, this could serve to inflate the contingent's operational activity when in reality, many of these "patrols" were not in the service of protecting the population, but getting an officer from Point A to Point B. Major Baba clarified, however, that typifying all vehicle movements as patrols is a command decision that is geared toward shaping troop behavior and keeping them safe in the city. Categorizing routine vehicle movements as operational tasks keeps soldiers alert to their surroundings and ready to defend themselves and the vehicle during what begins to feel like monotonous commutes and errands. Maintaining awareness during routine vehicle movements is also a principle of counterinsurgency tactics, Major Baba tells me.

When one thinks about vehicles in cities with a large international humanitarian presence, one typically thinks of the Toyota Land Cruiser or the Land Rover. Luxury class SUVs like these and other unspecified SUVs and 4x4s pepper scholars' accounts of urban areas impacted by humanitarian intervention. They are framed as part of the transnational assemblages that constitute humanitarian response (James 2020), are argued to reify the notion that interveners live in a separate world (Autesserre 2014; Jennings 2015; Smirl 2015; Jennings 2016), and are even argued to reurbanize postconflict cities (Hackenbroich and Vöckler 2010). Kurt Mills (2006) has referred to the Toyota Land Cruiser specifically as the postmodern tank, arguing that it is not only representative of the international community's response to conflict but to contemporary conflict itself. Yet, painting a vehicle landscape in Goma with the neat categories of humanitarians in Land Cruisers and militaries in armored vehicles overlooks the intricacies and nuances of peacekeeping conveyances in Goma. Understanding vehicles solely for the distances they create between those inside and those outside ends up reducing the complexities of journeying through the city. Goma's particular traffic profile is representative of the differences and nuances within international intervention and a shared diversity of vehicle makes and models present in many cities of the Global South more generally. For instance, French-manufactured Sides firetrucks blare their horn through the packed downtown streets as Malawian firefighters race to douse out a fire across town. Nissan Patrols with police lights on top are parked on the side of the road during speed checks by BANMP. Indian officers peel around town in their boxy Mahindra Scorpios. *Jawans* climb onto the benches installed in the cab of their TATA Xenons (or, as many pronounce it, *junoon*).[18] Hyundai buses, Toyota Hilux pickup trucks, TATA 2.5-ton trucks, Ashok Leyland Stallions, Ford Rangers, Mercedes 1720s, MAN rigs, and Iveco tanker trucks transport troops, water, and fuel around town daily. Soviet infantry carrier vehicles (ICVs) are brandished with the names of Indian warriors like *Sultan* and *Chandrashekhar* to motivate the *jawans* and are generally reserved for patrols in more high-risk areas or for COB defense purposes in places like Goma.[19] The diversity of vehicle makes and models circulating in Goma is a testament to the heterogeneous global profile of the contingent troops serving there and the long duration of the mission, which has engaged multiple vehicle contracts over the years in search of the most operationally appropriate and cost-effective options. If the Toyota Land Cruiser has become a symbol of Western elitism and exceptionalism in humanitarian response (Smirl 2015), perhaps the Mahindra Scorpio best signifies an overwhelming reliance on peacekeepers from the Global South in MONUSCO and other contemporary peacekeeping missions (Cunliffe 2013).

Even from the comfort of their vehicles, peacekeepers cannot maintain a clear break from the environment through which they are traveling. While officers are shuffled around town in enclosed, air-conditioned, guarded SUVs, troops fill the cabs or repurposed cargo areas of trucks with sunglasses and scarves to protect themselves from the equatorial sun and pervasive dust. Moreover, just as the voices of neighborhood youths transgress the gates of the peacekeeping camp, locked doors and rolled-up windows cannot drown out the sounds of the city as the local populations shout greetings and admonishments at the blue helmets passing by. When vehicles stop downtown, ambulant vendors rush to the guards in the truck cabs with everything from sunglasses to power banks. Peacekeeping vehicles can elicit the prospect of a sale from hawkers, the delight of children, and the ire of frustrated communities, some of whom have expressed their generalized anger with the mission by throwing stones at vehicles and wielding machetes. Most of the time, however, peacekeepers in vehicles only evoke verbal engagements from the local population. Senegalese soldiers have heard it all from the back of their patrol pickup trucks, including "Rentrez chez vous!" and "Vous n'êtes pas occupant!"[20] Insults, however, are often the exception rather than the rule. Often, residents of Goma address peacekeepers in their cars with an ambiguous albeit nonthreatening greeting. Peacekeepers' confusion around what people (mostly children) are shouting at them as they pass sheds light on the ambiguities and spaces left up to interpretation that emerge between peacekeepers' practices of encountering and distancing themselves from the local population.

Children run after the Guatemalans in their pickup trucks, Indians in their Scorpios, and MILOBs in their Land Cruisers with the same fervor, often shouting. They shout an ambiguous two syllable sound that different peacekeepers hear as different words. While riding in trucks with officers from different contingents, we've all heard the same refrain, albeit attributing very different meanings. On one occasion, the commander giving me a lift out to the Guatemalan Special Forces camp told me very matter-of-factly that the children were shouting "MONUC," the name of the mission that immediately preceded MONUSCO. On another occasion, in Saké, I rolled down the window while the officer next to me warned me that the kids wanted "money." Both interpretations reinforce troublesome tropes about the local population that nevertheless helped the peacekeepers I was with understand themselves and justify their presence in Congo. MONUC has not been the name of the mission for nearly a decade, and it seemed unlikely to me that these children and their families were as uninformed as this interpretation led some to believe. Media programs frequently speak of different developments within the mission and Goma residents, like my neighbor Didier's father and uncle, were avid listeners of the mission-managed Radio Okapi—frequently pairing their evening Heinekens with a program, followed by discussion. Others with whom I spoke regularly rarely (if ever) mentioned the old mission moniker. Meanwhile, to understand the children as asking for money reinforces images of Congolese poverty as desperate and aggressive. Where would these children have come to have this expectation? What peacekeepers have been doling out cash on patrols (except for perhaps those involved in the incident Major Hari described)? Wary of both explanations, I replied to one of the children who shouted the ambiguous M-word on the latter trip in Saké, testing my own interpretation. "Eh, mtoto, 'morning' ni asubui lakini saa hii ni muchana. Una pashwa kusema 'afternoon.'"[21] The child took a beat before smiling back and shouting, "Good afternoon!" Maybe other children chasing after peacekeepers in cars wanted money. Maybe they were simply acknowledging them by the old mission name MONUC. But maybe they just wanted to say, "Good *morning.*"

Room for Interpretation

The shared spaces that emerge between the dwelling places of the peacekeeping camps and the city, particularly those uncovered by journeying with peacekeepers in their vehicles across the thresholds of their camp gates, are often socially, culturally, and linguistically ambiguous. Such ambiguity lends room for Goma's residents and foreign peacekeepers to interpret their own meanings from various scenarios. For Goma residents, uncertainty about peacekeepers' ends, means, and mandate is one of the reasons that negative perceptions of the mission persist. As for peacekeepers, they often view misunderstandings as a threat to their own safety and security. Language barriers and cultural differences make misunderstandings more likely.

These barriers, however, also generate new spaces of opportunity in the peacekept economy, spaces filled institutionally by LAs and CLAs. Community liaising, in particular, is one of many tools and platforms put at the disposal of the mission by the Civil Affairs section.[22] According to Civil Affairs staff, a CLA must have skills similar to a community organizer and be able to analyze incoming alerts before communicating them up the chain of command. In this way, CLAs represent the civil component of the mission within various military formations. As such, different military officers have both downplayed and emphasized their role in shaping the camp-city interface. After budget cuts, Lieutenant Colonel Kamal's contingent was left with only two language assistants, whose main tasks, by his assessment, had been to give his boys some basic language courses, assist with daily reports, and facilitate communication with notables. Regarding CLAs, Lieutenant Colonel Kamal asserts that since they report to HQ, "Their main task is not for us." The job description of an LA is limited to translation in comparison to CLAs, but this doesn't preclude the feeling among LAs themselves that they do much more that merely translate.

Given many of the misunderstandings among Congolese civilians about the mandate and role of MONUSCO, LAs see the work of creating understanding between the population and the force as requiring more than converting words between French, Swahili, English, and Spanish. Christian and Albert, who have been working as LAs with Indian battalions since 2004 and 2005, respectively, concur that speaking English needs to be paired with open-mindedness and flexibility as necessary criteria for performing this kind of labor. Delving deeper into the space created by this linguistic interface reveals several additional dynamics at play within the positions of LAs and CLAs, such as the mobility, precarity, persistence, analysis, and luck that obtaining and performing such mediating roles necessitate. The personal stories of LAs David and Pierre, along with insights from a focus group discussion held with the LAs and CLAs of an Indian battalion, illustrate the complexities of bridging the lifeworlds of the city and the camp.

David has been speaking Spanish with Uruguayan soldiers since he was around ten or eleven years old. This period of his childhood corresponded with the deployment of Uruguayan marines to patrol the Congo River and its tributaries from two bases—one of which was in his hometown of Kindu (Guyer 2013). Around the age of seventeen, because his parents could not afford his secondary school fees, David moved to Goma to try to make some money so that he could finish his schooling and receive his diploma, staying in a *gîte* in Birere organized by and for people from Kindu trying to make it in the city.[23] This diploma was necessary to be hired by the mission through a proper contract. After making some cash in Goma and graduating back in Kindu, he became part of the "personnel" for the Bolivians who had been redeployed there from farther west after the national elections of 2006 (Young 2007). The contract David held with them was precarious to say the least. The contingent wasn't compensating him adequately and would primarily give him food in exchange for his language services. From 2008 to 2011, David worked for a private security company and was stationed at a MILOB team site that included an Uruguayan MILOB named Francisco, whom he credits with helping him get to where he is today.

In 2011, David moved back to Goma to live with Marc, another Kindusien working with the South Africans—or "les Sud Afs," as they called them—this time staying in the Virunga neighborhood. "I bugged the Uruguayans every day." David said.[24] After a year of pestering, he still had not managed to get any employment offers from URUBATT. Marc had even brought David's documents to a South African battalion supervisor who was looking to employ around twenty people in various roles in and around the camp. "All of Goma was there!" he remembers.[25] David's English wasn't as strong as his Spanish, however, and he wasn't selected. Furthermore, as he said, he didn't know the South Africans who were interviewing the candidates like he may have known some of the Uruguayans. Growing up in Kindu next to the Uruguayans, in particular, should have proved more auspicious for David in his job search: Uruguay being a small country with a small army wherein soldiers and officers often make several tours to the DRC. This should have perhaps increased David's chances of becoming familiar and recognizable to the various contingents over the years. David continued to pray.

He decided to switch tactics. Instead of trying to wear down familiar officers, David seized the opportunity given by troop rotations to try his luck with fresh faces. He found out the name of the second-in-command and approached the Uruguayan base in Goma, announcing that he had a prescheduled meeting with said colonel. The troops manning the reception were new to the job and hadn't yet worked out the protocols that govern access to the camp. They took him at his word and brought him to the colonel's office. David promised himself that he wasn't going to leave without a job and, thus, pulled out all the stops. He responded repeatedly "Sí, mi coronel," just as the troops would, and boldly exclaimed, "If you let me leave, I will die here in Goma."[26] The colonel caved. He sent him to the officer in charge of hiring help for the base, who told him that if he wanted to work with the Uruguayans, he'd have to go to Pinga. David replied that he would work wherever they sent him. The next morning at 04:00, with all the documents and belongings he had been instructed to bring, the officer handed him a helmet and a bullet-proof vest. Moments later, a convoy of Uruguayan troops based in Goma were off to Pinga, with David as their interpreter.

David is keen to note in the story's retelling that this was the era of Sheka, referring to the rebel leader and war criminal Ntabo Ntaberi Sheka. "I experienced two wars there," he said.[27] He first witnessed a confrontation between Mai Mai Sheka and the Forces Démocratique pour la Libération du Rwanda (FDLR) that delodged Sheka. A week later, he found himself in the middle of renewed clashes, as Sheka sought to chase out the FDLR with the support of Guidon, a (then) ally and equally repugnant militiaman. David received targeted threats from various rebels (including threats of decapitation) and gifts from the local population. Most importantly for David, he had gained the trust of the Uruguayans, and they proposed to pay him USD 100 per month. "For me, it was a lot of money and the gateway into MONUSCO," David qualified.[28] He returned to Goma with the Uruguayan company and was soon hired through the formal channel of the mission. Between 2011 and 2014, nine different interpreters were working with the battalion. When I spoke to David, he was the only one from among that cohort to still be employed by URUBATT.

The circumstances of David's eventual employment with MONUSCO may seem unique in their extremity, but his grit, patience, and perseverance and the risks he was willing to undertake are common to many LAs and CLAs currently employed by the mission. Many assistants, including David, have experienced animosity and threats directed at them from the local community for a variety of reasons, including a particular community not being heard by the contingent or mission, the general perception of inaction by the UN force, expectations of payment for information, suspicion of assistants colluding with armed groups, or simply by virtue of assistants' salaried social standing.[29] To manage threats as well as raise awareness of the mission's mandate, and in an attempt to avoid several of these misunderstandings, these assistants are often involved in conflict management in addition to the already complex linguistic and cultural translation work they undertake.

Pierre, a language assistant for the BANMP sees his key tasks as building bridges and managing emotions. Pierre sees "challenge number one" of foreign troops in the city as "skin color." He elaborated, "Locals see that skin and believe that if they cut it money comes out"—though as the vendors at Sunday Market illustrate, Congolese perceptions of the wealth of peacekeepers varies across national (and often racialized) identities. He is frequently explaining to his compatriots, "My brother, *ndamu moya!*" in an effort to quell local aggression and animosity toward the UN troops.[30] Pierre's defense of the foreign soldier's presence and position is professional. His personal opinions about foreign troops and the international presence in Goma are more complex. "MONUSCO needs to intensify its informal gestures to break that wall of frustration. Why should we [the mission] spend USD 25,000 for a flight to Bukavu?" he asked rhetorically, acknowledging local transport options of ships, trucks, and speed boats. "The cost of that flight can change the perception 100 times over." Pierre is someone at the front lines of perception management who feels inadequately supported by the mission. In his eyes, without Radio Okapi and the Public Information Office, a UN mission wouldn't be possible here, due largely to the frustrations of the local population. In Pierre's eyes, "you make peace with small actions, not BMPs."

Albert and his colleagues working with the Indian army share with Pierre many of the challenges of assisting the mission and simultaneous empathy and respect for the contingents they work alongside. During our focus group discussion in their small, wooden office, directly adjacent to the battalion leadership's prefab CORIMEC offices, Lieutenant Colonel Dev's assistants acknowledged the importance of the kinds of CIMIC activities that Pierre evoked but confessed that "the population expects too much." They interpret this expectation as symptomatic of a lack of information and awareness raising about what the mission does. Some community members they encounter, for instance, confuse peacekeeping with development. Others confuse peacekeepers with combatants. "They want to see an Indian shoot at a bandit," Serge said, before quickly explaining the mandate and describing why that simply can't happen (as discussed a few pages prior). They nevertheless applaud the efforts of the Indian peacekeepers and feel supported by their officers and commanders, who they describe as noble and delicate in their work. Their complicity and amicable relationship with the military contingent they work for comes through in shared frustrations over increased precarity in assistants' contracts and the slow response of military bureaucracies and chains of command as well as, most strikingly, reference to the contingent with the first-person plural—we.

When he's not working with his Bangladeshi counterparts, Pierre teaches and manages over forty volunteers at his language school and vocational training center in the Katoyi neighborhood of Goma. All four assistants working with one of the Indian battalions were also English teachers before working for the mission; Blaise originally studied English with dreams of working in regional economic integration, recognizing the influence of Tanzania and Kenya on business in eastern Congo. That all changed in 1994 with the humanitarian deluge into Goma, which quickly recruited many English-language speakers, particularly teachers. As this dynamic progressed, Pierre founded his own language school with the objective of "preparing the youth for the needs of the international." Pierre estimates that about thirty former and current language assistants for the mission were trained at his center. Despite local suspicions about Pierre's connections and resource conduits for the school, when asked if international contingents, agencies, and NGOs have supported his work in the community, he replied, "not a single piece of chalk." A couple MONUSCO contingents have given small gifts—the nonfunctioning clock hanging in his office, a painting, a few books in Spanish—but clearly the mission and the international community as represented by foreign agencies and NGOs have failed to meet his own, more personal expectations. He feels frustrated, for instance, that he hasn't seen a UN truck carrying benches for a classroom or other WHAM outreach activities related to education. Pierre is aware of Bangladesh's reputation in Sierra Leone but has not seen the same level of commitment in Goma.[31] Not only is the mission's humanitarian engagement limited, but potential support from international NGOs and development agencies in general seems misguided to Pierre: "There are so many international organizations pouring money in the mouths of crocodiles."

LAs and CLAs, in their mediating role, both quell community anxieties about the mission and provoke new ones linked to the population's expectations about the information they provide. As Lieutenant Colonel Kamal remembered his CLA once put it to him, "You [peacekeepers] are like the reporters—you come, get info, and then nothing happens," echoing one of the attendees at Lieutenant Colonel Prem's Urafiki Meeting. Kamal explained that Congolese civilians often want something in return for the information they provide, sometimes making monetary claims, sometimes crying out for action. This interface reveals a socially transformative dimension of the peacekeeping presence in shaping Congolese values around information in terms of its exchange value, generating a sort of information economy. Uruguayans, for instance see their generosity as an input to this economy. Colonel Martín noted that locals who see or receive their small favors are more likely to give them a heads up if they know something is going to happen. Multinational peacekeeping forces, unlike national military forces, lack and express aversion to codified intelligence-gathering mechanisms (Johnston 1997), therefore relying heavily on the LAs and CLAs for information. In addition to being linguistic and cultural translators, assistants also thus act as intelligence collectors. Blaise and his colleagues rely on expansive networks across diverse communities to be as informed as possible about security threats—leveraging these networks to verify information that comes from local and customary authorities like *chefs de villages* due to their variable associations with armed groups as well as reports of incidents that emanate from one ethnic group and accuse another. Like Lieutenant Colonel Dev, they struggle to reconcile and explain to the population that the mission is meant only to support national security forces, though the security threats facing certain communities emanate from the PNC and FARDC themselves.

LAs and CLAs wear several hats (and sometimes, helmets) with the aim of enhancing the security of various Congolese communities as well as the security of the peacekeepers themselves. As Lieutenant Colonel Dev was calling my phone for me to wrap up with his assistants, I closed my notebook before Albert started telling me about a direct encounter between an Indian commander and Ntabo Ntaberi Sheka. It is often when the notebook closes and the pen is already buried in my bag that the most illustrative anecdotes about a given topic emerge. Albert recalls that the encounter was extremely hostile from Sheka's side as he threatened the Indian commander to get on his knees or else be shot. It is ambiguous in Albert's storytelling in what language Sheka was making such pronouncements, but it was certainly not a language that the commander understood. Albert noticed Sheka's posture and behavior change in a way that encouraged him to take the threat seriously. He understands himself as acting professionally by not translating Sheka's threat but making some conflict management choices to deescalate. Albert turned to the commander and said, "This guy is mad and is insulting you." No violence ensued between the Indian battalion and Sheka's forces.

Conclusion: Camping on Common Ground?

At a first, material glance, the walls and gates of the peacekeeping camps in Goma reflect the efforts of military contingents to create a break with the city—to make of the camp a protected interior from the city as an exterior. As this chapter has illustrated in its narrative commitment to following soldiers and civilians in, out, and across the threshold of the camp gate, the social lives of camp and city dwellers transgress such strict divisions. The curiosity, gregariousness, and entrepreneurship of youngsters and neighbors transform gate spaces into sites of exchange (of goods, languages, ideas, and sometimes insults). These barriers become social spaces, acted on by men and women who have become accustomed to living among peacekeepers over the past twenty years and, like David or Sunday Market vendors, pin large portions of their economic futures on the existence of the camps. These relationships and the encountering and distancing practices of peacekeepers from the city and its inhabitants work to reshape our understanding of what separates and connects peacekeeping camps and the wider urban fabric of Goma.

Through WHAM initiatives, vehicle movements, or the multilingual conversations held through small cut-outs in the gates, camps leak into the city around them. For Lieutenant Colonel Ram, the way that you run a camp and the order and ethos that you instill in the boys in this space comes out in their tasking—through the performance of their duties beyond the camp. In this way, the ethos of the camp, its habitus, spills out into the city through the way soldiers conduct themselves.

This chapter has taken stock of several spillovers in both directions, focused on the spatial practices of peacekeepers and Goma residents that blur the bounded notions of a separate camp and separate city. Peacekeepers build bridges with urban society through different WHAM initiatives in different spaces across Goma as well as in the camp under weather havens converted into classrooms. Those same bridges can also work to create division and dissension when tensions flare up in an Urafiki Meeting hosted in the camp. While the UN peacekeeping force is mandated to protect local populations against war crimes and crimes against humanity, Congolese civilians often expect peacekeepers to protect them against criminality writ large. As such, encounters like Urafiki Meetings can foment negative perceptions of the mission across the city, perceptions that peacekeepers are doing nothing in the face of certain types of urban violence.

As illustrated throughout, the camp-city nexus is defined by practices of encounter and distanciation, which Till Förster (2013) has argued is a dialectical process in which the possibility of urbanity can emerge. In this understanding of urbanity, "distanciation is an attitude that to some degree complements and accompanies the encounter as another possibility of how to relate to the other" (9). Goma's particular brand of urbanity cannot be forged separately from the existence of peacekeeping camps but is co-constituted by the ways that people move in and out of, or toward and away from, these camps. Peacekeeping camps thus coconstitute the social urban fabric of Goma and the aesthetic of the cityscape. Markets emerge. Roads are paved. Schools are built. Children learn Spanish. Or English. Or Wolof. Residents curse the peacekeepers. Others kindly greet them. Mahindra Scorpios park outside Bombay Mart. TATA Xenons zip by with scowling *jawans* on the back, until one cracks a smile in response to a kid shouting *"Ram! Ram!"* Such a shift from thinking Goma against camps to thinking the city through these camps disrupts prominent narratives of peacekeeping camps as islands and of the whole peace-humanitarian-development nexus as a separate bubble (Autesserre 2014; Shoshan 2016). To miss the contiguity of these spaces is to miss out on important practices of entry, exit, and passing through that contribute to Goma's urban character and to the camps themselves.

Key figures whose physical mobility and sociocultural flexibility helps weave the different fabrics of understanding between peacekeepers and Congolese civilians are the LAs and CLAs who enter and exit the camp daily to work with the encamped contingents. Their mediation of information and encounters between peacekeepers, armed groups, and the peacekept population far exceeds their translation abilities. These assistants do not simply translate and repeat military discourses of security or community experiences of insecurity but internalize and analyze their meanings, building bridges of understanding that rely on skills in intelligence gathering, security analysis, and conflict resolution. Yet while it may be tempting to relate these assistants to the types of colonial middle figures that serve as the focal point for Nancy Rose Hunt's (1999) work on colonial medicine, Congolese assistants to the mission share a postcolonial subjectivity with UN peacekeepers from Uruguay, Bangladesh, and India that is particularly brought to the fore by the politics of the languages they work in. Unlike the children who loiter around the gates of peacekeeping camps learning and speaking Hindi or Wolof, the information that they transmit to contingents in Goma is conveyed in the standard UN languages of French or English. These are equally colonial linguistic heritages for the peacekeepers. In the day-to-day of peacekeeping, it is rare that officers from the Global South address each other in English or French—universal languages "from nowhere" (Garrido 2017). Congolese assistants and foreign peacekeepers alike mostly converse among themselves in the languages of the "somewhere" they are from, meeting through both the languages of colonial empire and official working languages of the United Nations. Moreover, just as these troops and officers serve their own postcolonial states, Albert and his colleagues aspire to be recognized for the competences and experiences they've gained serving MONUSCO's militaries and be put to use one day by the Congolese state to combat insecurity with diplomacy. English and French translator-interpreters will be of far less relevance in such a postmission future.

Discussing Fred R. Myers (1991) ethnography of the Pintupi, and in particular an Aboriginal conception of place, the geographical philosopher Edward Casey (1996, 15) astutely notes: "As an anthropologist in the field, his task is not to argue for space over or against place but to set forth as accurately as possible what being-in-place means to the Pintupi." The aim of this chapter has been to explore what being-in-Goma means to encamped peacekeepers as both a place and sociocultural urban space. It has done so by exploring efforts big and small to engage with the people of Goma as well as maintain a safe distance from them, embracing the ambiguity between these practices. The next chapter focuses more narrowly on what being-in-camp means to peacekeepers and how the surrounding cityscape continues to play a role in shaping the quality of space in individual camps. If this chapter has painted a picture of the urbanity that emerges between camps and the city through movement, the next chapter illustrates how urban life in Goma shapes peacekeeping camps as sites of restricted movement.

3

The (Extra-)Ordinary Spaces of Peacekeeping

Regard your soldiers as your children, and they will follow you into the deepest valleys; look upon them as your own beloved sons, and they will stand by you even unto death. If, however, you are indulgent, but unable to make your authority felt; kind-hearted, but unable to enforce your commands; and incapable, moreover, of quelling disorder: then your soldiers must be likened to spoilt children; they are useless for any practical purpose.

—Sun Tzu, *The Art of War*, 44

If the previous chapter approached the ways in which peacekeepers and their architectures join in the making of the city, this chapter flips perspective to consider the quality of space created within the boundaries of the base, often in conversation with the city. Its aim is to explore the various commands, interests, activities, and routines shaping the internal layout, amenities, architectures, and biopolitical orders of the camp. Foregrounding the exposition of camp interiors as spaces of dwelling allows this chapter to take seriously things that provide structure to life in the camps—from daily schedules and routines to physical layouts that mediate a variety of internal relationships. Yet despite homing in on the physically bounded interiors of the camp, describing the nature these spaces (particularly as they relate to peacekeepers' confinement) necessarily requires views of and from their exteriors as well. The sociality and spatiality of peacekeeping camps are constructed through a constant reconfiguring of an inside and outside at multiple and simultaneous scales. The way that these insides and outsides work to perpetuate a sociospatial tension and the ways on which that tension is perpetuated, cut, or resolved creates a kind of camp space that I argue is best understood as (extra-)ordinary.

Many features of peacekeeping camp life are literally and theoretically ordinary. Ordinariness, the everyday, and the mundane are hallmarks of southern urban scholarship that inspired the original conception and structure of this chapter to focus on the everyday realties and rhythms of life shaping the camp (Robinson 2006; Parnell and Oldfield 2014; Oldfield 2023). To posit that peacekeeping camps are ordinary camps also participates in the same kind of theoretical project as ordinary cities. "Understanding cities as ordinary," Robinson (2006, 2) writes, "opens up new opportunities for creatively imagining the distinctive futures of all cities."

While peacekeeping camps retain their ordinariness to the extent that they are variably comparable to the features of barracks around the world, the context of international peacekeeping in the DRC also distinguishes these camps and engenders new and different modes of inhabitation. It is this problem space that this chapter focuses on, particularly the biopolitical mechanisms and discourses that abound in peacekeeping camps as a matter of keeping troops and officers confined inside. These ordering logics of the peacekeeping camp distinguish soldiers' and officers' experiences of these spaces (and the city) from their experience of other barracks and postings, making these camp spaces not only ordinary but also (extra-)ordinary. The ways that the UN exerts its power on and shapes the governance of national contingents and their camp spaces impels a perspective of camp space that revisits how the bodies of peacekeepers from the Global South enter a machinery of power "that explores it, breaks it down, and rearranges it" (Foucault 1995, 138). Philosopher Michel Foucault's proposals of power as fragmentary and not the exclusive purview of the state sovereign have been crucial to framing understandings of contemporary refugee camps (Martin 2015; Oesch 2017). The foundations of his ideas on the military-body nexus and governmentality have equally been called into question in international relations debates when trying to understand international organizational contexts like peacekeeping (Powel 2017). Turning these insights toward the terrain of peacekeeping camps thus joins a marked, and continuing shift in camp studies toward post-Agambenian analysis of camp structures and agencies (Martin, Minca, and Katz 2019, 2). To do so requires unpacking the political anatomy of these camps to understand how seemingly ordinary amenities and commands simultaneously subject and support soldierly bodies.

Despite the frequency of their movements in and out (highlighted in the previous chapter), a significant portion, if not the majority, of peacekeepers' time in Goma unfolds within their camps. The interiors of peacekeeping camps are polyvalent, multilayered spaces shaped by global design standards and the particularities of the militaries that inhabit them. They are spaces in which myriad infrastructures and activities come together to sustain both the mission and individual human lives. Although peacekeeping camps serve to protect local civilian populations through their very presence, as well as through the operational assignments coordinated and launched from them, they also function as spaces that shelter and protect troops themselves (and military equipment). Inhabiting smaller barracks than many are used to, contingents come up with a range of activities and creative uses of space to fill and structure the time between operations. These internal activities are often framed by commanding officers as a matter of keeping morale high and ensuring that troops' bodies are ready for the physical demands of military peacekeeping. In (extra-)ordinary camps, command structures are at once concerned with looking on soldiers as one would look after one's own kin and looking on them in a surveillance sense, ordering and regulating their lives. While being regarded in these ways, peacekeeping officers and soldiers retain varying levels of agency in shaping social life and making camp. This tension between camp life as at once ordinary and anomalous (relative to more familiar ways of inhabiting barracks for contingent soldiers and officers) brings into focus some of the contrasting logics shaping the organization of peacekeeping camp space as well as peacekeepers' creative agency to work within these limitations. It highlights the inherent heterogeneity of soldiers in these spaces as they lay out the camp in ways informed by constantly redrawing the boundaries between different physical spaces, sexes, and ranks and, at times, erasing them entirely. Furthermore, the camp's internal urbanism constantly renegotiates the relationship between inside and outside, allowing this chapter to simultaneously describe camp practices and physical structures through internal and external considerations.

Troops' lives and different joys, frustrations, and consequences of their confinement within the (extra-)ordinary space of the camp are the primary concerns of this chapter. Scholarship and literature on peacekeeping to date has given us only fleeting glimpses into these camps and their internal rhythms, materialities, layouts, and everyday social life. The design of these peacekeeping camps is discussed not only as a consequence of UN and national military structures and standards but also as the outcome of social practices that reflect different scales of agency within the military hierarchy. Different scenes illustrate different meanings of being in the camp, many of which are related to restricting movement beyond its gates. Logics of providing security and leisure, control and care, discipline and reprieve, become increasingly entangled in the organization of camp life and space.

The first way that this notion of the (extra-)ordinary is explored is through the daily routine of peacekeepers. I describe the schedules, economies,

Bulletproof vests hung out to dry after laundry day at URUBATT. (Photo by author)

infrastructures, activities, and protocols that constitute everyday life as it unfolds. This day-in-the-life narrative is collated from the experiences of multiple
camps and national contingents, bookended by an extended weekend visit to
the Guatemalan Special Forces camp (GUASFOR). Second, I turn to consider
the ways in which the camp is conceived as a bounded entity motivated by soldiers' confinement. I show how the peacekeeping camp can be understood as
a barracks of defense conceived of to protect soldiers from the assessed threats
of the mission area *and* to protect the surrounding environment from potential
misconduct perpetrated by soldiers. Camp perimeters and their boundedness
act as biopolitical mechanisms that function to keep other bodies out as well
as to keep peacekeepers' bodies in, though they do not always succeed. Third,
I discuss the role of women's inclusion in peacekeeping as it has transformed
the space of the camp both materially and socially. Women's presence in peacekeeping affects the spatial layout of the camps as well as male soldiers' perceptions of this exceptional environment as more ordinary. Lastly, I deepen my
discussion of welfare activities, features of the camp that boost morale, and

rituals that illustrate the ways in which peacekeepers reimagine ordinary occasions as extraordinary events.

A Day in the Life of a Blue Helmet

Life in a peacekeeping camp adheres to a precise schedule as a matter of the
military culture of ordering, controlling, and disciplining individual troops to
increase the collective's strength, a culture underpinned by understandings of
the nature of war.[1] Order in the form of daily routines is an important part of
military life for soldiers on duty as well as off duty to maintain and strengthen
operational efficiency, even when the operational mission is not war but peace.
While officers' duties are generally carried out in the administrative offices of
the camp or another MONUSCO compound, a personnel officer determines
the duties of the contingent troops and keeps track of who is doing what at
any given time. Major Baba frequently repeated the adage—"Busy troops are
happy troops." Peacekeeping camp schedules ensure that troops always have
structured times during which to keep busy, not least to keep them happy. At
GUASFOR, busy, happy troops wake up at 05:30.

The morning I woke up at GUASFOR, like all Guatemalan mornings in
Mubambiro, began with a jog around and through the compound garrison. The
run was scored with call-and-response chants throughout, an inspirited way to
greet the day and the surrounding militaries. "¡Bue-nos dí-as! [¡Bue-nos dí-as!]
¡Sud A-frí-ca! [¡Sud A-frí-ca!]" Good morning, South Africa! Good morning,
Tanzania! Good morning, India, Malawi, and Bangladesh! Over the course of
the run, the chants changed into more purposeful reminders about why the
troops were in Congo and why they had come to fight for peace. We turned at
the Tanzanian Level I hospital, where a group of children peered through the
fencing with shouts of "Kaibil! Kaibil!" that drifted away as we ran downhill to
GUASFOR's gate. We covered two kilometers before the sun was up, though
I'm guessing that without an out-of-shape anthropologist in tow they would
have increased both their distance and speed. After a brief cooldown, everyone
on the pitch joined in a unison chant of the Kaibil motto: "Si avanzo . . . sígueme.
Si me detengo . . . apremiame. Si retrocedo . . . mátame. Kaibil!"[2] The young
special forces had more than enough energy left to sprint happily to the showers. I could not say the same for myself and remained on the parade pitch, lying
on the gravel looking skyward. The flags had been raised in the camp while we
were running—the UN flag to the left, the Congolese flag to the right, and the
Guatemalan flag (twice the size of the others) in the center.[3] They would come
down twelve hours later at 06:00 and the Kaibil motto repeated while everyone

in the camp stood at attention. This ritual rallying cry every twelve hours may be the most familiar thing about camp life in Congo for the special forces, as it is the same performance that opens and closes the day of a Kaibil in Guatemala. I headed to my CORIMEC for a shower.

CORIMEC is the name of the Italian company that acts as the primary supplier of modular, prefabricated, semipermanent structures to MONUSCO but has become the preferred eponym to refer to the individual and collective dwelling areas of the camp.[4] CORIMECs are the building block of the company operating bases (COBs) and other administrative compounds of MONUSCO and are arranged and assembled into different configurations to serve as accommodations, as well as offices, dining areas, and storage units, among other purposes. Lieutenant Colonel Shoora thought someone should add "CORIMEC" to the dictionary as no single definition could justly account for the myriad ways it is put to use in the camp. The repartition of a camp's UN-allotted CORIMECs is up to each contingent but in most camps, officers have their own CORIMEC or share with one or sometimes two other officers. The CORIMEC I stayed in was large and comfortable. It belonged to the deputy commander of the unit who had been deployed to Beni. His only personal touches included a makeshift hat rack made of wire fencing for all of his caps, berets, and boonie hats and some letters from his children taped on the wall. Several letters from his daughter were prayers for her father's safety in "faraway Africa." Furnishings in the room were sparse. There was a large table next to the bed, where troops kept placing plates of fruit, juices, and yogurt throughout my stay. The reappearing snacks reminded me that there was no key for the door; most keys to camp CORIMECs have gone missing over time and over the course of multiple rotations. The perimeter of the room also had a locker for clothing, a small shelf with books and toiletries on it, a folding chair, and an improvised recliner made from an old bucket seat posed on a wooden base with armrests. A private bathroom had been built off the back of the CORIMEC with concrete blocks, tile, and corrugated galvanized iron sheets for a roof. I was told to keep the bathroom door always closed, as birds had been known to fly in through the bathroom windows. I showered quickly before meeting with my host, Captain Mario, for breakfast.

Most troops had already gone through the serving line with their personal trays and tin cups as the Guatemalan women staffing the camp kitchen dished out scrambled eggs and black beans and ladled up sweet, piping hot coffee from an enormous cauldron. Captain Mario and I sat in the open-air mess with a few straggling soldiers and took in the view of the lake and the Masisi and Walikale hills emerging from the early morning mist. At 07:45, officers and troops reassembled on the parade pitch. The sole female officer of the contingent sprinted out to brief the commander of the day's activities. Each contingent has its own order of the day, shaped by their operational mandate as well as cultural practices from their home countries. In some camps, the day is broken down into intervals as short as forty-minutes, beginning at 05:30 for most—as it had at GUASFOR. The day generally begins with a run combined with some other physical training (or as most officers refer to it, PT) like push-ups, sit-ups, stretching, or, in some Indian camps, yoga practice. Morning training is followed by breakfast or preceded, in Indian camps, by a "bed tea" from 04:30 to 05:00.[5] Breakfast is usually wrapped up across the camps between 07:00 and 08:00 before troops set to work on their daily duties to sustain the camp and everyone in it.

Food—in its growing, storing, cooking, serving, eating, and disposal—is a key temporal and spatial organizing logic within the peacekeeping camp, and a key component through which soldiers' bodies are cared for and controlled. The UN itself provides and manages the food supply chain for peacekeeping camps through a dedicated contractor.[6] Bases are outfitted with storage units, kitchens, and mess halls to move meals from the ration delivery trucks to soldiers' mouths. Rations constitute a key flow in and out of the camp and are constantly changing from camp to camp depending on contractors, contingents' palettes, and calorie quotas. For the Indian battalion in Kiwanja, for instance, one refrigerated truck arrives per week from Goma. Dry rations are stored in a container near the kitchen, equipped with shelves, labels, and samples of everything to indicate where it should be placed. Based on the ration stocks, the mess staff make a weekly menu around a 4,500-calorie-a-day diet. Once a week, antimalarial medication is distributed while soldiers and officers step on the scale to ensure that they continue to meet their military's weight requirement. Cooks additionally make a visit to the doctor weekly to be examined and to give a stool sample as a matter of ensuring that they are healthy and do not compromise the health of the contingent. Once the menu is made, the cooks and the mess staff set to work preparing hot meals on diesel stoves and fires. Because of the diet of Colonel Samir's particular troops, there is a separate area in the kitchen for cutting meat. Vegetables are always cooked first. At the end of the meal, food waste is handled carefully and tactfully. GUASFOR disposes of its food leftovers in the back of its camp (facing the lake), since disposing of leftovers in the front of the camp, with only fences and gabions for a perimeter, would allow nearby families to see the scraps and leftovers.

Meal timings are designed to take into consideration the duty rotation schedule, ensuring that everyone can eat either before or after their shift and that all stations remain manned for everyone's protection. Lunch constitutes the second of four meals in the day for the four hundred troops in the Uruguayan battalion and is served within the space of one hour. Colonel Pablo emphasized this short lunch period as an example of how he sought to balance welfare and discipline in his command of troops; discipline being essential to making sure that all on- and off-duty soldiers in his camp were fed. Across peacekeeping camps, troops, noncommissioned officers (NCOs), and officers dine in separate mess halls, space permitting. Back at the GUASFOR camp on the day of our run, officers and NCOs exceptionally dined together to celebrate the newfound fatherhood of one of the NCOs. A particularly well-loved soldier known as "the Russian" had spent all morning killing and cooking hens for a *caldo*, a Guatemalan broth soup.

Camp maintenance duties were generally carried out in the afternoon in GUASFOR, with the morning reserved for military and vocational education and training. GUASFOR's location on Lake Kivu enhances the training opportunities available to troops. As a special forces unit, Kabiles are charged with some of the most difficult and complicated tasks in the mission. They can and have been called on for various rescues and advanced reconnaissance missions and thus need to be familiar operating by air, land, and water. As such, they are keen to take advantage of their lakeside location to sharpen their skills in swimming and helocasting. In the GUASFOR camp as well as the other camps in and around Goma, operational training can also include weapons handling, shooting practice, slithering, and emergency evacuation drills in case of a volcanic or limnic eruption caused by the symbiotic, tectonic relationship between Mount Nyiragongo and Lake Kivu. In addition to these drills, MONUSCO civilian personnel visit the camp for different UN "trainings of trainers" on the rules of engagement, political affairs briefings (particularly around elections), child protection, human rights, conduct and discipline, and other topics related to different mission sectors. Training rounds out the intellectual plane of the soldier's well-being, as Colonel Samir once phrased it, complemented by the physical plane (ensuring the soldier has food, water, and shelter) and the spiritual plane.

Maintaining contingents' spiritual well-being is a priority across the diverse religious backgrounds of troops serving under MONUSCO and is reflected in dedicated services and facilities within the camps of eastern Congo. Even before reaching Goma, several Senegalese gendarmes sought out the guidance of their marabouts to mystically prepare them for the mission. Once deployed, the Senegalese fashioned an empty Rubb Hall in the camp into a mosque. Bangladeshi and Tanzanian faithfuls pray together on Fridays at the MONUSCO

Muslim Community Mosque built near the gate of their combined garrison in 2015 and renovated in 2017. GUASFOR benefits from the presence of Spanish-speaking priests and pastors in eastern DRC, who assist in conducting their Catholic, Protestant, and Evangelical tent services on Sundays and other religious holidays. Tuesday mornings in the Indian camps are reserved for the Mandir Parade and its variations. The concept of *sarv dharm sthal*, or a common worship hall, helps maintain the secularism of the army and accommodates men and women of all faiths—acting as a mandir, masjid, gurdwara, and church for Indian soldiers. Shona George (2017, 118) writes in his semiautobiographical novel about the (post)colonial legacy of the Mandir Parade and how its ceremonial aspect has been mocked in Indian army names for other military routines: "In the olden days, Britishers used to have Church Parade, where the entire garrison used to march out together to church every Sunday. When they commanded Indian troops, Church Parade was replaced by Mandir Parade. The troops continued with this penchant and named almost every routine activity a parade. So mealtimes were called Cookhouse Parade, if someone was unwell, he would report for Sick Report Parade, the evening orders were called Roll Call Parade, so on and so forth. I once heard one of the new recruits refer to the morning job as Latrine Parade."

Infrastructure for many of these camp-based utilities, services, practices, and "parades" have been built from scratch on a temporary basis, frustrating some commanders like Colonel Martín, who see such short-sited, incremental constructions and constant improvement projects as costing contingents and the UN more money in the long run. Yet, maintaining physical infrastructures and assuring the smooth flow of materials essential to sustaining these systems constitute the very activities that keep troops busy throughout the day. For instance, utilities like water, waste, sewage, electricity, communication (mobile, radio, and internet), and transportation require dedicated facilities and operators to run smoothly in each camp. Tradesmen soldiers, a particular category of troops in the Indian Army, provide specific support services in all camps, like the tailor, cook, washerman (for laundry), housekeeper, drivers, and the barber. These services are thought to enhance not only the well-being of the individual soldier but also to maintain order. Details like having a short, well-kempt haircut and wearing a clean, ironed uniform are related to discipline—"the soul of an army"—and rely on tradesmen and their dedicated spaces in the camp.[7] In addition to basic services, the camp provides its soldiers with health, hygiene, and subsistence services; each camp operates its own medical office as well as convenience stores for hygiene essentials, souvenir shops, and libraries. Despite the presence of an Indian-run Level III hospital in Goma, Uruguay comes with a particularly large medical team to accommodate its larger battalion, including doctors, nurses, dentists, and a psychologist. Most of the contingent's female peacekeepers were employed in the medical unit—including the head doctor during Colonel Pablo's tenure, a woman in her late sixties on her seventh peacekeeping tour.

On top of the everyday tasks of keeping the camp's "interior economy" working (as Indian officers call it), camp maintenance and improvement projects are popular ways to occupy troops. These projects fill the mornings at the GUASFOR camp—from building a new gazebo to redecorating the mess hall. Every battalion that comes through these camps leaves their mark. Commanders would take particularly pride in showing me the constructions and improvements that they had initiated during their respective tenures. During one of my stays in Goma, Colonel Luis was in charge of coming up with improvement projects for URUBATT and had already remodeled the Officers' Mess, or Casino, in his first three months. On the morning of one of my visits, troops were busy painting the letters of "URUBATT" on the backs of the steel sheets at the edge of the camp. The deputy had particularly wanted to beautify this part of the base because of the adjacent airstrip, making the camp one of the first things people see when they land in Goma. Colonel Luis framed most of the other improvement efforts as a "fight with the soil"—an attempt to tame the dark brown dust that covers everything in the camp and requires troops to clean their boots and CORIMECs up to four times a day to maintain an acceptable and orderly personal and camp appearance. Luis's strategy of attack had been to install flooring in the kitchen, plant grass in front of the offices, and pave the vehicle path on the western side of the camp. Two years later, this latter initiative was still being negotiated with mission leadership. Colonel Martín highlighted his ongoing battle with the soil in the URUBATT camp as a key site of internal mission politics and inequality; it is not lost on him that MONUSCO provides the resources to pave the compounds where civilians work but not parts of the camps of the contingents.

After maintenance projects or any requisite UN or operational trainings are finished for the day, sports and games are organized in the dual perspective of maintaining operational readiness and troop well-being. Commanders place great importance on the recreational spaces in the camp and frequently complain when they are lacking in quality or quantity. Even the smallest camps, such as those inhabited by Bangladeshi military police, are not without a badminton court at the very least. Peacekeepers play organized matches of badminton, volleyball, football (soccer), and basketball in the late afternoon, either on dedicated courts and fields or by delimiting space in a parking lot or parade pitch. In some of the larger camps outside of Goma, contingents even have enough room to play cricket, enormously popular among the Indian battalions. Back at the GUASFOR camp, a soccer match had begun around 16:00. The Kaibiles who weren't playing soccer or on guard duty were working out in the gym, which was little more than a few bench presses and concrete-poured canisters for barbells and dumbbells. After game time, which generally ends between 18:00 and 18:30 with the sunset, there may be a roll call or an evening briefing before dinner is served. Dinner is generally wrapped up by 20:00, followed by one of the main "free time" slots in the day for most soldiers before bed. Many soldiers from the Latin American contingents stay up late despite early wake up calls, particularly older troops who want to speak to their children after school is out in Guatemala or Uruguay (GMT-6 and GMT-3 respectively, compared to GMT+2 in Goma).[8] The general lack of downtime in peacekeepers' schedules is reflected in the response many peacekeepers give when asked what their favorite place in the camp is. Their bed.

The Guatemalan troops that I ran with in the morning had congregated in the Kaibil Club after dinner, a recreational and polyvalent space for different activities among the ranks. The club can function as a lecture hall for presentations made by UN staff or a computer lab for troops' vocational training by day and a video game room, after-hours cafeteria, cinema, or party venue by night.[9] Adjacent to this rec room was the club store La Cueva del Kaibil, or Kaibil Cave, where some of the young men had come to purchase a ramen noodle packet, still hungry after the UN-issued, ready-made lasagna rations they were served for dinner. Soldiers were receiving an allowance of USD 38 per month that could be used on food or snacks from the store, the proceeds of which returned to the camp and financed small improvement projects. My first night in the camp was movie night for the troops, and the club had transformed into a cinema with *Whiskey, Tango, Foxtrot* being projected onto the wall.[10] The spectator soldiers roared with laughter as an Afghan man shot his gun into the air to light his cigarette from the barrel. The following night there was no movie. A couple guys hung out in the small TV/video game room off the club while "the Russian" made french fries in the club's deep fryer. One soldier sat in the now empty club having a beer while he called home.

Before retiring to my CORIMEC, I watched Captain Carlos address his company before night patrol. Captain Carlos's boys were one of two companies inhabiting the camp at the moment—the others, including the deputy commander whose CORIMEC I was staying in, were deployed to Beni. I was simultaneously reminded of the respite the camp affords from these arduous forward operations and the operations necessary to sustain life in the camp.

Captain Carlos loomed large over his boys, a fact that reflected the rural-urban divide along race and class lines in Guatemala, a divide that is perpetuated in the military hierarchy and was now strikingly visible in the shadows being cast in the camp. Most GUASFOR soldiers were from Indigenous backgrounds and from the rural parts of the country, while officers like Captain Mario and Captain Carlos came from upper-class families in the cities.[11] On a prior visit to GUASFOR, the then-deputy commander had insisted that in his camp, "todos son iguales"—all are equal. I now questioned how the social gestures of sharing meals and dining halls across ranks, as well-intentioned and hierarchy flattening as they seemed, could possibly undo the inequality embodied in the stature and position of Captain Carlos in front of the rows of youngsters. At Captain Carlos's command, the Kaibiles checked their guns, emptying the chamber of their rifles to prevent accidental fire before going out to patrol the camp perimeter. When most troops and officers go to sleep, guards on camp perimeter posts rotate as frequently as every two hours. As Captain Carlos and his men marched out the gate, their boots crunching the gravel in step, I could hear the call to prayer coming from the neighboring Bangladeshi camp. It was dark—the time of the Isha prayer; it couldn't have been later than 19:30 though it felt like midnight; 21:00 was the flexible, earliest bedtime at the GUASFOR camp. I was already back in my CORIMEC by then, the camp audibly hushed out of respect for those who would have to wake up for various guard and patrol duties throughout the night. Goodnight South Africa, Tanzania, and Bangladesh. Goodnight GUASFOR.

"We are a small city," Colonel Martín tells me about the URUBATT camp. "We have the same problems as a small city has." Keeping the camp running like a small city is not only a matter of sustaining the camp in ways that provide for the individual soldier's well-being, but are inherently laced with logics of control and the disciplining of bodies—values underpinning military notions of success. This dual perspective of control and care underpins the rigidity of routines related to the maintenance of the camp's basic infrastructures, services, and interior economy. A commander's responsibility to discipline his troops *and* to ensure their well-being is clearly elucidated and simultaneously expressed in such daily activities as beautifying the camp, organizing physical training/games, and managing rations. The ritual of distributing antimalarial medication and conducting weigh-ins after Mandir Parade in the Kiwanja camp illustrates the tight entanglement of care and control of the soldier's body, mind, and spirit in camp logics. A day in the life of a peacekeeper thus highlights the orderly yet ordinary nature of the camps in which they live.

Despite significant amounts of time spent staying in the camp, peacekeepers always need to be ready to move out—a consideration that comes through in the time dedicated to activities like physical and educational training organized in the name of operational preparedness. Inhabiting a camp in Goma in this way may be considered by a solider as a "field tenure," both because of the attention to physical and mental readiness to deploy, as well as his or her distance from family and country. Similarly, many of the duties, patrols, and deployments are reminiscent of tasking orders in combat zones. In tenures such as these, the camp, like the city, never sleeps and is at work 24-7. However, because of Goma's distance from the primary battlespaces of conflict in eastern DRC and the nature of the military mandate under MONUSCO, it is also understood by soldiers as a "peace tenure," meaning more down time necessitating thoughtful structure. In such tours, soldiers' and officers' ability to focus on physical and educational training is a key privilege of being deployed to a "peace station." The way the camp is organized and space dedicated to enhancing the physical, intellectual, and spiritual plane of the soldier reflects the lived realities of a tenure between war and peace.

In troop-contributing countries with active conflicts like India, field tenures and peace tenures are mutually exclusive. One either is on the frontlines of war or given reprieve from battle in a peace station removed from the war zone. In Goma, the distinction between these two kinds of deployments through which a soldier cycles in and out throughout his military life are blurred. The combat zone and peace station collapse into each other in ways that shape the activities and possibilities in peacekeeping camps. If Goma has been understood through the conceptual continuum of "no peace, no war" (Richards 2005 cited in Oldenburg 2015 and Büscher 2016), peacekeeping camps in the city have collapsed the two points of the spectrum in practice, shaping a sort of "at war, at peace" environment, giving rise to an (extra-)ordinary camp. The spatiality of personal and professional life also collapses or at least overlaps in a peacekeeping camp, creating an "at home, at work" environment. Different administrative offices in a camp can be located only a few meters away from an officer's CORIMEC or directly next to it. The Club Kaibil can act as a cinema one week and host a presentation from MONUSCO's human rights section the next. Several work and recreational activities take place in the same place at an Indian Rapidly Deployable Battalion base, where the vehicle parking lot serves as a basketball court, roll call area, badminton court, and prepatrol briefing point. The tradesmen category of soldiers, like the washerman and TV man, live with the

Guatemalan troops invite neighboring Malawians to the camp for a volleyball match. (Photo by author)

equipment they operate. Everything to sustain the life of a peacekeeper is all-together, in one place.

Life in a peacekeeping camp draws on distinct features of soldiers' national cultures—from the kinds of games that are played to the ways that the spiritual well-being of troops is accommodated—while also adhering to international and institutional standards and regulations. Camps are equipped with modern appliances and weaponry and follow a system of standardized planning principles for a military base. The mission ensures compliance with such standards and the proper functioning of all camp equipment through frequent inspections of contingent-owned equipment. (See UNGA 2017 for complete procedures and standards.) Nonetheless, infrastructures decay, equipment is decommissioned, and things break down, driving peacekeepers to innovate and improve camp services, spaces, and activities. Commanders order their troops to undertake near constant maintenance and construction projects not only to develop their camps but also to "keep Joe busy." Joe is kept busy through ordinary tasks in a way that reminds us that peacekeeping camps are dynamic. Always changing. Always in the making.

While Major Baba's oft-repeated adage of busy troops being happy troops appears over and over again as a shared foundational belief structuring the temporal and spatial structure of the camp across national contingents, an American staff officer working at the force headquarters had a slightly more sinister way of phrasing the maxim: "If you don't keep Joe busy, Joe will find something to do." The following section describes key confinement protocols and the ways that they frame the threat of Joe finding something to do. It delves deeper into how the camp works to keep bodies apart (from the city and from each other) in line with overlapping juridical orders. To do so, some brief returns to the city are necessary to understand the rationales and consequences of confining peacekeepers to the camp.

Confinement, Zero Tolerance, and Porous Peripheries

Orders related to the "conduct and discipline" of UN troops not only affect peacekeeper's interactions beyond the camp but also shape the environment and practices in the camp. Since controlling the conduct and discipline of all ranks is, in large part, exercised through restrictions on movement outside the camp, various provisions are brought into the camp to limit the necessity for soldiers to leave. Shops like the La Cueva del Kaibil are ubiquitous in peacekeeping camps, purchases for which are made in downtown Goma on a weekly basis by a single officer. On one of my visits to a camp at Mubambiro, the officer in charge of stocking the camp store had been away in Goma for a little too long one morning, eliciting suspicions from his commanding officer that he was doing more than simply purchasing goods to stock the store shelves. There was sexual innuendo in the commander's suspicion that would have been lost on me had it not been for another officer telling me directly that the officer was suspected of having a girlfriend in Goma—possibly even one of the women working at the store where they bought their provisions. I excused myself before the officer returned to camp.

Not only do most camps run these kinds of canteen stores departments, many have also established souvenir shops and workshops within the bases. Congolese woodworkers with long ties to different battalions have an assortment of souvenirs for sale in most bases, reflecting the tastes and cultures of different contingents. These artisans create carvings of African wildlife, water-fetching women, or the famous Goma *tchukudu* alongside national military seals, figures of soldiers, battalion iconography, commemorative plaques, and culturally specific images like depictions of Hindu gods. The memorabilia on offer in each camp combines the aesthetics of Congolese space and those of troops' home countries to create popular souvenirs for the soldiers.

The store at the front of Lieutenant Colonel Shyam's camp is a container filled floor to ceiling with different masks and wooden handicrafts. Near the doorway were more practical everyday items like toothbrushes, shoe polish, and sneakers. The shop even sold women's jewelry "for the romantics in the brigade." Shyam described the interest of having such a wide assortment of products available for sale in the camp as making it so that troops "don't have to roam around the countryside." He sees this as both a security and welfare measure: "[we] don't have to go out"; Shyam associated going out with "taking chances." Few officers consider trips to Sunday Market, which takes place weekly in an enclosed sports field belonging to the Institut Technique Industriel de Goma (ITIG) across from the URUBATT camp, as "going out" for goods. The small, open-air environment and proximity to the camps in Goma make Sunday Market a welcomed alternative shopping experience for peacekeepers, who prefer these market features for the security and controllability they provide. While contingents do make trips to Virunga Market (the city's primary market), officers complain of its large size, crowdedness, rats, and high prices. Many feel less comfortable in Virunga and are required to go in uniform to enhance their security, which is not always the case at Sunday Market.

Interior shops and mini-marts are not only created for convenience or a more ordinary atmosphere but also as a result of the biopolitics at work in the camp. The "chances" Lieutenant Colonel Shyam and many other officers

allude to when they talk about efforts to keep soldiers in the camp are less related to perceived threats of violence against the peacekeepers and more often
framed in terms of the UN's zero-tolerance policy for sexual exploitation and
abuse—or, as it is known throughout UN peacekeeping, SEA. The chance that
the peacekeeper takes when he or she steps out of the base is thus framed as a
chance to commit or be accused of SEA.

The UN defines sexual exploitation as "any actual or attempted abuse of a
position of vulnerability, differential power, or trust, for sexual purposes, including, but not limited to, profiting monetarily, socially or politically from the
sexual exploitation of another." It defines sexual abuse as "the actual or threatened physical intrusion of a sexual nature, whether by force or under unequal
or coercive conditions" (UN Secretariat 2003). Posters remind contingents
of this zero-tolerance policy at every turn. Wherever soldiers congregate in
their peacekeeping camps or MONUSCO office compounds, one can expect
to see posters addressing the UN code of conduct, the rules of engagement,
and SEA, which spell out the repercussions of such a violation. Committing
acts that constitute SEA work to break trust between peacekeepers and the
host population, compromise the reputation of the United Nations, jeopardize
the success of the mandate to protect civilians, and can negatively impact civil
society by increasing the vulnerability of certain population segments (UNGA
2005; Burke 2014). While there is no disagreement about the negative outcomes
of such reprehensible conduct among peacekeeping officers and commanders
that I spoke to, the level of fear that contingents face over even being accused
of SEA has led to preventative measures, such as those related to confinement,
that some feel are excessive.

Strict restrictions on movements outside of the camp are often seen through
the lens of SEA prevention, in large part due to the wide scope of the policy.
Lieutenant Colonel Juan has previously lived in Goma as a military observer
(MILOB) (in the city) and now as a contingent officer (in the camp). The juxta-
position of these experiences allows him to feel the weight of such restrictions,
particularly in light of having lived beyond the camp freely and safely. He understands the fact that he can no longer ride his bike around town, go jogging
in the city, or stay out late at a restaurant as a result of SEA policy being "overdimensional." "Any relation is SEA," he laments. And in any relation, "we lose."
The overdimensional nature of SEA policy that Lieutenant Colonel Juan senses
is one that Olivia Simić (2012), coming from an international human rights law
perspective, would understand as an overinclusive definition of sexual exploitation.[12] Simić writes about the lack of nuance in the policy between exploitative

sex and consensual, adult sex as producing a discourse that strips participants of their agency and shapes perceptions of peacekeepers as sexual predators and perpetrators (5). Kathleen Jennings (2008) also takes a critical approach to the zero-tolerance policy interpreted as a total ban on sexual relationships and agrees that the lack of distinction between types of sexual behavior is problematic. The *inherent* power imbalances on which the zero-tolerance policy is predicated are understood as imbalances in vulnerability, power, and trust, as fixed, nonrelational objects. This framing, Jasmine-Kim Westendorf (2023, 1665) argues, "restructures paternalism in ways that entrench imbalances of power between local communities and the organizations mandated to 'protect' them." This has the attendant effects of "reproducing colonial patterns dealing with sex and sexuality" and "reinforcing racist dynamics that have long characterized how the global North has perceived and policed the personal and sexual choices of the people in the global South" (2023, 1665).

As Lieutenant Colonel Juan's superior Colonel Martín put it, "an allegation is a fault." While an allegation may not result in a substantiated case or prosecution, the troop-contributing country's military and national reputation takes such a hit that many peacekeepers feel the repercussions of unsubstantiated allegations against their contingent are equivalent to actual cases of exploitation and abuse.[13] Because of the different reputational interests of the UN and troop-contributing countries (Daugirdas 2019; Karim 2019), mission leadership is less concerned with curbing allegations than it is in preventing actual misconduct that impinges on the security and protection of civilians. SEA allegations carry particularly high stakes due to the international media attention given to UN peacekeeping missions. As Brigadier Kabir put it, "while deployed here, if something goes wrong, it will immediately be on CNN or BBC." Many contingents are not ready to risk an allegation of such high-level misconduct getting back to their families or host country headquarters, let alone circulating the globe through the international press. As a way of curbing allegations, many contingent commanders have responded by keeping their troops in their camps as much as possible. Keeping soldiers in camp and bringing different services and provisions into the barracks as a reactionary measure adds an extraordinary layer to life in the camp. Such confinement measures implemented by contingent commanders are also often evolutive over the time of their tenure. Officers in the Indian army use a common saying—"There are more causalities on the descent from the summit of Mount Everest than the ascent"—to convey the necessity for increased vigilance toward the end of a mission and to make sense of the stricter policies toward the end of the tenures. If security is not the main priority of the peacekeeping camp, complacency and comfort set in. Major Siddharth, a dedicated conduct and discipline officer, confirmed that he saw a clear trend of contingents having more cases of misconduct and SEA allegations leading up to their deinduction from the mission area.

Colonel Martín, Brigadier Kabir, and several lower-ranking officers throughout Goma understand their heightened visibility and the risk of allegations as operational challenges. Major Neel feels the military is under a microscope and that contingents are so afraid about SEA and other allegations of misconduct that they refrain from even doing their job: "There's so much I could do if I'm allowed to and supposed to." He even went so far as to frame a quick impact project implemented by one contingent as being rooted more so within a logic of putting troops to work to create less downtime—less time during which they could potentially misbehave—than actually building infrastructures and institutions for the benefit of the Congolese civilians. Colonel Martín admitted that there was a time during his tenure when he considered removing the nametags from the uniforms of his troops before they went out of the camp, lest someone sees an opportunity to make a false accusation in an attempt to obtain some financial compensation. In this way, officers and commanders alike see the impact of such an overdimensional SEA policy of the UN as limiting their capacity to engage with the Congolese community in ways that would benefit the project of peacekeeping.

The legacy and international media attention around military contingents in the DRC that have been involved in serious misconduct in the past may play a role in the overwhelming targeting of SEA prevention campaigns toward military contingents in Goma today. In Bunia in 2004, peacekeepers were reportedly sexually exploiting and abusing women from a nearby internally displaced persons camp, engaging in sex for money, sex for food, and sex with persons under eighteen-years-old (UNGA 2005; Dahrendorf 2006; Neudorfer 2015)— reports that made international press (K. Holt 2004). The UN reacted with a comprehensive report aimed at eliminating SEA (known as the Zeid Report) and a dedicated Office for Addressing Sexual Exploitation and Abuse, the first of its kind (Dahrendorf 2006). This did not stop cases from occurring, however. Former mayor Roger Rachid Tumbula recalls having a "serious squabble" (une prise de bec sérieuse) with the South African contingent based in Goma over allegations of sexual abuse committed against local children during his tenure. The UN does not disaggregate SEA data on a subnational level, so knowing how many cases occur in Goma is difficult.[14] Considering the spatial and urban dimensions of SEA may help scholars better understand place-based factors that shape the persistent phenomenon. It may also help individual contingent commanders restore some balance to overdimensional policies that restrict where and when their soldiers' bodies are allowed in the city.

Today, allegations are investigated by troop-contributing countries in tandem with the Office of Internal Oversight Services or the Security Investigation Unit, and several redressal mechanisms and victim assistance programs have been implemented. MONUSCO's Conduct and Discipline section has established three centers for SEA victims in and around Goma in partnership with a local nongovernmental organization. In Saké, victims grow mushrooms and run a bakery. In Bujovu, there is a school for children who have been born out of SEA, and in Munigi, women run a *salon de coiffure* and a *patisserie*. Not coincidentally, these centers are in neighborhoods and communities near active peacekeeping bases.

Just as variable rates of SEA have been associated with variations in the national and military cultures of different contingents (Kovatch 2016; Moncrief 2017), so too do prevention and disciplinary measures vary across peacekeeping camps. While Uruguayans and Senegalese peacekeepers generally adhere to the strictest UN curfews, South Africans have been known for looser timing restrictions. Indian peacekeepers have sought a balance between the 18:00 contingent curfew and the 01:00/02:00 UN-wide curfew, requiring officers to be back in the camp by 23:00. Discipline is necessarily dependent on each national military, since they dictate the orders of the camp and have the exclusive jurisdictional right to prosecute their soldiers for crimes committed on a peacekeeping mission. The fact that national militaries (and not the UN) are responsible for taking disciplinary action is repeated by scholars as contributing to the ongoing problem of SEA through rare, nontransparent, or unfair trials or a lack of will or capacity to prosecute on behalf of the military of the accused (Kanetake 2010; Burke 2014; Neudorfer 2015). The UN as the employer can terminate and dismiss civilians for serious misconduct and can only repatriate soldiers, barring them from future work with the UN (Kanetake 2010).

The way that previous misconduct in the DRC has driven SEA policy reform over the years, that current policy's aggressive rollout, and its overwhelming translation by national contingents into measures, facilities, and architectures of confinement coalesce to produce a strong biopower that operates in peacekeeping camp space. Routines, physical trainings, camp maintenance works, strict curfews, shops, and welfare activities that decidedly take place within the camps can all be seen as military matters of discipline and regulation, the two poles of power over life distinguished by Foucault. If the daily routines of peacekeepers served to highlight the disciplining of the troops' bodies in the name of order and operational efficiency, it is the confining, regulatory control of the peacekeeper's body, and particularly his sexual conduct, as a "target of intervention" that produces a biopolitical current to life in the camp (Foucault 1978, 26). Looking at soldiers' security as it unfolds in the logics, rules, and amenities of peacekeeping camps highlights the idea that while peacekeepers act as the enforcers of humanitarian and neo-imperial modes of power in the name of peace, they also become the subjects of such modes of power.

A peacekeeper's subjugation to the biopolitics of peacekeeping camp space is a voluntary act that stems from his or her choice to join the armed service of their respective country as well as their ability to abstain from participating in peacekeeping (even if selected). Nevertheless, during their tenure of service in the DRC, the peacekeeper's biological and sexualized body is confined and governed through multiple, overlapping juridical-political orders regulating life in the camps. These include the UN's code of conduct and definition of SEA, the status of force agreements that legitimize the presence of a foreign military in a sovereign state and the laws of the sovereign state itself, the national military law and penal law of troop contributing countries, and the orders of the contingent commander. This means that even if certain sexual behaviors or transactions are legal in the DRC, peacekeepers are beholden to the laws of their own country and armed forces, in addition to the policies of the United Nations, while participating in military peacekeeping. The biopower of the camp thus emerges not through an exceptional suspension of rights (as Agamben has posited in vastly different contexts of encampment) but in the (extra-)ordinary overlapping of juridical orders regulating camp space and peacekeeper mobility and behavior in the DRC (1998).

For all that is ordinary about peacekeeping camps, natural life and politics become intertwined in (extra-)ordinary ways. These bases are built and function to sustain the lives of the troops living in them by imposing certain rules on their bodies and are places in which discourses, layouts, and disciplinary practices limit and interrupt different possibilities in the lives of soldiers. At the same time, peacekeeping camps accumulate war materials that destroy life. Ammunition is stored next to the library. Armored vehicles with light machine gun mounts are parked behind places of worship. Rifles are kept in a securitized CORIMEC or container armory, known as a *kote* among Indian contingents. Each rifle is coded by number and assigned and adjusted to an individual soldier's body. Two separate signatures are required in the log book before a rifle is removed from the *kote*. Just as the peacekeeper's body is conceived of as a threat to the environment beyond the camp and is thus subject to strict regulations and confinement, so too are the materials of the camp controlled, checked, and double-checked even. The UN's mandate and rules of engagement reserve the intended use of such equipment for extremely particular circumstances on the battlefield of peace.

Much of what brings into focus the (extra-)ordinary quality of camp space and limited mobility beyond it is underpinned by the built-in assumption (in SEA reduction measures, for instance) that peacekeeping camps are exclusively male spaces that uphold a culture of hypersexual, military masculinity. Control of the male body through regulated confinement to the camp and strict accountability mechanisms for the handling of weapons has been the overwhelming coping strategy of the UN and various contingents. To counteract the irregular living conditions of strict confinement during a relatively safe deployment, contingent commanders have re-created certain city services and amenities within the camp, bringing in souvenirs, hygiene products, and other consumer goods for purchase. They are also, increasingly, bringing women with them on missions.

Camping with Women

According to Major Olivia, an officer working in the mission's gender section, having women around in the camp can make it feel more "normal." The women Olivia has in mind are not civilian, foreign nationals such as myself (though my presence has also been interpreted as normalizing social spaces in the camp in addition to exposing and familiarizing troops with women from other countries and cultures than their own). Rather, Olivia is referring to an often-overlooked benefit of increasing the recruitment of women in military peacekeeping. The UN has made increasing women's participation in military peacekeeping a priority, particularly since the Women, Peace, and Security Agenda of 2000. A disciplinarily diverse academic and policy literature has discussed the operational advantages and limitations of women serving in peacekeeping missions (Beilstein 1998; UNSC 2000b; Sion 2008; Simić 2010; Karim and Beardsley 2017; Alchin, Gouws, and Heinecken 2018; DPKO and DFS 2018). Efforts to include more women in peacekeeping are widely framed and perceived in terms of the positive impact they bring to a mission's community engagement and outreach. MONUSCO included around twenty-two "mixed engagement teams" across different contingents by 2020. The advantage of such mixed teams (and particularly women's role in them) is seen as being able to unlock pieces of society that would "otherwise be inaccessible to the military," according to Olivia. She highlights this benefit with anecdotal experiences of Western forces in Afghanistan being constrained by cultural norms from searching women's living quarters for weapons. Having such

teams, particularly among some of the more culturally conservative contingents in Goma, is already seen as a "big step forward" given gender norms in
these militaries, according to her. As Sabrina Karim and Kyle Beardsley (2017)
argue, however, barriers to gender equality persist in peacekeeping, in part,
due to women's relegation to and unique recognition for community engagement initiatives within peacekeeping missions. Straying from the concerns of
gender (in)equality in peacekeeping for peacekeeping's sake, I am interested
here in discussing the ways that women's presence in peacekeeping intersects
with the space and place of the camp and the views of different contingents
regarding this nexus.

Given the spatial constraints and limited resources allocated to many peacekeeping camps in Goma, both men and women in the mission can view accommodating women as a challenge. Arno, whom we met earlier, served in
the United Nations Operation in Burundi with his girlfriend (now wife) and
recalled some of the demands this put on his contingent and the ways that
they innovated. During that mission, Arno's partner was the only woman on
their team, and the contingent could not justify spending its self-sustainment
resources on a separate ablutions space. Instead, the contingent bought a small
painting of a lady, which his partner would hang on the door of the ablutions
unit so that men wouldn't enter while she was using it.[15] Arno ran into a similar
accommodation problem in Goma, despite the UN being responsible for providing accommodation in the camp. Arno recalls that in 2010, a female pilot
joined the South African Air Force contingent in Goma. In military aviation
practice, it is common to have aircrews sleep together, making command and
control easier. Because of the number of CORIMECs the UN had allocated for
their camp and the types of hierarchical divisions that the air force was used
to, the female pilot would have been expected to sleep in a room with three
other men. The pilot was willing to do so, though "unisex" is not a particularly
popular concept for South Africans according to Arno, let alone for the military. Since the camp also hosted a female doctor and other support staff, the
female pilot was accommodated with them instead. While the men of the air-
crew already felt cramped sleeping four to a CORIMEC (instead of three), the
women's CORIMEC now hosted five sleepers, including the female pilot. Arno
added a sexist comment about the chaos that can ensue by having five women
living in a tight space together before saying, "The UN is not up to this gender/
persons thing." In camps with few female officers (including certain rotations
of BANMP and GUASFOR, for instance), this practice of forgoing norms that
dictate organizing accommodation in line with the military hierarchy is typical. When accommodation divisions by rank become untenable because of a

lack of dedicated CORIMECs or ablutions facilities, women tend to live with more people or in different parts of the camp than their male counterparts do. In this way, organizing accommodations for women does not privilege their rank in the same ways it does for men.

Gender considerations in terms of the camp layout and shared spaces are not only an issue in terms of lodging. Contingents with more frequent and larger groups of women, such as the Uruguayans and Senegalese, still face challenges accommodating women in other ways. When I asked Uruguayan NCOs what they would change or improve about their camp, the men overwhelmingly wanted to see improvements or additions to sports facilities, such as the renovation of the defunct swimming pool, planting grass on the football field, or even adding a *frontón*, or court for playing Basque pelota. The sole woman in the group raised the issue of the gym, suggesting the need for more privacy for women who want to work out in the camp. While each camp reflects the different cultural gender norms of the national militaries present in Goma, women overwhelmingly expressed the need for greater collective privacy in their peacekeeping camps.

For the Senegalese gendarmes and other militaries from countries with more conservative gender norms, separate social spaces for men and women become more important. Women constitute the cooking staff of both GUAS-FOR and the Senegalese Formed Police Unit (SEN-FPU), making the kitchen a predominately female space in these camps. Part of the importance of such gender-segregated areas is because many women in peacekeeping camps experience leisure differently than men. The Senegalese women of SEN-FPU have created quite a comfortable and joyous sisterhood among themselves over late-night ludo games, *sabar* dances, and gossip sessions. Even in spaces and events organized within a logic of welfare, gender considerations become important to troops' sense of comfort and normalcy. Often, however, materials and resources are unable to make these kinds of adjustments in peacekeeping camps. Part of this issue stems from the troop-contributing countries themselves, who should stress the gender component of their camps and the associated material needs in their memorandums of understanding (MOUs) with the UN Department of Peacekeeping Operations. When MONUSCO provides accommodation, it does so based on how many people the camp needs to accommodate, not how many men or women. When MOUs are signed, it is difficult to know the number of women who will join any given troop rotation. Nonetheless, Arno believes that a better understanding of how gender works in the military, especially when it comes to cohabitation with women, could help resolve some of the problems they face when they reach their camps in Goma. So far, efforts to feminize the mission space have overlooked the necessity to feminize the camp (Higate and Henry 2009; Kronsell 2012; Karim and Beardsley 2017).[16]

More gender-sensitive camp planning has emerged as a seemingly unintended consequence of moving the SEN-FPU camp from an industrial site owned by a coffee estate to public land next to the airport runway. Senegalese women saw the transition from accommodation in the permanent structures on the site of the former Camp Jambaar to accommodation in semipermanent, prefab CORIMECs as a marked improvement of their living conditions. In addition to better living areas, the new camp allowed them to gain more space and more privacy due to a greater distance from the male living quarters. In this new camp, the women even have their own refectory and TV room. Such spatial considerations were part of the norm back home in Senegal, where the layout of barracks adequately reflect Senegalese gender dynamics. They found Camp Jambaar, to put it politely, "a little strange" commenting on the morose atmosphere given by the darkness inside many of the concrete buildings and the cramped living quarters.[17] It is also worth mentioning that when men were asked to compare Camp Jambaar with their new camp, gendered space was also an issue—not with the women of the contingent, but with local women. They mentioned the promiscuity present in the old camp during a focus group discussion. It was relatively well-known in Camp Jambaar and the adjacent neighborhood that local women were entering the camp from a hole in the perimeter abutting the neighborhood. The very location of the COB is often seen as a factor that can impact the incidence of SEA cases, with a staffer at mission support praising the move of the Senegalese across the street so that they would be adjacent to the airport and not near places where the local population lived. Major Siddharth was charged with conducting assessments of all COBs to ensure that their architectural perimeters were intact, lest physical "leaks" between the camp and the city gave rise to such incidences.

I never directly observed these kinds of illicit and gendered intrusions at the perimeters of the peacekeeping camps but rather was around and aware of several informal liaisons happening between peacekeepers and Congolese or Rwandan women in the national houses mentioned in chapter 1. Large residences where MILOBs or civilian staff of MONUSCO from a particular country find accommodation in Goma offered a sort of bridging space between the confinement of the camp and the city at large for encamped peacekeepers. Officers from various camps were frequently invited or would drop by the residences of their compatriots who had much less restricted mobility in the city and thus, more frequent possibilities to encounter people living in Goma. These houses sometimes offered a refuge for a romantic rendezvous between

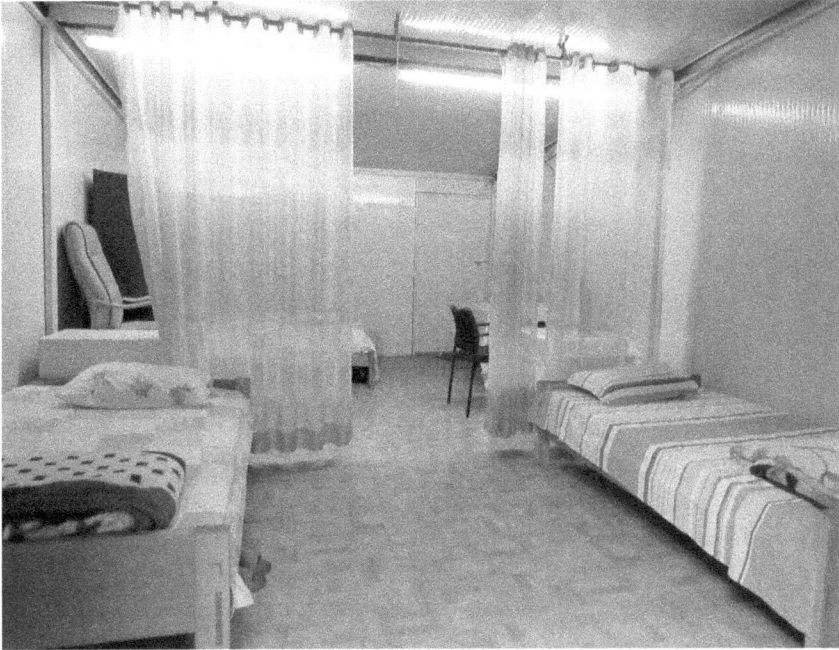

While most officers are accommodated two to a CORIMEC, three female officers at BANMP share a single accommodation. (Photo by author)

encamped peacekeepers and women in the city. This role for such houses, however, was much more of an exception than a rule. On many, if not most occasions that I was invited to gatherings at national houses, if Congolese or Rwandan men and women were also invited, they were presented as friends or mission colleagues.

Special accommodations and other spatial considerations for women within the camps are balanced by an ordinary sense of camaraderie in peacekeeping camps between military men and women. Many women attribute their level of comfort and familiarity serving in overwhelmingly male spaces to their collective training and their shared objective of supporting the peacekeeping mission. The conviviality of gender relations in these camps come through in the way that women of SEN-FPU often refer to their male counterparts as uncles or brothers. Khady, one of two female officers at SEN-FPU during her rotation (and the more outspoken of the two), even called some of the men in the contingent her sons, since she had been their instructor during training. Some of the highlights of the women's time in Goma have been their football matches against the older, male veterans of the squad and the late nights they have spent among themselves in their shared CORIMEC. Whether in their own quarters or socializing with men, the women of the camp feel a close, nonthreatening camaraderie with those with whom they share their camp.

According to Major Olivia, increasing gender equality in peacekeeping is not just a matter of improving the performance and outcomes of such missions but also of shaping military cultures and spaces of troop-contributing countries, including their camps. Many officers believe that serving alongside women can serve to normalize the camp environment for the overwhelmingly male force—countering the otherwise more exceptional circumstances that can negatively affect officers' morale and conduct. Major Olivia has witnessed for herself "a breakdown of normal relationships" in her own army when women are completely absent in certain military spaces. She adds that women in the camp can help remind male troops of familial relations. They can help remind them of home.

Welfare, Morale, and Affinity in the Camp

In addition to a female presence in peacekeeping camp space, Major Olivia points out the significance of sports, lounges, and temples in terms of making camps look and feel "normal." Milestones and occasions, for instance, activate different places for socialization within the camp. Birthdays, anniversaries, military achievements, and holidays are often magnified in the camp for the opportunity they offer to break what can otherwise become a monotonous daily life. Many ordinary social events and milestones are seized on to bring all camp dwellers together and take on a more elaborate tone in peacekeeping camp life. Back at the GUASFOR camp, where we began this chapter, only two companies were left back in Mubambiro: one was actively guarding and patrolling the camp while the other rested. The quiet of the camp was nonetheless broken up several times during my stay. I had arrived in camp on All Saints' Day—a day celebrated in Guatemala with a large colorful salad known as *fiambré*. The commander had invited other Latin American UN staff as well as a group of Spanish-speaking priests from a nearby mission to join for the famous lunch as well, followed by karaoke in the conference room that went well into the evening. Immediately after the morning briefing (following our run), troops celebrated a fellow soldier's birthday by throwing flour on him and blasting him with the hose straight from the back of the water tanker. The Uruguayans similarly seized on the All Saints' holiday, celebrating Halloween with an elaborate party the Saturday before. They transformed the URUBATT base into a haunted camp with the décor and detail that has come to exemplify the commercialized American idea of the holiday. Ripped and recycled mosquito nets made convincing spider webs. Clear garbage bags tied in just the right spots became ghosts in a graveyard full of cardboard box tombstones. Black garbage bags wrapped with duct tape became a sort of corps placed in the "tomb" of the *barbacoa*. Creative credit for the evening went to the women of the camp.

In more religiously diverse camps like SEN-FPU, religious holidays are particularly strong moments to enhance the esprit de corps of the contingent. Back in Senegal, in more religiously mixed communities, Christian and Muslim neighbors frequently spend their respective religious festivals together—with Muslim families hosting Tabaski and Christian families making *ngallax*, a peanuty millet porridge, for Muslim friends on Easter. The Senegalese gendarmerie is one such mixed community, and the gendarmes in Goma reflected fondly on these holiday moments when looking back at their tenure. One of the women described feeling among family during such celebrations.

The feeling of being a family, of serving as brothers- and sisters-in-arms, is important to troops' welfare and morale. Sporting games, previously discussed, constitute a sort of mandated leisure activity that have real and perceived benefits for the soldier's physical fitness, for breaking the monotony of daily life, but also for the way that they encourage bonding. As Colonel Pablo says, "The best psychologist is the soldier next to you." His understanding of social support in the camp starts with the smallest scale and lowest unit of military organization. In URUBATT, that unit is the squad level of nine or ten people—an ideal size for many of the team sports played in camp like soccer and volleyball. Sporting events also tend to leak out of the camp in controlled settings, such as the ITIG field that hosts cricket matches between Indian officers and businessmen from the diaspora living in Goma. Lieutenant Colonel Dev even combined the benefits of fitness and outreach in organizing a friendly volleyball match at one of Goma's central sporting grounds for one of his units of *jawans* to play against a local youth team. With the attendance of the head of the Sports and Leisure Division of the provincial government, the sporting match equally became a civil-military coordination activity. By holding the match out in the city, rather than in camp, Lieutenant Colonel Dev proudly declared, "This is my Urafiki Meeting!"

Despite the various scales at which togetherness can be forged in the military and the array of sporting events that can foment teamwork, the space of the camp is organized in such a way as to be the great equalizer among troops

in creating, as the Senegalese put it "benn morale"—a singular and encompassing morale. That morale has as much to do with the creation of a metaphorical
family in the camp as it does to ensuring that the individual soldier and officer
feels connected to his or her family back home. For that reason, rosters of officers in any given Indian camp often list the officer's name, birthday, phone
number, wife's name, and anniversary date. Features of camp life that seek to
build camaraderie within the contingent and remind soldiers of their domestic
attachments both contribute to fomenting familiarity against the backdrop of
an unfamiliar environment.

Despite strict attention to rank hierarchies and general spatial separation
between cohabiting regiments, rank troops, junior commissioned officers
(JCOs) and NCOs, and the officer class, different militaries have different
traditions of bringing everyone together and building collective spirit. The
Indian army tradition of the *bara khana*, literally meaning "big food" or "feast,"
is a common occurrence in Indian military life and has followed the Indian
battalions to the DRC. Officers attend these events, but it is the soldiers themselves who organize the evening and put on the show. As the protocol goes,
when all the officers have their drinks, the senior-most JCO says a toast before
a series of performances commence. Different acts take the stage: one soldier
may recite a poem; another may perform a stand-up comedy routine peppered
with patriotism and jabs at the officers for not revealing information about their
promotions. Yet another may lip-synch and dance. All the while, the barman
and drink registrar make their way through the rows of troops with an alcohol
issue, making sure no single soldier goes over the limit of pegs (thirty-milliliter
shots) he is allotted for the special occasion. Strict distinctions and segregations
between the various ranks, who sit in different sections of the audience, often
collapse into joint dancing by the end of the event. During a *bara khana*, there
are not multiple ranks or multiple regiments but a singular morale making the
camp. Rotations out of the duty station are one of the reasons to hold a *bara
khana* but can also be celebrated with different military rituals across different
ranks. The two *bara khanas* I was graciously (and rather exceptionally) invited
to attend served to celebrate Indian Republic Day as well as the rotation of
units. In one camp, the *bara khana* was also the occasion to celebrate the honorary promotion of a JCO to an officer for thirty years of honorable service.[18]
Toward the end of a given unit's tour in Congo, Indian officers sometimes take
small groups of *jawans* and NCOs out for dinner and drinks in Goma (usually at one of the Indian-owned restaurants). These outings are one of the few
exceptions made during soldiers' tenure when they can go out into the city for
fun (always with and under the supervision of an officer or JCO). Throughout

their time in the mission, several battalions rent swimming pools at large hotels in Goma or organize small group trips to beaches or hotels in Gisenyi on Sundays and holidays. These are the only leisure or welfare events that rank troops partake in beyond the camp walls. Even during such outings for the soldiers, spatial control and confinement to specific sites, as well as the presence of one or more officers, provide a strong sense of discipline built into the exercise of leisure, rest, and relaxation.

Conclusion: Controlling and Caring for Peacekeepers

The insides and outsides of the peacekeeping camp are in constant tension on multiple scales, resolved through ordinary and extraordinary measures that often underpin even the most leisurely activities with a degree of control in the name of troop security. Camp scheduling and routine is similarly as much a matter of ensuring troops' welfare as it is about controlling their bodies. Leisure activities are underpinned by the logic that comfort is one of the keys to a soldier's utility. Because of the operational link this understanding creates, troops are disciplined into having fun. Care becomes a commander's responsibility. Welfare activities become a command. Busy troops are happy troops. And happy troops are viewed as the most effective in battle.[19]

Many of the welfare amenities, services, materials, configurations, and jobs that exist in a peacekeeping camp call to mind salient features of cities. Like cities, camps are relatively dense clusters of people and agglomerations of resources to sustain life. They offer a scale at which we can identify an independent (albeit interconnected) economy, settlement pattern, and set of decision-making logics that shape their politics. Like cities, the visual and material environment of the camp also acts as an expression of the social relations contained therein and operates as a function of serving those relationships (Mumford 1937). The peacekeeping camp is a way of life (Wirth 1938). The ways that peacekeepers tend to speak about their camps, as shown throughout, reinforces the experiential aspects of these spaces as urban.

As a place of respite from the operational theaters of military peacekeeping and seclusion from the wider urban landscape, however, the interiors of these camps and the lives peacekeepers live inside of them are shaped by multiple, institutional power structures. The "developmental and humanitarian modes of power" studied in refugee camp settings and that have come to constitute the genre of relief anthropology (De Waal 2002, 252) become blurred when we home in on a specific population that is too frequently lumped together with other interveners in humanitarian discourse. "Blue helmets" are not only the object of these modes of power in their operational requirement but become the subject of it themselves as UN standards, rules, and restrictions impact the architectures, amenities, and workings of the camp. The zero-tolerance discourse and SEA prevention measures (as they are understood and internalized by contingent commanders), for instance, create an overwhelming emphasis on measures that further confine peacekeepers to their camps and keep them "out of the city." Even the most banal and domestic scenes are underpinned by logics of control and confinement that engender different sociospatial developments, acting as an undercurrent in organizing peacekeepers' possibilities during their free time.

Understanding peacekeeping camps as (extra-)ordinary camps proposes two things at once. First, the orthography of (extra-)ordinary camps suggests that the "extra" prefix in parentheses could be left out without compromising the veracity of the phrase. Acknowledging peacekeeping camps as ordinary camps adopts the kind of comparative gesture that has been at the heart of much of Jennifer Robinson's (2002, 2005, 2006, 2016, 2023) scholarship over the last two decades, which has sought to transgress the categorical divisions that have come to characterize the study of cities and, thus, inform urban theorizations. In such a move, peacekeeping camps are recovered and included in a world of camps and camp scholarship, currently dominated by the study of camps accommodating refugees and migrants. Second, however, the (extra-)ordinary qualifier distances itself from the production of exception (in Agamben's sense of the word) while nonetheless acknowledging the ways that power operates through multiple layers of order to govern bodies in the peacekeeping camp. While many of these orders are internal to the national armies inhabiting each camp and their own regimes of military justice, others are imposed externally through discourses and regulations of the supra-sovereign United Nations. The (extra-)ordinary quality of space in these camps thus draws our attention to the experiential and governmental similarities and differences between peacekeeping and other types of camps.

As several of the activities illustrated throughout this chapter have sought to show, entangled logics of control and care pervade the space of the camp. Physical training and games are conducted following a rationale that is between physically disciplining the soldier's body and providing him with recreational opportunities. Shops pop up in the camp to offer troops small comforts and souvenirs as well as to discourage trips outside of the base. Camp leaders furnish and arrange their camps in ways that seek a balance between caring for their soldiers and controlling their bodies. Troop discipline and welfare also frequently collapse into a single rationale for organizing various activities and amenities in the camp. Furthermore, different rituals in the camp make ordinary events and celebrations more extraordinary. These ritual occasions are not only associated with particular places in the camp where these events occur—such as the parade grounds of the *bara khana*, the flagpoles in front of the parade pitch, or the officers' mess—but mark the peacekeeping camp space as a whole and, at times, leverages the city as a privileged space of escape for special occasions. Events that mark an entrance to a liminal state with a ritual, such as those associated with promotions and rotations, are particularly ripe for human bonding and of cultivating communitas (V. W. Turner 1977; E. L. B. Turner 2012). Commanders build these moments into a peacekeeping tenure and operationalize them to enhance sociality, soldier welfare, and morale, not as ends in and of themselves, but as means to achieve overall operational success. Within the Congolese context, these camps occupy a liminal space of intervention between the devastation of war and the hope of peace. Here, work lives and social lives are intertwined, and both are seemingly strengthened because of it. As Victor W. Turner (1977, 96) points out, liminal phenomena present us with a "moment in and out of time." Peacekeeping camps as liminal entities present us with a space that is both in and out of the city, both frustrating and joyful, both ordinary and extraordinary. The following chapters pick up on the space of this productive tension to discuss how peacekeeping camps emerge in a liminal space between home and the world.

4

At Home in the Camp

Experientially, home was a matter of being-at-home-in-the-world. It connoted a sense of existential control and connectedness—the way we feel when what we say or do seems to matter, and there is a balanced reciprocity between the world beyond us and the world within which we move.

—Michael Jackson, *At Home in the World*, 154

Major Baba ate something to line his stomach upon returning to camp. The festivities got underway early as his fellow officers began offering him libations. He wasn't in the mood for making a late night of it and paced himself. With his deinduction in two days, it was the night of his "dining out"—a traditional and elaborate farewell party replete with rituals that insist on the outgoing officer's liminal position between being here and being elsewhere. Despite the social and celebratory nature of the event, it retains a level of decorum and dress marked by formality and follows certain military protocols and customs that prevent friendly anthropologists from attending. Major Baba and I instead texted throughout the night while his fellow officers took photos and videos.

Out on the lawn of the officers' mess, a sound system had been set up for the occasion. After receiving his commanding officer's glowing commendations, it was Major Baba's turn to take the mic and reflect on his tenure. Major Baba was leaving Goma after witnessing two rotations of officers and troops, which had come with "many drunken speeches." He admitted being slightly inebriated himself but kept his remarks sober and sincere, save the kind of witty and self-deprecating humor that so endeared him to his cohort. The gratitude he expressed for those he'd met in Goma made evident that he had been changed by the experience, that colleagues had become much more over time. After thanking "Sir" for all the kind words and for everyone who organized the evening, Major Baba became more sentimental. "In that I would also start by saying, I consider myself to be very fortunate to have served with the best of the Indian army. I did not do much to deserve it, but I do value that." He paused for a beat before continuing, "And also, I would like to thank everyone here for their professional help, more importantly their friendship, which I hold close to my heart. I would always value that and I could never repay." He thanked his seniors for their guidance and love, his "brothers in arms"—including those who had since returned to India but who he asserted were always with him—and the civilians whom he'd met in Goma. "They changed everything," he said, adding, "even the way I think." He reminded his fellow officers of where his next posting would be, extending an invitation that reiterated his affection: "My house is your house."

After the dinner following his speech, Major Baba wrote some farewell remarks in the Visitor's Log, a registry of those who have come through the officers' mess. The log stays in the camp until it is dismantled and all troops are repatriated. For the final act of his dining out, fellow officers sang a rendition of "For He's a Jolly Good Fellow," hoisting Major Baba into the air on a chair and carrying him out the door. From that point forward in an officer's tenure, they are no longer a member of the mess. Major Baba remained in camp to finish handing over his duties to the officer replacing him but was no longer allowed to pay for any meals or drinks. In a night, the officer moves from being able to host to becoming an exclusive guest. Removing this person from the ordinary rights of dwelling in the camp relegates them to the same position of those just passing through, making the tradition of an officer's dining out akin to a liminal rite (Arnold van Gennep in Thomassen 2014, 3).

Major Baba remained in the camp for a day or two, but, as his dining out intimated, he was no longer at home in the camp; the farewell fanfare was rooted in acknowledging his return to a home elsewhere. Yet his affectionate remarks for the men in his camp who had once been strangers reflected a way of inhabiting camp as one inhabits a home. As anthropologist Michael Jackson (1995) has written, home can be a place, but it can also be "a group of *people* without whom your life would cease to have meaning" (66, emphasis in original). Major Baba's dining out brought to the fore aspects of home as places and as people, as well as an appreciation for the camp as a place made with notions of home as simultaneously here and elsewhere.

This chapter focuses its attention on how peacekeeping camps are made with and complicate notions of being at home. I illustrate the personhood and place of home through an attention to camp-based eating practices, architectural and aesthetic features, and the multiple temporalities along which time in a peacekeeping camp is structured. These elements of camp life across different national contingents reveal that the principles, people, and places underpinning notions of being at home in the camp are both proximate and distant, at times more fluid than fixed.

Camps have become privileged sites through which to unpack and problematize the relationship between concepts of home and displacement (Beeckmans et al. 2022). As Nasser Abourahme (2020, 41) writes on the nature of the camp as an urban concept, "it is the camp that most forcefully returns the home—in all its contradictions from affective attachments and belongings to experiences of utter squalor, from security threat to a built container of memory—back to politics." While home is central to politics in camps inhabited by the forcibly displaced, Thomas Hendriks has shown how homemaking in camp spaces inhabited voluntarily can also resist stability and centrality. In his ethnography on Congolese logging camps, he writes, "Loggers . . . made their homes especially through objects and images that *referred to elsewhere*" (T. Hendriks 2022, 132, emphasis in original). Hendriks goes on to argue that displacement lies at the heart of homemaking practices in the logging camps (ibid., 136). Yet recent work in urban geography has highlighted that the term *displacement* "is less well equipped to depict the variations and contradictions in outcome and experience of relocation" (Meth et al. 2022, 2). This chapter draws inspiration from this burgeoning literature in its consideration of deployment as a lived experience between dislocation and relocation, taking seriously the ways in which peacekeepers understand, experience, and engage with the particular place of the latter in making a home in the camp.[1] This chapter also most sharply insists on deployment as a mode of dwelling, revealing how peacekeeping camps become a home made up of references to elsewhere that are simultaneously relocalized in ways that insist on the significance of peacekeepers' actual location in Goma and thus allow the city to shape senses of home in their camps.

A Taste of Home

The men in the kitchen were busy preparing *canelones* for lunch on one of my first visits and tours of the URUBATT camp with Colonel Pablo and his deputy, Colonel Luis. To reach the kitchen, we had passed through the adjoining bakery where bread and biscuits were being prepared according to recipes from Uruguay, the warm and yeasty smells following us. As Colonel Pablo saw it, we were at the epicenter of not only the camp's provisioning but also its morale.

Full stomachs gave his troops full hearts, he thought, believing that familiar foods were one of the most effective ways to ward off homesickness among his soldiers. Across peacekeeping camps, different recipes and provisions are brought along for the same remedial effect. In GUASFOR, bars of pressed cocoa (*tableta*) sustain troops' sweet tooth as does *ayote en dulce*, a sweet pumpkin dessert that makes a frequent appearance on the mess menu. Senegalese contingents have brought enough bags of dried *kinkeliba* leaves to share so that visitors can also enjoy *sexaw*—a tea well-known back home for its health benefits. Strong and sweet chai appears steaming on a silver tray (seemingly out of nowhere) at an outpost on Eastern Hill in Munigi, as if one had just arrived at an Indian *dhaba*. The appearance and familiar taste of strong and sweet chai retains, regardless of the base or place, an element of intrigue for even the most senior officers in the Indian army—an anchor to something familiar in less than familiar places.

For the Second Battalion of the Jammu and Kashmir Rifles, who chronicled their 2009–10 MONUSCO peacekeeping tour in Kiwanja with a unit memoir, familiar food was viewed as a more specific mechanism with which to cope with the year-long celibacy of the 850 "grooms" deployed abroad. Reflecting on their preinduction preparations, they write, "A simple guesstimate indicated more than five thousand items on the shopping list and if due diligence was not paid, life with bare minimum comforts in the mission area would become mission impossible." As such, they ensured that the unit had a "perennial supply of lassi, soups, and boiled eggs" to complement UN-issued rations (Avasthi 2010, 12).

As decades of anthropological and sociological research has shown, the preparation and consumption of food account for vital architectures and human comforts of home as a place in addition to being processes for group identity formation.[2] One of the reasons food is so central to feeling at home is that it can "evoke the experience of home as a sensory totality" (Petridou 2001, 89). In peacekeeping camps, food is perhaps the most visceral way peacekeepers maintain connections to homes elsewhere. The material culture of food—including its growing, storing, cooking, eating, and disposal—is also a key organizing and design logic of the camp. Central in this schema is the mess, the privileged site of food's preparation and consumption and, thus, home's reimagining.

The centrality and importance of the mess is reflected in part by its location and situation in peacekeeping camps across Goma. Mess halls tend to occupy primary architectures and locations such as permanent buildings (if there are any on site) or places with a view. Yet the mess is not just a privileged place in the home of the camp; it is an institution, one that requires codified management and demands a certain level of decorum by those who enter that space.

Institutionally, the officers' mess is distinct from the mess for rank-and-file soldiers and is governed by a committee of officers (led by a mess secretary), has a dedicated staff, opens and closes at certain hours, and follows its own specific rules and protocols. It is also the main place in the peacekeeping camp where outside guests are hosted and proudly served dishes from the peacekeepers' home country and where officers celebrate their own milestones, achievements, and deinductions with familiar and favorite meals. In the room adjacent to the dining room in many messes, the locally made furniture, coffee tables, and bars give one the sense of entering a living room, creating a sense of domesticity adjacent to where the dishes that evoke a home elsewhere are prepared.

Whether with guests or among one another, peacekeepers value the mess as an important social space in the camp for its connection to "the communitas of food" (E. L. B. Turner 2012, 68). That communitas lends it the power to undo many of the strict hierarchies governing military life. Indian officers treat the word *mess* as an acronym for "maintenance of equal social status," reinforcing its identity as an unalienated space. In the mess, rank should not act as a barrier to forming strong social bonds among its members. At the same time, messes are multiple in most camps. The existence of several mess halls within any individual camp reifies the notion that "consumption rituals mark social relationships of inclusion and exclusion" (Valentine 1999, 491). In the mixed brigade camp for instance, the infantry and signals units have their own mess halls. Given the space constraints of BANMP, everyone below the rank of officer dines in the same mess hall, though at different tables. While spatially segregated along rank or unit lines, the mess halls often serve the same meals to all—officers as well as contingent troops. In URUBATT, the meals even require inspection from the commander himself before they are served to the rest of the troops in the camp. Sharing the same menu, albeit in different spaces, is viewed as an important component of the officer-soldier relationship, momentarily and minimally cutting across the unequal power relations between soldiers of differing ranks for the time it takes to enjoy a warm meal.

Food in the camp is also, at times, a serious source of complaint. The frequency with which officers discuss or raise issues with rations points to the ability of food to ease or exacerbate the frustrations of everyday life—reinforcing its import to morale. Over a coffee with Lieutenant Colonel Ram and Major Baba at their office, our chat was interrupted by the dinging of group messages reaching their phones in rapid succession. In the WhatsApp group they shared with other officers from their camp, the mess secretary had initiated a debate about dried fruits and nuts, arguing that orders should be discontinued because they were taking up too much of the calorie count that the contingent

Familiar flavors across peacekeeping camps in Goma.
(Photo by author)

was afforded in their rations order. Major Baba could not help but laugh at the minutiae with which he and his fellow officers had become preoccupied. Cribbing about comestibles was practically a pastime in and of itself in the camps, partly for lack of other things to talk about but also to suss out what tasted like home and what did not. The Uruguayans for instance were unimpressed that the maté from the ration contractor came from Brazil, and officers could frequently be spotted roaming the mess with their personal *matera* and supply of yerba maté leaves. Changes to the supplier holding the rations contract for MONUSCO do not go unnoticed by troops. Between 2017 and 2018, when the ration contractor changed from ES-KO International (Monaco) to Hashi Energy (Kenya), so did the brand of rice being delivered to the camps. The Indian contingent at Mubambiro considered the less appealing taste of the new rice a high-priority problem. If brigade officers were to begin cribbing about food, the mess secretary would subject the cooks to a written menu test (naming a dish and asking for the recipe) to determine whether the problem lay with the ingredients or the cooking.

The diverse diets and different tastes of peacekeepers from different countries make the job of provisioning the multinational mission that much more difficult. For the rations contractor, the challenges of feeding peacekeepers come down to trying to balance cost efficiency and the maintenance of UN standards in delivering on the food preferences of individual contingents. A group of South African men working for ES-KO, the rations contractor in 2017, spoke to me at a mutual friend's house about some of the competitor firms that they saw trying to enter the market created by MONUSCO. They understood one of the biggest challenges for their competitors as being able to source meat from a single supplier that could provide halal and non-halal options, a key dietary consideration given the demographics of peacekeepers in the mission; Pakistan and Bangladesh, two majority-Muslim, halal-eating countries, are among the top countries in terms of troop contribution to MONUSCO. The men saw ES-KO's advantage as a ration contractor in the preestablished contacts with suppliers that they had developed over the years. Many of the suppliers or vendors used by ES-KO also run small shops and grocery stores in Goma. It is a testament to their longevity with the mission that many shop owners or employees refer to the imported eggs that they sell as "ES-KO" eggs—that is, eggs that are usually sold to the ration contractor or procured from their same supplier. Despite the ready availability of locally sourced food in Goma, the mission sources very few ration elements from DRC growers and farmers. An acting MONUSCO Head of Office in Goma chalked this up to the necessity of ordering rations "in bulk" with a stable and certain supply chain and to the negative economic consequences on local markets of the inflation that local ration procurement could entail.

Before the public health crises of Ebola and COVID-19 halted their ability to travel to and purchase from local markets, many camps chose to supplement their familiar ration orders with local foods and flavors. Individual officers in particular, with more freedom of movement, are keen to shop for fresh vegetables for the occasional salad or to buy fresh fish from the Rwandan women on the side of the road between the lakeside mission compounds and the border. The SEN-FPU contingent in particular was keen to venture out to procure fresh vegetables, local snacks, and goats for slaughter. For many of the women of the SEN-FPU camp (who work in the kitchen and thus assume gender roles that mirror those in Senegalese domestic spaces), they only leave the camp to visit either the Birere or Virunga market for additional and fresh ration provisions. Local food has also enabled the Senegalese gendarmes stationed in Goma to develop new social practices. During downtime in the early evening, those in the Senegalese camp can choose from several different leisure activities to stay busy and relieve stress. Some play billiards or cards in the courtyard space they've created between their CORIMECs. Others head to the sports fields or Rubb Hall to work out, riding exercise bikes with missing pedals or using a cut piece of linoleum flooring as a yoga mat. During this downtime, a new leisure activity has also been invented that uses a local snack to organize sociality. The men and women call this gathering a "*mboq* party" (*mboq* being Wolof for corn). Tempted by the smells wafting over the walls of the camp, these gendarmes have taken to buying several cobs of corn from the women grilling them on the street across from their gate—engendering a new practice that uses local flavors to thicken the social ties between camp dwellers. Similar experiences of local food spark the creativity and imagination of foreign contingents in other ways. In Kiwanja for instance, avocados represented a new piece of produce not found in that regiment's particular region of India. Soldiers have taken a particular liking to avocado shakes due to the belief (that they have developed in the DRC, far from their wives) that avocados are an aphrodisiac.

The Indian battalions are in a unique position with regards to the familiar foods and flavors that they can find during their deployment thanks to a small, yet significant, Indian community in Goma. Indian presence in Goma dates back over a century. Congolese citizens of Indian origin, as well as more recent waves of Indian migrants, still live or have landholdings in the general vicinity of what the colonial administration inscribed on the 1931 C.I.M. map as the Quartier Asiatique, located at the then-northern edge of town near the *cité indigène* and the border with Rwanda.[3] Members of Goma's Indian diasporic community socialize together, organize informal savings clubs (kitty parties), and attend each other's religious festivals across regional, cultural, and religious differences, often inviting their military compatriots to join. This community, which overwhelmingly originates from Gujarat, is particularly active in Goma's food and beverage services sector, and many of its members own and operate bars, restaurants, nightclubs, and supermarkets frequented by members of the mission and Congolese civilians alike. A Congolese businessman of Indian origin, whose great-grandfather was brought to Kenya from Gujarat as an indentured laborer by the British to build the infamous Lunatic Line railway, described the contemporary Indian community of Goma as creating steep competition in the services sector despite not being able to cheat the tax system, for instance, in the same way that locals can and do. At the time of this study, several new Indian-owned restaurants opened next to the lakeside MONUSCO compounds while others were expanding in the downtown area.

Indian-owned establishments were the preferred venues for outings among the Indian peacekeeping officers, not least because of the familiar menu offerings and the discounts they were able to negotiate based on a shared nationality. One of the younger Indian restauranteurs in Goma, Amit, went into business with a friend whose cousin owned the parcel across from one of the MONUSCO compound gates, which quickly became a popular drinking hole for officers. I asked him what he thought the future held for Indian-owned and operated restaurants in Goma, and Amit made an important caveat about the community's continued success: "UN needs to be here. Once UN is gone, Goma will be ten years back. They are playing a huge role in the economy." In addition to his new restaurant venture, Amit was a partner of the company who had recently won the contract for restaurants within the civilian bases of MONUSCO. The scale of this contract surpasses everyday restauration on site to include catering for special events. "We are getting many parties," he says. "Minimum fifteen parties per month." When members of the Indian diasporic community host their own parties, they often also invite the Indian officers currently deployed to Goma. The Goma Hindu Mandal's Navratri festivities for instance brought together the diverse Indian diaspora (including members of the Shia Ismaili Muslim community in Goma numbering around fifty people), members of the Indian army, and Indian civilian staff of the mission. The officers who were not from Gujarat stumbled about for a bit learning the Garba dances but enjoyed the rituals and variety of dishes offered to guests so much that many attended several evenings, bringing me along to three days of the nine-day festival. On one of the nights, the peacekeeping officers had a spirited discussion about their childhoods, prompted by the *jalebis* being served.

Peacekeeping contingents bring their favorite foods and spices from home, expand their culinary repertoires with the flavors of Goma both new and familiar, and bring or nurture seeds to generate a recurring supply of garnishes to meals that create a sense of communitas and a sense of being at home. Camp kitchen gardens are a common feature of foreign contingent bases. Different Indian bases grow a variety of herbs and vegetables—from cilantro to mint and spinach to eggplant. With the transition of the Guatemalans from tents to CORIMECs in their base, they also decided to build elevated plant beds behind the showers to grow different ingredients used in their cooking. Space constraints in peacekeeping camps do not deter the appearance of such gardens. The BANMP camp is the smallest camp in Goma yet has still managed to squeeze in a small vegetable garden underneath a MONUSCO radio tower to grow chilies, cucumbers, and tomatoes. Colonel Samir puts it thus, "The garden is not sustenance, but it makes a difference." Gardens gesture toward home as food and flavors that come from beyond and within the camp. Contingents bring their faraway homes here, growing and eating the herbs they have come to know and love. They also embrace their new environment, supplementing their home flavors with new ones or physically planting them in the earth. Echoing the small gardens planted by encamped refugees and captured by Dutch photographer Henk Wildschut in *Rooted*, these peacekeeping camp gardens may tame the uprootedness experienced by deployed individuals: "For individuals displaced—garden making is one way of placing oneself" (Helphand and Wildschut 2019). Even a small garnish coming from the kitchen garden can make the notion of home mobile and multisited. Adding a garden for herbs and vegetables or supplementing UN rations with a locally purchased goat for a special occasion situates the sense of home felt in the peacekeeping camp between experiences linked to the "here" of Goma and the "there" of troops' origin countries.

Bringing flavors, recipes, and dishes from there to here—thereby collapsing the distance of disparate places through the mobility of foodstuffs—helps combat homesickness and feelings of otherness that troops may experience in such a prolonged deployment. Food, in this instance, not only sustains the soldier's body as nutrition but also reinforces and adds to his identity as a member of a group in an otherwise foreign place. Nickie Charles and Marion Kerr (1988, 17) write, "Food is important to the social reproduction of the family in both its nuclear and extended forms and food practices help to maintain and reinforce a coherent ideology of the family throughout the social structure" (cited in Valentine 1999, 492). Just as food plays a central role in family ideology, so does it play a similar role in military ideology, in which soldiers' identities are narrated as kinship relations to other members of the military institution with whom they serve (Græger 2019) as well as through their service to the nation that the institution represents and defends. During deployment in a peacekeeping mission, that military identity is split, however, between one's national colors and the blue beret, allowing new foods, flavors, and practices to produce new notions of belonging to a broader group identity and a new place. Food maintains a palpable connection to a shared nation and foments social and kinly relationships in Goma, reimagining home between here and elsewhere through taste.

Images and Imaginations of Home

Expressions of the place of the peacekeeping camp between here and elsewhere are also materialized through architecture and aesthetics. Aesthetic features of camps are keen to make use of images, icons, and decorations from peacekeepers' respective countries as well as nearby materials and vernacular design elements. Signage around URUBATT orients visitors to the Área de Recreación or the Lavandería but are made by an in-house craftsman who incorporates his own motifs into the wood-carved signposts. In larger formats, images from the countries of UN peacekeepers collide with images of "Africa," as seen by foreign contingents, to bring life to the walls of the camp itself and the individual CORIMECs arranged within. These surfaces act as canvases to express peacekeepers' perspectives of their home countries and the host country that acts as their home away from home. As exterior walls act as the face of the camp, many contingents decorate outward-facing walls and gates by combining the images, colors, and symbols associated with their nation of origin, the host nation of the DRC, and the United Nations organization under which they serve.

URUBATT lives in a highly conspicuous camp, visible from the airport runway and airport road leading north out of the city. This visibility paired with the creative flair of officers and troops who have passed through the base have also made it an artful camp. Two murals on the walls flanking the gate were a testament to this artistic agency and penchant for projecting images from different places together. Entering the camp, a collage of Uruguayan cultural symbols greeted you on the right—a couple dancing tango, a maté and *bombilla* set, a gaucho atop a bucking bronco, and various flora and fauna. The wall facing it on the left featured a panorama of African wildlife including giraffes, zebras, elephants, and rhinos. These murals facing each other at the entrance orchestrated a visual prelude to the experience of place behind the gate, an experience of camp made with and between two places.

Artwork inside peacekeeping camps plays many variations on the theme described at the URUBATT camp entrance. Decorations big and small jointly arrange references to "here" and "there." VIP guestrooms in larger Indian bases feature locally made masks or artwork side by side with traditional prints or textiles from India. In the GUASFOR camp's religious spaces, several locally handcrafted figurines sit in the Christmas nativity set against a backdrop of the Guatemalan flag (with three gorillas occupying the places of the three wise men). In several camps, Swahili is superimposed onto spaces and images that are culturally significant to the encamped contingent. Watching over one Indian mess hall is a poster of an Indian woman with her hands pressed together in namaste pose with "Karibu" written in an arch over her head.[4] The grill in the URUASU camp near Bukavu is labeled "Parrillero Kitoko Mingi" in a handmade woodcarving—"the very nice barbeque" in Spanish and Lingala.

Handicrafts made and languages used in Goma join simulacra of "here" understood at an urban or regional scale. In the brigade camp, objects that symbolize the city, such as replicas of the Nyiragongo volcano and the *tchukudu* intermingle with images of Indian architecture, dance, and festivals.[5] In the URUBATT camp, references are even more local and literal, with a mural of Fidel (whom we have met in chapter 2) painted on the side of a CORIMEC, peering through a cut-out in the gate. Another mural portrays a woman releasing a dove of peace over Goma, with Nyiragongo towering in the background of the urban landscape at night. In many contingent camps hosting non-African troops, however, most of the visual references to peacekeepers' actual location are made at the continental level of Africa. Near the troop TV at the URUBATT base, a painting of a savannah of wildlife at sunset stretches along the wall. On the back of another CORIMEC—a rhinoceros. Further along down the path, paintings of faceless African figures wearing animal prints or playing ambiguous instruments flank a replica of a widely circulated stock photo face with the continent superimposed upon it. In another camp, a painting of two topless African men sitting amid mud huts drinking out of a shared pot adorns a wall near the entrance. It is as if some in-camp artwork is a translation in paint of Binyavanga Wainaina's essay "How to Write About Africa" (2005). These more essentialized representations of Africa reify some of the homogenizing and reductive ways that the continent is represented in global media, images, and discourse (Wainaina 2005; Gallagher 2015; Bunce, Franks, and Paterson 2017).

In addition to specific and simplified African imagery, peacekeeping camps are keen to incorporate local materials and vernacular architectures. Wooden window slats found on many residences across Goma have been incorporated into more permanent, self-built structures in the camps, while bamboo fencing collected and assembled by Congolese civilians hired directly by contingents serves multiple decorative and architectural purposes. Latticed fencing helps keep goats from roaming into the BANMP camp in Mubambiro. The Indian contingent in the same garrison has used bamboo as low, decorative fencing to delimit the gardens and walkways in front of the CORIMECs. In Himbi, it helps demarcate different paths throughout the INDRDB camp. GUASFOR has used it to extend the awning of the Kaibil Club and encircle the smoking hut near the entrance, enhancing the privacy of these areas.

While many camps incorporate images, symbols, and materials that express various, perspectival meanings of being located in Goma, all camps incorporate images that reflect meanings of being from a particular country. Essentializing images from the elsewheres peacekeepers come from appear in the camps though always at the national scale, and often blending imagery associated with tourism, patriotism, and militarism. National colors, flags, and country outlines are near ubiquitous features of peacekeeping camps. For a while, GUASFOR's mess featured images associated with their national military identity as Kaibiles, including a display of nautical knots, the Kaibil motto, and images of their emblem—a skull wearing a maroon beret clenching a knife between its teeth. The following rotation lightened the aesthetics of the mess, repainting the interior with the country's national bird (quetzal), flag, and flower (*monja blanca*). In addition to painting these national objects on various surfaces of the camp, GUASFOR adorns the spaces where it hosts visitors to the camp with pamphlets and posters from the Tourism Board of Guatemala.

The Indian camps in Goma are also keen to display their country's various cultural assets through posters hung inside and outside of the camps. Posters with titles like "Incredible India" (also the name of their country's official tourism campaign), "Unity in Diversity," and "Tastes of India" depict images of varied architectural, ethnolinguistic, and culinary heritage. National monuments of military significance, such as the India Gate war memorial in New Delhi, make multiple appearances in Indian peacekeeping camps. URUBATT has re-created the monument that stands at the center of their own Plaza del Ejército (Army Square) in Montevideo, the nation's capital. Replicas of monuments found in contingents' home countries are particularly important in military milieus for the sense of patriotism that they help curate in the camp, one that has been positively correlated with soldier readiness and retention in the service (Griffith 2010). Lieutenant Colonel Juan was keen to attune me to the pillar's hyperbolic shape, symbolizing an infinite and gradual increase in power. The monument stands at the center of the camp's own sort of national plaza, which juxtaposes emblems of national victories with symbols of the humble livelihoods of Uruguayans near the administrative and strategic offices of the camp. In front of the Army Square monument are the three official flags of Uruguay (the flag of Artigas, the national flag, and the flag of the Trienta y Tres). In front of those flags are a few models of the national bird, *el tero* (the southern lapwing). Behind the monument on the lawn is a model of an *aljibe*, a type of well used by Uruguay's early farmers, many of which can still be found on various *estancias*, or ranches, across the country. The lawn is landscaped with various tropical flora from around Goma. Around it, the African figures painted on the back of one of the CORIMECs cast their faceless and global gazes over the lawn.

In addition to these national military monuments, signposts erected in the camps act as a visual acknowledgment of peacekeepers' distance from home. Such signposts point toward different cities deemed important by different contingents and are common in touristic cities, often indicating the direction and distance from one's current location to world cities like New York, London, Paris, and Tokyo. The Kitona Base during the United Nations Operation in the Congo in the 1960s even featured one such signpost, indicating distances to places significant to the mission, such as Kamina, New York, and Stockholm (due to the presence of Swedish peacekeepers). The signpost in the Central Sector Brigade camp has kept this logic, indicating only Kinshasa and

URUBATT's replica national plaza. (Photo by author)

New York—the cities through which the mission hierarchy travels upward. The Uruguayan and Guatemalan bases have taken a slightly different approach. The Uruguayan signpost is similar to more touristic signposts, though instead of world cities, most arrows indicate cities in Uruguay (except for Moscow and Entebbe—the latter of which hosts a house rented by the contingent for troops' R&R). The GUASFOR camp features a single arrow indicating the azimuth degree and distance to Guatemala.

Peacekeeping camps incorporate real and imagined images of "here" at various scales and replicate images of the home country through landscaping and gardening, statues and murals, building materials and decorations. Both types of images enter into the single "visual language" of the camp and become properties of its physical space (Berger and Dibb 1972). They express values and meanings of place important to peacekeepers through past, present, and future localizations. The camp as a space of images allows peacekeepers to embody the environment of the nation state they serve *and* to collect and negotiate experiences of and ideas about their temporary localization in Goma, the DRC,

From left to right: "Distance to home" signposts in
GUASFOR; URUBATT; Central Sector Brigade camp;
and Mediterraneo—an Italian restaurant in Goma with a
completely localized version that indicates landmarks in and
around Goma itself. (Photos by author)

and Africa, illustrating how the home of the camp becomes a site of creative practice (Lenhard and Samanani 2019). In this way, the materiality of the camp reproduces relations of place and identity and extends them, with the aesthetics of peacekeeping camps serving to remind soldiers of home while replicating it and adding new visual repertoires to it.

The names people who call Goma home give to different places in the city mirrors the combination of references to here and elsewhere that we find in the peacekeeping camp, particularly when it comes to spaces of leisure, comfort, and relaxation. The names given to such spaces often reference the rural home spaces of many of the city's inhabitants. Some appeal to the universality of village life, as in Planète Village Bar or the Resto-Bar Mon Village. Other places are given specific village names, like the Ihusi brand of hotels and gas stations or the Ishovu Cyber Café named after an island in Lake Kivu. These spaces exhibit heterogeneous demographics—the Ihusi hotel catering to some of the wealthiest people in the city, while Planète Village in the western neighborhood of Ndosho attracts a more popular crowd. The commonality, however, in the bars and restaurants that reference other Congolese village names is that the owners are often from the places they reference. Many of the hand-painted signs on such businesses seek to attract their clients with bucolic images of a place removed from the hustle and bustle of the city—a place to call home. Such a brief and partial urban toponymy nonetheless highlights similar tendencies both in the camp and the city to bring together images and place-names from elsewhere to enhance feelings of comfort in situ.

In addition to naming bars, restaurants, salons, and boutiques after people, prayers, and local landmarks, people in Goma often make naming about home as it is perceived to be here or elsewhere, for instance, with the salon called "New Start" and the resto bar called "My Village." (Photo by author)

Camping around the Clock

The ambiguity and tension of dwelling between here and elsewhere is not only expressed visually in the camp but also has an important temporal dimension. Given the places that peacekeepers come from, personal and professional life in a peacekeeping camp is constantly coping with and negotiating the simultaneity of different times of day. This element of everyday life is often materialized in various offices and gathering spaces as adjacent clocks set to two different times or a single clock with a different set of numbers taped next to the original hours. This plurality of clocks in peacekeeping bases is one of many material reminders of the ways that the time of elsewhere works on the camp, shaping the ways peacekeepers relate to their homes abroad and their temporary home in Goma. While signposts like the directional arrow in the Guatemalan camp acknowledge the space between camp and country as a distance, dual clocks and other, unexpected architectures of the camp reflect the temporally in-between quality of that space.

Multiple temporalities coexist in the base that shape the routines, activities, and spaces of the camp. For troops in URUBATT, the end of the school day in Uruguay delays bedtime in the camp. Despite the 05:30 wake-up call for Uruguayan troops, it is typical for parent-soldiers to stay up until 22:00 or 23:00 to speak to their children after school. Indian troops have to deal with time differences in the other direction, often milling around the basketball court after games and eating dinner a bit later so they can call their families before they go to sleep. All bases take into consideration the working hours of their colleagues back home when making phone calls or mailing documents from the in-camp field post office. Practices and daily life routines in the camp are thus structured by the synchronous elsewhens of Uruguay or India—the rhythms of life back home. With the near ubiquitous use of mobile messaging and calling apps on peacekeepers' smart phones, internet connections are crucial for individual peacekeepers to communicate with family and friends across great distances and disparate time zones.

For Colonel Pablo, the internet is rivaled only by food as the camp feature that is most critical to warding off homesickness. Just as sharing familiar foods can provide a relational and sensory experience of home for the soldiers, so too can a WhatsApp video call with a loved one. Internet provision in UN missions has emerged as a topic of concern among several troop-contributing countries, as reflected in numerous issue papers from a 2020 UN Working Group on contingent-owned equipment. Internet access for peacekeepers is considered a welfare component and thus operates contractually under the category of self-sustainment, meaning that it is the troop-contributing country's responsibility to provide internet access, which is then reimbursed at a specified rate by the UN. Member State Issue Papers for the 2020 Working Group from Bangladesh and India (both troop-contributing countries with peacekeeping camps in Goma) have addressed their concerns with the current scheme based on an inadequate reimbursement rate (USD 3.16 per soldier per month) compared to the actual costs of internet provision (calculated to be around USD 30) (Bangladesh 2019; India 2019). India's justification for seeking to revise the reimbursement rate stands out, highlighting the necessity of peacekeepers to interact with families and friends in order to stay connected and to access the internet to make purchases and money transfers for their families back home (India 2019). Commanders in Goma frequently raised the issue of internet access as one that has cost the contingent a great deal of money but has made it easier for the camp to feel like home itself. Lieutenant Colonel Janeeb went so far as to personally invest in individual SIM cards for his small contingent with subscriptions of two gigabytes of data per month for the military police to communicate with their families back home. He also initiated a VoIP facility in his base, as some of his soldiers' relatives live in remote villages without access to smart phones.

The significant investments that contingents have made in establishing Wi-Fi in their bases have led to new architectures and sociospatial practices in the camps themselves. In mid-2017, URUBATT leadership noticed that soldiers were gathering in a particular corner of grass in the camp at all hours of the day, including under the midday equatorial sun. All of them were on their phones. For troops who want to catch someone back home in Uruguay before they head to work or school, they must call from Goma around noon, which can come with the hottest and sharpest sun. It turned out that this patch of grass was close to a recently installed router, giving troops a strong internet signal through which to reach out to loved ones. Soon after the officers took notice, they ordered the construction of a small gazebo to provide shade and seating near the router. As it came into being and began to be used, the gazebo began to express new meanings. According to a group of noncommissioned officers (NCOs), a soldier entering the space of the gazebo can be a clear signal to others that he or she is homesick and wants to be left alone, whether they manage to reach their loved ones on their phone or not. Later, it would not be uncommon for a fellow member of that soldier's platoon or company to reach out and check on the person.

In Uruguayan military jargon, extreme homesickness can bring about a feeling known as the ax (*el hacha*), expressed in the body as hanging one's head low and in the mind as a more acute awareness of the burden one carries. Of great concern to military leaders, *el hacha* compromises troop health and welfare as it can make soldiers prone to developing physical illnesses. As such, the installation of power outlets, landscaping, stone pathways, and nearby murals stand as efforts to lift the spirits of those who retreat to this gazebo, aptly named the Rincón del Hacha (The Homesickness Nook). The Rincón del Hacha is not a space of immediate and proximate sociality to quell feelings of loneliness or detachment but one where soldiers make connections outward, beyond the camp, in an effort to make life within it more livable.

Improvement projects like that of the Rincón del Hacha follow a shift in the Uruguayan battalion's understanding of time over their sustained peacekeeping tenure in the DRC, one that is inspired by and begets an increased permanence of the camp. In the early years of the mission, Colonel Pablo and

Colonel Luis tell me, the Uruguayan battalion was deployed all over the DRC in tents. By 2009, the Uruguayans had settled into the current URUBATT camp in Goma, from which they coordinated their deployments further afield. The commander at that time saw the camp as a "home base" that troops would return to after camping in less comfortable conditions in standing combat deployments. CORIMEC accommodations were installed the following year, literally and figuratively solidifying the commander's intentions, which were carried forward by subsequent commanders who adopted the mindset of continuously improving the camp with more durable building materials, no matter how long they might actually live there. Colonel Pablo credits the 2009 commander with setting the tone of the camp as a more permanent and ever-evolving home. Improving the camp and creating a more comfortable, homey environment also advances other military logics discussed in the previous chapter, such as keeping troops busy as a matter of maintaining welfare. With camp beautification and solidification projects in particular, the outcome of an improved living environment can also enhance the performance of the troops. In Colonel Pablo's words, "if the soldier is comfortable, you can ask more from him."

A similar mentality has more recently been adopted in the GUASFOR camp in Mubambiro. The demounting of tents and appearance of greater permanence began around March 2017 at the insistence of the contingent. The deputy commander in 2017 recognized that troops' accommodation in tents was the result of their force's operational logic of mobility—their ability to be deployed across the entire country for special operations. This mobility over time, however, concretized the notion that a central, home base should provide comfort and reprieve from frequent, highly mobile, and more distant missions.

In looking at the evolution of the URUBATT and GUASFOR camps, renovations that instill a greater sense of material permanence are underpinned by their relation to places where troops conduct more temporary operations and standing deployments—proximate elsewheres. Making URUBATT into a comfortable home is particularly important juxtaposed against the taxing and temporary living conditions of field deployments in active conflict zones like Bunia, where Major Alonso, my closest in-camp connection at the time, was heading with his company shortly after we had made each other's acquaintance. As Alonso's friend and colleague put it, Alonso should have a great interest in continued improvements back at URUBATT: "You don't want to come back to a shit camp or your troops' morale will go down."

The perceived and real dangers of operations as far as Bunia and as close as Saké enhance the sense of home felt in the peacekeeping camps in Goma and heighten the stakes of making the space of the camp feel safe and comfortable. Captain Tarek knows this all too well and appreciates the beautification projects taken up by his camp's youngsters even more since being shot twice in the leg during a patrol near his camp in Mubambiro. I had been at one of the Indian restaurants in town with several Indian officers when they received the call about the incident. Captain Tarek told me the story of that night almost a month later in the relaxed atmosphere of his camp, where he was still walking around with a slight limp.

He had been in the lead vehicle crossing Kimoka village just outside of Saké when about fifty bullets were sprayed in a few bursts from about twenty meters away on his left. Four bullets hit Captain Tarek's vehicle and two hit his leg before he could give orders to move out of firing range and split the patrol. No one else from Tarek's battalion was injured, though in a previous engagement, an FARDC captain had been killed. Tarek explains how their operational response would have differed if the FARDC had made MONUSCO aware of the situation. Because of this lack of communication flowing between local and foreign security forces, Tarek has reason to believe that the bandits firing on them thought that his patrol was reinforcement for the FARDC. While apt, Tarek's battalion nonetheless interprets these reports of armed bandits coming from the Virunga National Park as a law-and-order problem (see chapter 2). The officers still believe it is important to move out of camp and show their presence in areas where such banditry is reportedly happening, careful not to let fear set in after Captain Tarek's injury. Even though he was relatively camp-bound during recovery, he was convalescing comfortably in the new and improved camp. Other Indian contingents nonetheless took it upon themselves to invite him to their camps for a change of scenery or to accompany other officers from his base so he wouldn't be left alone in the camp, relegated to his CORIMEC with the Miley Cyrus poster he put up over his bed.

Captain Tarek's camp is adjacent to the BANMP camp at Mubambiro, which is viewed as a comfortable camp and a marked improvement in the living conditions of the military police that inhabit it relative to bases in Bangladesh. The commanding officer showing me around praises the camp for its health, hygiene, and water facilities. There is even air-conditioning in all of the CORIMECs, which prompted him to tell me, "It is very much homey in this place." The existing and relative "homeyness" of the BANMP camp did not stop the 2018 contingent from improving the camp further, however. Their "administrative achievements," as they called them, included the construction of a new visitor's shed, dining hall, and generator shed as well as the installation of a new low-noise block downconverter for the satellite dish. For peacekeepers

deployed to Goma, likening the camp to a homelike environment is predominantly about comfort. To build on the popular adage from chapter 2: busy
troops are happy troops, happy troops are comfortable troops, and comfortable
troops are able to feel more at home in the camp.

Yet, not all peacekeepers feel at home in their camps all the time. "We have
come to help a country, and they put us in *these* conditions!" one of the Senegalese men who had joined a focus group rebuked when asked about the camp.[6]
The other members of his platoon seemed to affirm the man's disappointment
and position on the matter. Many of the Senegalese peacekeepers felt that
their dignity and their willingness to serve in a peacekeeping mission were not
matched or respected by the living conditions to which they were subjected.
The other men in the room chimed in, mentioning the lack of basic elements
(without elaborating); the presence of rats, snakes, and cockroaches in the living quarters of their former camp; and the dust everywhere.[7] Over the course
of 2017, these gendarmes had shifted out of the permanent buildings in Camp
Jambaar and into a new camp site down the road furnished with CORIMECs.
While still seeming to have some trouble adjusting to the new living environment, many conceded that the new camp was more spacious and airier. The
SEN-FPU took the initiative to create new spaces within the camp to a degree,
making use of tarpaulin to create suspended ceilings between dwellings. This
once empty space quickly became a weather-roof recreational space with a billiard table and television. The improvements needed to make the space more
livable, comfortable, and homey by their own standards, however, were out of
the unit's own budget. "Mënul xalaat caserne"—one cannot think of this as a
barracks, another man said of the new camp. "Caserne mooy sa kër"—a barracks is your house (or home). Home is thus a moving target in a peacekeeping
camp, one that relies on multiple and overlapping socioenvironmental conditions as well as resources.

The increasing permanence of peacekeeping camps in Goma and the home-
making opportunities that such durability affords is built into many of the
agreements between the UN and individual troop-contributing countries. The
eventual hardening of accommodations and amenities is a stipulation of most
of the rental schemes for camp locations in and around Goma. Most MOUs
stipulate that the UN pay a tentage reimbursement to contingents for the first
six months of their initial deployment. After six months, if the UN can't provide
"permanent, semi-rigid, or rigid accommodation" to a contingent, then they
will need to reimburse the self-sustainment rates for both tentage *and* accommodation (UNGA 2017). Several camps in Goma accommodated soldiers in
tents for several years before receiving prefabricated CORIMEC dwellings.

Juxtaposed against such hardening measures across camps and the incorporation of more permanent structures, peacekeepers deployed between 2017 and 2019 increasingly spoke of the temporality of the mission as a whole, particularly in light of budget cuts and murmurs of an eventual withdrawal of MONUSCO from the DRC. By 2019, one of the first things that the force commander (FC) said when I entered his office one afternoon was that the FARDC wanted the UN force out in less than a year. He recommended completing the withdrawal of the force by July 2022. An independent, strategic review of MONUSCO was carried out in light of the UN's ambition to begin thinking about an exit strategy for the mission. This review recommended that the phased withdrawal be completed in three years at a minimum (instead of the FC's proposed maximum). North and South Kivu were recommended as the last regions from which to withdraw (Mahmoud 2019). July 2022, the FC's preferred withdrawal date, has since come and gone, but MONUSCO forces remain at the time of writing. A drawdown strategy was set in motion in 2020, with a Transition Plan formulated in 2021 that plans for a full withdrawal in 2024 (UNSC 2021). That strategy has since been revisited, however. Revisions to the withdrawal plan already began at the end of July 2022, which saw violent protests targeting MONUSCO personnel and installations in the cities of Goma and Butembo that left four peacekeepers and thirty-two civilians dead (Bukajera 2022).

"My plan for the COBs [company operating bases] is to hand over to the country," the FC told me. He reassured me that he had spoken about this plan with the director of Mission Support and the special representative of the secretary-general (SRSG), the most senior civilian position in MONUSCO. By "the country," he was referring to Congolese security forces—primarily the FARDC. "They are not deployed as we would like to see them deployed. They do not have barracks. They are in huts or tents." The FC clarified his view that the FARDC are not bad as such; they have good troops and many of their colonels and generals are intellectually prepared for the security threats the country faces. But their own camps are not up to the task. He saw the benefits of handing over UN military bases to the national military in terms of comfort, training, and discipline. Even the furniture will stay, he said. The camps themselves thus have a potentially important role to play in MONUSCO's support of Security Sector Reform in the eyes of the FC. The force's plan was to hand over all the bases that it had built on public lands, while bases on private lands would have to be dismantled as per agreements with the landowners.[8]

In Goma in particular, a city that hosted over twenty different peacekeeping camps in 2018, the FC's intention to leave as many mission installations and infrastructures as possible for use by Congolese security forces could have a number of positive or negative consequences. On the one hand, part of Goma's reputation as a safe haven has been predicated on the concentration of Congolese army bases and police forces (Büscher 2020). That same concentration, however has led to a pronounced military footprint in the city, contributing to the dilapidation of the urban architectural landscape (due to a lack of state resources) and heightened insecurity near the bases of Congolese security forces (Pech, Büscher, and Lakes 2018). Evidence from five MONUSCO base closures in Walikale and Masisi Territories in 2017 also raise several concerns in terms of the security consequences of withdrawal for the city. Persisting and worsening dynamics in rural towns experiencing mission base closures included increases in reports of weapon possession by civilians, banditry, and the continued threats posed by armed groups of armed clashes, sexual violence, recruitment (including among children), and the reignition of ethnic tensions (MONUSCO 2018). The same base closure report cited several incidences of abuse committed by Congolese security forces themselves.

Architectures and improvement initiatives in the peacekeeping camps of Goma, however, tend to disregard the elsewhen of an eventual withdrawal of the mission and subsequent closure of bases in the near future. Learning about the eventual wind-down and withdrawal of the mission has not seemed to stop contingents and civilian sections from making substantial, permanent changes to their living and working spaces. The 2018 rotation of officers in one Indian camp, for instance, built a *machan* as a second-floor to the officer's mess, completed in 2019 with a price tag of several thousand US dollars. Unsteady bar stools dotted the bar around the perimeter and wooden chairs and couches with overstuffed cushions provided another place for officers and guests to enjoy drinks or dosa brunch. Such improvements are primarily financed with a contingent's own resources and purchased locally. The increasing permanence and investments in concretizing different dwelling spaces of a camp repeatedly trump increased awareness about the temporality of the mission, often in the name of making the camp feel more hospitable, more like a home.

While peacekeepers themselves will return to their home countries, many of the constructions in the COBs that were built by contingents themselves will remain, as many infrastructures and projects built by earlier rotations of troops have. Over time, the mission has accumulated many materials, physical infrastructures, and equipment. Containers in particular pile up in the mission's Logistics Base or in the camps themselves, often acting as foundations on which sentinel posts are built. The containers that arrive in the Indian bases in and around Goma have taken a ninety-day sea and overland route from Mumbai to

Mombasa to Goma. It is not financially viable for individual forces to send them back. The work of time on many of these imported (and never to be exported) materials creates opportunities for improvement projects as things decay and break down over the course of a mission that, as many commanders I've spoken to acknowledge, was not anticipated by national forces to last as long as it has. As such, the materiality and activities of peacekeeping camps in terms of maintenance, investments, improvements, and renovations express coexisting temporalities rooted in endurance and expiration. The shifting notion of home as at once a component of the present place-making of the camp and as a place at a distance is central to the temporal indeterminacy of the camp.

Longer-term thinking about individual life futures rather than the future of the camps themselves returns the notion of home back to the country from which the peacekeeper was deployed. As deinduction becomes more imminent in the Indian camps, officers begin to quantify time by calculating their DLTGH—days left to go home. Once home, peacekeepers often invest the salaries they've saved in Goma in building a better future and a better home for themselves and their families. During a focus group with Guatemalan Special Forces, the troops agreed that while their motivation for participating in the mission was surely economic, they had each linked that financial benefit to a more personal, concrete objective. Of the twelve soldiers I spoke with, eight were planning to purchase or invest in land, housing, and home renovations once back in Guatemala.[9] The remaining four were going to invest in starting businesses. The troops of GUASFOR are relatively young compared to other military units (in part due to the physical requirements of special forces), a fact that helps contextualize these intentions for how to spend their peacekeeping earnings in terms of starting a family and gaining more independence or supporting older family members. In a similar discussion at URUBATT with a group of NCOs (most of whom were much older than the Guatemalan troops), the majority agreed with one officer who spoke of investing in housing to bring more comfort to his family, in particular his children.

Bangladeshi soldiers equally share a desire to invest in land purchases or housing construction with the extra money they earn in the mission, though they often also purchase amenities and furnishings like motorbikes and TVs. Lieutenant Colonel Janeeb notes a clear and significant lifestyle change among former peacekeepers in Bangladesh, relating these changes to the way that the UN is indirectly helping "developing countries" like his own. Senegalese gendarmes were equally looking forward to putting their earnings toward either a car or a house when they returned. In the recreational area of their camp, investment opportunities back home and for future homes are posted on

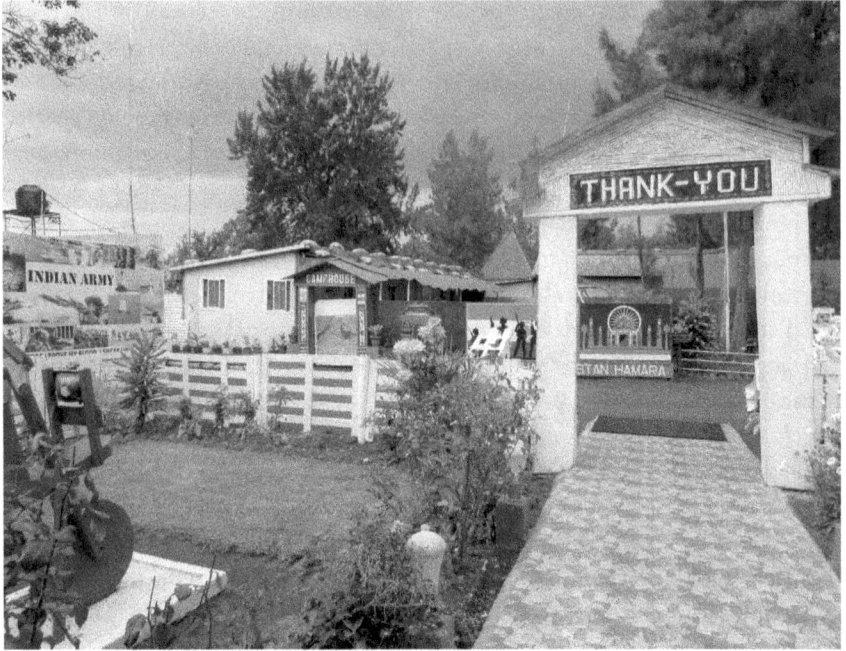

The view upon exiting the officers' mess of one of the Indian camps combines images of home as India and home as here. (Photo by author)

CORIMEC doors, such as one that reads, "300m^2 plots available in Diass," with a contact person and phone number for those already thinking about acquiring land back in Senegal with their earnings from being deployed to Goma.[10]

Conclusion: No Place Like

"When you look at [our] camps," Brigadier Kabir began matter-of-factly before trailing off, first clarifying that the places I was visiting and spending time in in Goma were operating bases, spatial considerations for which were based on a number of determining factors. In our first formal sit-down together, he was pressed for time and left little room for questions, launching headlong into a monologue about what *makes* a peacekeeping camp. For him, determining factors included intent, level of force, definitive threat levels, support infrastructure, troop strength, logistics, and duration. Duration rang dissonant to me when I thought of the night before.

The evening before we met to talk about camp factors, Brigadier Kabir had organized a little get together on the occasion of a mission-wide conference going on in Goma and his own immanent return to India. The anteroom that normally hosted Ping-Pong matches had been set up as a special dining area reserved for most high-ranking officers from several countries to dine with him. Cocktail hour was hosted on the lawn off the back of the officer's mess— the same place where Major Baba's dining out was held. The lawn had been renovated during Brigadier Kabir's tenure with new structures and landscaping and enclosed by crisscrossed bamboo fencing. The night of the get-together, the new bar, made of stone, was well-stocked to keep guests' drinks refreshed. In the corner of the lawn, a tiled stage covered by a slatted wood trellis hosted the brigadier's welcoming remarks. These new improvements, laid in concrete, seemed to defy Brigadier Kabir's and his contingent's limited duration in this place. The architectures and aesthetics of these camps had a durability to them despite their hopefully limited duration. Concretizing the camp was perhaps a matter of "bringing some space under control" as a way of making it home (Douglass 1991 cited in Kusenbach and Paulsen 2013) instead of allowing the materiality of the space to constantly defer to a sense of home as elsewhere.

Peacekeeping camps express a notion of time that is between now and then and between an underpinning logic of endurance and a fixed duration. In the latter tension, temporariness and permanence compete and collide in shaping the environment of the camp, as does a multisited notion of home as both here and in the countries to which peacekeepers ultimately return. On the one hand, the notion that home is back in Bangladesh or Senegal or Uruguay can have an impact on the types of features that come up in the camp, such as the Rincón del Hacha in URUBATT. At the same time, contingents' efforts to incorporate more durable features into the camp are valued for their added comfort and for the meanings and affects they add to the camp—namely, that the camp is a home, however temporary. Making the camp into a home is not all about favoring the "here and now" over the "there and then" but is an exercise in selectively relativizing a plurality of elsewheres and elsewhens. It is between these uneven temporalities and disparate places, I argue, that peacekeepers make themselves at home in the camp.

Prita Meier's (2016) powerful concept of the architecture of elsewhere is helpful to thinking about the material culture and aesthetics of the liminal space of the peacekeeping camp as they relate to notions of home. She argues that Swahili coast architecture, while seemingly fixed, encapsulates mobile practices—materially translating "the desire to claim belonging to a range of elsewheres" (2). That this particular culture of things collected from faraway has come to define Swahili port cities themselves has not been a matter of bringing the elsewhere to a specific here in a localizing process. Rather, Meier argues, this architecture and material culture hold mobility and rootedness together in a productive tension—in an architecture of elsewhere. The architectures of a peacekeeping camps are neither completely fixed nor entirely mobile. They are made of a mix of durable materials that can add a sense of comfort and settledness to the camp and objects that are more makeshift or ephemeral. For peacekeepers, the architectures of elsewhere are not those that translate into aspirations of belonging but those that remind them of the places to which they already belong and the places in which they actually are. Living with images, recipes, and temporal calibrations from their countries of origin explicitly works to foment the types of feelings, practices, and states of being associated with peacekeepers' distant homes. It is rather the culinary, visual, and temporal repertoires of Goma, the DRC, and Africa that are incorporated into the camp, arranged in relationship to the things from faraway and incorporated into daily practices in ways that challenge the idea that home is purely elsewhere. The use and appropriation of these different repertoires in camp beautification projects, improvement initiatives, and soldiers' leisure activities often function in ways similar to the repertoires of elsewhere. In Swahili coast architectures of elsewhere: "Exotic objects fulfilled a desire to possess and amass the materiality of the far away. This culture of things encapsulated the port city itself, and these objects paid tribute to mobility and the ability to make the exotic one's own" (Meier 2016, 10). In a camp context, the exotic is often not that which is far away; it is that which is close by or right here. And yet, it takes a creative desire to be at home in that place to make it one's own.

In his own "Ethnographic Notes on 'Camp,'" Thomas Hendriks meditates on the nature of camps from an industrial logging camp in the Congolese rainforest. He writes, "Although home-making and self-making conventionally suggest the production of a stable center, camp centrifugality constantly undermined these centers, up to a point where 'home' and 'self' were produced in and through the very displacement itself" (2015, 168). As this chapter has argued, the production of "home" and "self" in the space of a peacekeeping camp is a matter not only of displacement but also of *emplacement*. Not only do encamped peacekeepers adopt and incorporate the stuff of their immediate surroundings in Goma—a foreign and faraway context to most peacekeepers—these things have an impact on how officers and soldiers are able to feel at home in the camp. As Major Neel reminded me on the phone while I was writing this chapter's introduction, he met Major Baba and the other officers in his camp for the first and last time in Goma. During their short time together, they had managed to become close enough that Major Baba would refer to him as a "brother in arms" in his dining out speech and a "bro" on most other occasions. The nature of the exchanges they had that began to bind them to each other had everything to do with the nature of the place they were in. Major Neel got to know everyone in his camp through their individual affects shaped by the initial discomforts of being far from home and specific reactions to the foreign cultural, material, and linguistic context of Goma. Kinly ties then, it seems, are knitted faster among those who share a national notion of home that is elsewhere and experience heretofore unknown places together. Matters of place became matters of sociality, of building relationships, of creating a sense of being at home with a group of erstwhile strangers. To return to Hendriks, camp centrifugality does undermine stable centers of home and self. Such undermining, however, leaves them open to reinvention through the camp's centripetal forces, which impel its dwellers to draw upon new and relative centers between dislocation and relocation, to world their homes.

5

Being Global in Goma

Eagerly, musician.
Sweep your string,
So we may sing.
Elated, optative,
Our several voices
Interblending,
Playfully contending,
Not interfering
But co-inhering,
For all within
The cincture
of the sound,
Is holy ground
Where all are brothers,
None faceless Others, . . .

—W. H. Auden, "A Hymn to the United Nations"

W. H. Auden's poem "Hymn to the United Nations" was first performed at the UN headquarters in New York in 1971. Today at the URUBATT camp, set to music by Spanish composer Pablo Casals, it is blaring out of an Indian-manufactured sound system. The hymn is preceded by an enthused rendition of the Uruguayan National Anthem, "Orientales, la Patria o la Tumba!" sung by the battalion to a backing track as they march around the camp parade pitch holding hand salutes or rifles at port arms position. The troops now stand in front of a row of UN trucks and armored personnel carriers. Once their rifles are at left shoulder arms, a troop inspection is carried out to a live drum beat, which produces a distracting but exact backbeat as the drum resonates off the Italian-made CORIMECS within the base.

I am seated next to a crew of Ukrainian helicopter pilots and behind two newly arrived Indian officers, Major Baba and Major Neel, whom I would meet for the first time at the ceremony's reception. Hundreds of Uruguayan soldiers stand before us on the brown gravel parade pitch, waiting to be honored with a medal to mark six months of service to MONUSCO. Before the medals are distributed however, Colonel Pablo approaches the podium. "Free countries must live in peace," he begins, clarifying that peace is "not just the absence of war" but "the presence of stability." Uruguay has a long and proud history of answering the call for peace, which the commander dates back to 1936. He speaks proudly of Uruguay's military service under the UN flag and commitment to peace from Cambodia to Colombia, and from Angola to Afghanistan. Despite six months of successes in the DRC, however, Colonel Pablo insists that the Uruguayan battalion has much more to offer. His battalion, he says, has the "means, the training, and the will to operate." I could have sworn he shot a glance at the force commander (FC) seated to his left. The weekend before, I had heard him raise his voice in the officer's mess—frustrated that his battalion was not being deployed more frequently. Frustrated at having to wait for commands from above to fulfill the protection of civilian mandate. Sick of sitting around and drinking whiskey to bide the time. Colonel Pablo concluded his remarks with an instruction to his troops about to receive the UN medal in recognition of each individual soldier's hard work, professionalism, and dedication. "Bequeath it to your sons to show what you can achieve on behalf of the world."

Material and personnel from across the globe were gathered at URUBATT on the day of their medal ceremony. Days like this, when contingents open up their camps to host military counterparts and select civilian acquaintances are pinnacle events that foment peacekeepers' sense of being in an "international environment." This emic phrase and supposed space is the single, most repeated benefit of joining a UN peacekeeping mission, according to the officers and troops I spoke with in Goma.

Like Michael Jackson's (1995) notion of home, this international environment can be a place, but it can also be a group of people. As the understandings and experiences of the global detailed in this chapter attest, peacekeepers notionally place and personalize the international environment both in Goma and within an imagined community made up primarily of peacekeepers from the Global South (Anderson 2006). For many of the troops deployed to Goma, their participation in MONUSCO is perhaps one of the only international deployments they will see in their military career. Given the limited active foreign conflicts in the countries that peacekeepers come from, Goma gains value in the eyes of troops as a unique and novel foreign posting. Framing and discussing local experiences of place as "international" is not unique to military peacekeepers; as Lisa Smirl (2012) has written, it is also a feature of foreign humanitarians' liminal subjectivity. Unlike other, globally mobile, foreign interveners however, a military mission abroad is often a once-in-a-lifetime opportunity for a national soldier to see the world. Many of the perceived opportunities of this international environment are rooted in interpersonal relations within and beyond experiences of Goma as a place. Acquiring new technical expertise and intercultural competency is a value of the environment for military personnel, particularly with respect to learning from others within the mission. Brigadier Kabir has seen his officers mature professionally throughout their tenure, citing how they have learned to use and rely on networking to achieve certain goals. His contingent has also strengthened its problem-solving abilities by his own assessment, having creatively dealt with various mission constraints (such as a lack of financial and political support for operations) and analyzing the pros and cons of what they do with greater tact in light of the greater diversity of actors affected (both in situ and across wider political landscapes).

Within the purview of peacekeepers' explicitly military mandate, joint trainings and operations are another valuable opportunity afforded by this international environment, though these types of exchanges are more prevalent between certain contingents than others. Given the mission's structure and geographic articulation, the brigade headquartered in Goma and staffed by the Indian army is only responsible for operations conducted by their own battalions; professional intramilitary interactions are most often limited to support from South African or Ukrainian aviation units. The Uruguayan and Guatemalan contingents, on the other hand, are under the direct comment of the FC and have more frequent operational collaboration with each other and with other contingents from the Force Intervention Brigade. According to several Indian officers, joint operations for their battalions need to be linked to both strategy and capacity and are, in their words, hardly achievable. Their value has less to do with operational efficiency and mission success than they do with military-to-military diplomacy. For encamped peacekeepers, such diplomacy in this international environment is overwhelmingly maintained through intramilitary social events like sporting matches, demonstrations, cultural festivals, parties, and celebrations—such as Medal Day ceremonies.[1]

Having reviewed peacekeepers' modes of encounter in Goma, experiences and logics of confinement in their camps, and the ways they feel at home in their camps and the city, this chapter turns its attention to how military personnel understand and inhabit this discursive international environment. While the metaphorical world of Peaceland notionally locates peacekeepers within the same everyday lifeworld as other international interveners (Autesserre 2014), the ways that militaries live and work, the places they come from, the ways they relate to people living in Goma and other foreigner interveners, and the meanings and values they ascribe to their participation in intervention differ significantly from their civilian counterparts. Guided by officers' voices, experiences, and concerns, I illustrate peacekeepers' own perceptions about their place within the working environment of the mission and broader space of international intervention. Doing so helps provide important social texture on which to situate intermilitary encounters and from which the camp can come into higher relief as the primary site where national contingents at once distinguish themselves and express belonging within a multinational mission space as it is made to seem like an entire world. Through the lens of the peacekeeping camp as a performative space, I conclude this penultimate chapter by illuminating some of the practices and relationships that national contingents take up among one another and with different groups of Congolese civilians. An Indian Republic Day celebration and a multinational karaoke night among military personnel each illustrate different ways in which peacekeepers understand their own and each other's individual and collective modes and practices of being global in Goma.

A Less Than United Nations

In 2010, the Second Battalion of the Jammu and Kashmir Rifles chronicled their time in the Congo with a unit memoir. The battalion was based in Rutshuru and served the MONUC mission as INDBATT II for thirteen months. The commanding officer, Lieutenant Colonel Aabhas Avasthi, provided a prologue to the coffee table book I borrowed from the brigade commander's office in Goma: "As I pen down my thoughts for this souvenir, my mind goes back more than a year when we set foot on Congolese soil with trepidation just like a pugilist has before entering the ring. The mental conundrum we faced was a maze of an unknown terrain, indifferent foreign faces, perceived animosity of armed elements and a complete change in the working environment under the aegis of the UN" (2010, ix).

Nearly a decade after Lieutenant Colonel Avasthi's battalion arrived in the DRC, Major Guru was nearing his departure—still trying to come to terms with the everyday politics of working under the aegis of the United Nations.

The sector of the country that Major Guru's brigade is in charge of is dealing with about a quarter of the armed groups in the DRC with only three battalions (as opposed to five in the southern sector of the country, he highlights). His sector is the smallest but the busiest, with 40 to 48 percent of the country's reported human rights violations taking place in North Kivu alone. Major Guru doesn't call them human rights violations. He calls them HRVs, reflecting the military penchant for acronyms.

Major Guru's frustration is growing over our beat coffees by the lake as he lays out this situation for me and in an attempt to understand the logic himself. He had recently learned that the mission was planning to repatriate another Indian battalion within the next year. This troop reduction would come on the heels of another battalion repatriation following the closure of multiple peacekeeping camps in Masisi Center and Nyabiondo in August 2017. Major Baba is with us, having invited me to lunch at the office compound. He interrupts Major Guru, asking in earnest, "But, do you think the Indian Army has done anything to decrease HRVs?" Major Guru rolls his eyes. "Don't talk like mission civilian leadership *na*." Major Guru understands this reduction as a political decision made by such civilians instead of being based on evidence from the frontlines, evidence that, by Guru's assessment, would suggest the need for a continued presence. "These people earning 10,000, 15,000 dollars [per month] ... they're self-serving. They have no idea what it takes to take care of an area. They don't give a shit about the force."

Military officers, particularly those commanding various formations, experience many social asymmetries within the working environment of the UN, discernible in part by the way they often speak of the UN or MONUSCO as a separate entity, a "they" that Major Guru distinguishes from a categorically military "us." For many peacekeepers in Goma, when they speak of the UN or MONUSCO, it is in reference to a specific civilian section of the mission or civilian offices in general. Within the mission, military peacekeepers frequently feel marginalized in a structure in which civilians hold the greatest decision-making power. While the military component of the mission consists of those men and women on the frontlines, they can feel constrained by the command structure of the force and othered by the institutional decisions made by the civilian mission leadership. Lieutenant Colonel Ram saw things slightly differently. A few days after meeting up with Major Guru, Ram and I were back in the same spot by the lake when he asked if I knew the difference between "black UN" and "blue UN." While military and civilian personnel working in various sections of MONUSCO drive cars with black UN lettering, members of UN subsidiary and related organizations, like the World Food Programme and International Organization for Migration, drive cars with blue logos. According to Ram, "blue never talks with black."

Within MONUSCO (black UN), social and professional dynamics between its civilian and military components is often a point of tension from the perspective of contingent leadership. Officers are quick to highlight the challenges of working together and the disparities they recognize between themselves and nonmilitary mission staff. Brigadier Rawat, ever the diplomat in his interactions with foreign nationals, was one of the few to laud the working relationship between these groups. "We have come a long way," he says, which may say more about his personal professional trajectory in peacekeeping than anything else. Brigadier Rawat went from working strictly with military personnel in Kinshasa to working as a brigade commander, which requires more liaising with civilian-run institutions. He recognizes that both components seek to achieve the same goal with different approaches. He acknowledges that civilians are "specialists in their field[s]" and support his contingents' training in disarmament, demobilization, repatriation, resettlement, and reintegration; interrogations; and quick impact projects (QIPs), for example—areas in which the Indian army is not necessarily trained. For him, these examples of support are illustrative of UN peacekeeping's integrated approach.

Most officers, however, relate more to the sentiments touched on by Major Guru and are keen to point out the challenging realities of working in an integrated fashion with various civilian sections of the mission. Brigadier Kabir works with fifteen or so different civilian program officers and calls the disconnect between the military and civilian sections one of the biggest problems of MONUSCO. This disconnect leads to contradictory information being circulated in the mission, with higher-ups often receiving and even favoring information that comes from civilian sectors over military contingents. By Lieutenant Colonel Dev's frank assessment, "civilians feel that they control the mission." While pointing out this attitude of superiority he senses, he is keen to point out that civilians depend on the military for their security and for support in many of their activities and operations. He equally echoes Major Guru's perception of a self-serving attitude, saying that civilians share a concept of working that is focused on self-preservation: "Everyone has created their own cocoons." For Lieutenant Colonel Janeeb, mission resources do not seem to prioritize the security and comfort of his military police. In a mission that he also recognizes as "dominated" by civilians, he believes that a maximum of support should be provided to the military troops since "they are taking the risk of their life." Colonial Martín has come to expect that he will have to work with fewer resources than many of the civilian sections of the mission, as the unequal politics of paving between civilian compounds and peacekeeping camps highlighted in chapter 3 attests.

The FC himself believes in the necessity of an integrated approach but none-theless acknowledges that integration is not a neat and tidy process. "Protection of civilians is not just for the military," he says. Different expectations about the roles and responsibilities of civilians and militaries to carry out the mission's mandate have left tensions between the two groups that the force commander has sought to resolve. "I have tried to make arrangements to put them together at the negotiation table." He cites many examples of situations that produce these tense working relationships with civilian mission components. Many of them involve the civilian sections not showing up. He's seen and orchestrated several risky and expensive deployments during which "nobody came from civil sections to do their job." During a standing combat deployment to Bijombo, he tells me, colleagues from the human rights section did show up and the force asked them to speak with community leaders who were "begging for help to avoid danger." The civilian colleague's alleged response? "I didn't come here to do that." Human rights colleagues were there to report on killings that happened near the standing combat deployment two weeks prior. These types of situations visibly frustrate and confuse the FC as a matter of principle. It seems that civilian sections sometimes take the military presence for granted. "They don't know what we do," the FC lamented. He expects civilian sections of the mission to have the cultural and linguistic competencies to "understand their minds and speak their language." While he is referring to Congolese ci-vilians, one could say the same about understanding the military components of the mission.

From the force's perspective, civilian sections also do not know how militar-ies think. Major Olivia, a military advisor to the FC, sees the space between civilian and military ways of working as a misunderstanding between how either side conveys and processes information. For instance, civilians' in-depth knowledge on different topics often fails to culminate into prescriptive, action-able decisions about what military partners should do. This creates ambiguity for institutions like militaries whose knowledge politics are oriented around seeking certainty. Understanding the epistemological priorities of each actor group and adjusting communication across them not only is critical to military effectiveness but could also reduce some of the outstanding civilian-military tension in the mission.[2]

Blue Helmets and Humanitarians

This "black and blue" distinction is not only a palpable professional divide between the mission and different UN-affiliated organizations that affects ways of working and the emotive states of officers but is also paralleled by a divided social landscape among international interveners in Goma. MONUSCO's institutional inability to remain neutral to the conflict helps sow a social divide in everyday life between military peacekeepers and humanitarian professionals, as the latter group's interventions are based on principles of noninterference. The military component of the mission, particularly the operational mandate of the Force Intervention Brigade and their ability to launch offensives creates several ambiguities with respect to international humanitarian law (Sutton 2020). MONUSCO's Security Sector Reform also undermines the mission's supposed neutrality and creates for problematic partnerships, as it can be understood as a capacity building program for the national army (FARDC) and police (PNC) (who are often the most egregious violators of international human rights) (Mobekk 2009; Hirschmann 2019). As such, UN policy itself requires a visual distancing between military personnel and humanitarian interveners in their operations so as not to compromise the latter's neutral stance. According to UN guidelines on civil-military relations: "A clear distinction must be retained between the identities, functions and roles of humanitarian personnel and those of military forces—i.e., travel in clearly marked vehicles, clearly marked offices and relief supplies, etc. Weapons should not be allowed on the premises or transportation facilities of humanitarian organizations. Humanitarian personnel should not travel in military vehicles, aircraft, etc., except as a last resort or for security reasons" (United Nations and Inter-Agency Standing Committee 2008). Beyond professional life and in their rare social encounters, humanitarians in Goma are required to follow these guidelines, often refusing even the most innocuous offers for a lift back to their compounds in UN vehicles or an invitation to the camp for a friendly match of badminton. Several organizations equally restrict their staff from entering a peacekeeping camp regardless of the occasion and only permit them to be in a civilian MONUSCO compound if necessary for work meetings.

Given the protections of international humanitarian law and the policies promulgated to ensure the clarity of those protections, it is perhaps unsurprising that social interactions among humanitarians and military peacekeepers in Goma would be limited as well. When I would invite Major Baba and others to attend the occasional humanitarian house party with me, few other guests would engage in conversation or network with the contingent officers.[3] Simi-larly, at a particularly raucous party billed as Gomapalooza Festival at the Inter-national Rescue Committee house, the Indian officers overwhelmingly stuck to themselves and socialized with very few foreign national acquaintances or Congolese guests present. A month or so after the party, I was talking to Major Ayush during a break in our rehearsals for the Indian National Day celebration. He had attended the party as it doubled as a farewell for a civilian colleague in the mission. Despite a lack of sociality across various identities, it was the first time he really felt a part of the UN mission, a part of the international environment.

Social and professional distancing practices within foreign, interventionist circles are not new and have appeared in complex conflict zones with a UN peacekeeping presence since the early 1990s (Minear 1997). Recent work by Rebecca Sutton (2020) is prolific in detailing how civilian NGO actors negoti-ate and jostle for certain statuses and labels in relation to other actors in conflict zones and even other civilians in everyday encounters. Her empirics, drawn from South Sudan, illustrate how humanitarians distinguish themselves from the peacekeeping mission as a matter of affirming their status as a civilian, often relying on notions and levels of combatantness in peacekeepers that need to be avoided. These distinctions made by humanitarians are felt by peacekeepers in ways that make them cautious of interactions with these actors.

Colonel Martín frames his contingent's engagement with international NGOs as more explicit confrontations, whereby the NGOs they encounter in their field operations purportedly ask, "Why are you here?" "What are you looking for?" Colonel Martín understands the subtext of these questions as accusations that his troops are somehow engaged in foul play. Brigadier Kabir feels similarly to Colonel Martín. His view of the humanitarian and develop-ment sector is that they are highly critical of the mission and quick to accuse the military force of wrongdoing. He has the impression that if the mission or a specific contingent undertakes a project within the specific domain or sector of an international nongovernmental organization (INGO) operating in the region that the INGO will have a problem with it. When he orders a standing combat deployment, his soldiers not only need to know the grievances of the local population and the conflict dynamics of a given area but also take stock of the humanitarian actors operating in that place. Organizations and their staff are viewed from the military perspective as a part of the human terrain—an object to take into consideration while planning operations—a "them" juxta-posed against a deployed military "us."

These perceptions from different commanders illustrate how civilians' fear of peacekeeping encroaching on "humanitarian space" (both in work and in everyday life) affect peacekeepers themselves and shape their attitudes about those operating within said space.[4] Humanitarianism as an ideology (Benthall 2017) effectively allows humanitarian actors to conceptualize their own place in the world in ways that understand military peacekeepers as "out of place" (Cresswell 1996). In their own work, this often leaves peacekeepers, like Colonel Martín, feeling "damned if we do, damned if we don't." To speak of a single social lifeworld of intervention like Peaceland, then, is to ignore the ways in which peacekeepers are discursively and effectively excluded from it.

In relation to their identities as soldiers, peacekeepers do, however, feel more "civilian" in peacekeeping, despite the ways in which their colleagues and other international interveners may view them. In an illustration by Anne-France White titled "The Spectrum of Expat Facial Hair in Eastern Congo," she distinguishes between UN peacekeepers and diplomats on the "very clean cut" end of the continuum, juxtaposed against staff from specific nongovernmental organizations (NGOs) on the "full beard" extreme. Within the outline of the spectrum, she writes what these facial hair styles (correlated with different organizations) denote in terms of different actors' identities and ideologies. While UN peacekeepers and diplomats are characterized by "seriousness" and a "more traditional world view," most INGO staff fall on the side of the spectrum that denotes "field cred," an "anti-establishment vibe," and a sense of "closeness to the people" (White n.d.). This illustration, while satirical, is indicative of the sorts of factors and understandings of self that humanitarian actors use to distinguish themselves from military peacekeepers. Yet, from the military peacekeeper's perspective, the most "human" or "civilian" face they will ever be able to show in uniform is the one they show under the blue beret on a UN mission.[5]

The diversity of their encounters with Congolese civilians are a point of pride for many peacekeeping commanders. In particular, seeing the more direct benefits of community engagement activities and voluntarily engaging in additional outreach enhances peacekeepers' ability to identify with a more civilian, humanitarian identity.[6] Lieutenant Colonel Mona is a civil-military coordination (CIMIC) officer at the Force Headquarters in Goma. CIMIC projects, as well as QIPs conducted by contingents, are a part of her professional responsibility in MONUSCO. They particularly help her understand herself as a more-than-military peacekeeper because people can see, touch, or feel that MONUSCO has done something upon completion of one of the many projects she helps manage. These activities are juxtaposed against the operational mandate and military strategies deployed in eastern DRC, which Lieutenant Colonel Mona implies have a more indirect impact on the everyday life of the Congolese people. Humanitarian assistance is not within what peacekeepers consider to be their operational requirement (beyond assisting in securing areas in which humanitarian assistance is delivered). Yet, many contingents leverage their military deployment to Goma to participate in more humanitarian endeavors such as making donations and volunteering at orphanages. Peacekeepers justify these activities in ways that go beyond the necessity for militaries to win hearts and minds, instead appealing to shared sociocultural traits and recognition of a shared postcolonial subject position.

At the English Club encounter between Major Baba and Goma youths detailed in chapter 2, Baba made several parallels between India and the DRC as a means of relating to the students in the room: high levels of linguistic diversity, ongoing ethnic tensions, land reform and challenges in promoting gender equality specifically regarding land rights, and a shared history of colonization by a European power. Officers and commanders in Goma not only allude to common postcolonial subjectivities and shared cultural traits and societal values between themselves and Congolese civilians when expressing feelings of closeness, but also the more proximate geopolitical positions of their countries (relative to Euro-American interveners, for instance). "Uruguay is not a first-world country," Colonel Martín said, alluding to a greater sense of solidarity between Uruguayans and Congolese people than soldiers from other, more powerful countries. A European soldier, he ventured to say, would "see them more primitively." The UN's reliance on troops from the Global South, while perpetuating imperial and colonial patterns and logics of military deployment, also helps downplay perceptions of the mission as a renewed, neocolonial occupation (Cunliffe 2013). This political dynamic translates into personal feelings of affectual and structural solidarity based not only on the more embedded nature of contingent camps in Goma neighborhoods (relative to civilian compounds), but also a shared experience of being from a postcolony.

Among the broader circle of interveners operating in Goma, the professional necessity of division between humanitarian actors and military actors to maintain the former's neutrality and impartiality spills over into a social distance that is not easily reconcilable. While humanitarian actors understand themselves as relatively "closer to the people," military peacekeepers also construct ideas about their proximity to Congolese people as a matter of understanding themselves, albeit from different geographies and histories. Through the transformation from soldier to peacekeeper, officers are afforded a new level of civilian-ness. Their proximity is also understood through recognizable cultural dispositions and a shared postcolonial subject position. In his critique of Séverine Autesserre's argument, Adekeye Adebajo (2011, 92) comments on the diversity of backgrounds from whence actors grouped together in the metaphorical space of Peaceland come, calling Autesserre's brushstroke a bit broad and naive. The socioeconomic, cultural, and racial differences between encamped peacekeepers and other, predominantly white, Euro-American members of Peaceland cannot be overlooked when seeking to understand how military personnel understand and live the international environment.

For a variety of reasons highlighted here and throughout this book, contingent peacekeepers participate only partially in the customs, rituals, and routines that constitute the everyday life of civilian interveners living in Autesserre's Peaceland. The military nature of their participation in peacekeeping and the structure of the camp entrench social distance from civilian counterparts while simultaneously thickening sociality between officers from different national militaries. The remainder of this chapter focuses on how peacekeepers curate a sense of belonging to the international environment they so highly value through culturally and nationally specific performance and spectacle within their camps.

National Days in an International Environment

Following Indian independence from British rule, Republic Day celebrates January 26, 1950—the day on which the Indian constitution came into effect. I first got word that the Indian brigade was organizing a celebration in Goma for the occasion from Lieutenant Colonel Shoora, who was the main point person for the event. His camp would physically host the festivities due to its large lawn and premium location on the lake. The brigade in Goma has an annual budget from their army to organize celebrations for what they prefer to refer to as "National Day." Unlike past years however, this particular brigade staff decided that instead of disbursing funds to each battalion to celebrate separately, they would pool most of the resources to have one big, blow-out celebration in Goma. Lieutenant Colonel Shoora was stressed for weeks, if not months, in advance.

Rehearsals were held at Himbi every day for a week leading up to the event. Throughout the week, forklifts and soldiers filled the camp, building different installations, paving a dance floor, and hanging posters to welcome guests. Congolese subcontractors came into the camp with what they called the "honeysucker" to empty the septic tanks that week, leaving large truck tracks that spoiled the well-manicured and arranged lawn. Lieutenant Colonel Shoora and

Lieutenant Colonel Madari had a good laugh about it, which broke a bit of the tension and pressure mounting in the run-up to the big day.

Performances were to take place in various places across the vast lawn. The jazz band set up atop a container that acted as a sentinel tower. Individual singers would perform from a *machan*, and the MCs would keep the program going from a makeshift stage in front of a wooden sign that read #LacKivu, which proved to be a popular place for guests to take photos before and after the official program. Fountains were built in the lake itself, along with a gate and water curtain reflecting the colors of the Indian flag across the water. Congolese ICs that usually work in the Mubambiro garrison were brought in to build bamboo fencing all over the camp to create new backstage areas on the lawn and to protect the privacy of accommodation areas. Large UN tarp tents needed to be erected for the spectator area and dining areas, in addition to different serving stations—such as the Delhi Bazaar, where guests could taste various *chaats* and *tikkas* throughout the evening.

Resources from each battalion had been brought to Goma to contribute to the party—all of the tableware, for instance, belonged to a battalion headquartered in Rwindi. Each battalion also brought soldiers in to decorate and staff regiment-specific bar stations around the seating area. The mess staff from the Himbi contingent were busy creating an "Indian village" area that doubled as a hookah lounge, complete with sand mandalas and a replica water well found in rural parts of the country. Guests would be encouraged to try on a traditional headpiece for a photo op on the night of the event.

As Saturday evening approached, preparations reached a fever pitch. From Wednesday onward, performers rehearsed twice a day. The MCs, Captain Seema and Major Ayush, revised and rerevised their script in attempts to incorporate all inputs. Performances were timed and perfected, chairs wiped down, tables draped, and lanterns hung. Costumes were being changed up until the very day of the celebration. Not five minutes into Seema and Ayush's introductory remarks during Thursday night's rehearsal in front of Brigadier Rawat, the power went out across the camp. The Congolese DJ they had hired for the event installed a new sound system that day, which needed ten times the watt load of the jazz band's system (with which we had been rehearsing all week). While people scrambled around to fix the problem, Lieutenant Colonel Dev and Major Baba started talking about the whole production. "You are welcoming people to have fun," Dev remarked, "but you end up making it a drill." The National Day drill was indeed an enormous exercise. The budget for the event was around USD 13,000, a reported $5,000 of which had been spent on alcohol alone. Several officers and I shared warm glasses of *buddha sadhu*, as they taught me to call them, or Old Monk rum and water after the rehearsal, reassuring each other of the old theater adage that a bad dress rehearsal is a good omen for opening night. Major Raju and I, who had made a habit of making music together in his officer's mess, were set to perform a mash-up of Rahat Fateh Ali Khan's "O Re Piya" and Adele's "Rolling in the Deep" with our mutual friend Vaani, an Indian national working with the United Nations Mine Action Service (UNMAS). Vaani's and my vocals would be accompanied by Major Raju on electric guitar with backing from another battalion's jazz band.

The guest list for the event was limited and required an RSVP from the mission personnel (overwhelmingly from the force) and Indian nationals who had been invited. Several Congolese mission counterparts, including the host battalion's assistants—Blaise, Albert, Christian, and Serge—were also in attendance, as were different Congolese performing artists. The invitation stated a dress code of "Formals/Traditional" and asked guests to arrive at 19:20 so that the program could start promptly at 19:30. Major Raju fetched me around 16:00 on Saturday so that we could rehearse once more before the guests started to arrive. Members of the Indian contingent that weren't directly participating in the event arrived over an hour early—the men dressed in suits and women in immaculately draped saris. A long line of officers greeted guests before they descended down to the lawn, grabbed a drink, and took their places under the spectator tents for showtime.

Captain Seema and Major Ayush opened the program, welcoming guests and explaining the significance of Republic Day. Their introduction was followed by a three-part video projection. The first part, set to A. R. Rahman's song "Maa Tujhe Salaam," consists of a slideshow of different cultural, economic, and natural features of India.[7] The video shifts its tone to highlight India's military prowess and strength over the song "Aarambh"—a Sanskritized, motivational battle song.[8] The last part of the video spotlights India's contribution to UN peacekeeping, emphasizing the "expertise, courage, and single-minded dedication" of Indian peacekeepers. Following the video, the first performers to take the stage are soldiers from the Gorkha Rifles.

Performing groups came from all Indian battalions and were selected to create a diverse program that showcased the military and national specificity of different musical traditions as well as their worldly associations. The Gorkha soldiers were up first, performing a victory dance with their famous *khukris*. The *khukri* dance was followed by a subtle display of interregimental unity, as members of the Gorkha regiment's jazz band climbed up onto the *machan* to sing the patriotic Sikh anthem "Deh Shiva Var Mohe" (Bless me Lord). Members of the Sikh regiment themselves came bounding out onto the lawn next accompanied by members of the Goma Street Dancer Company. The men in colorful *kikwembe* tunics were interspersed with Sikh soldiers in equally eye-catching *vardiyaan* to perform nearly six minutes of high-intensity choreography that combined their respective dance styles and traditions and demonstrated both groups' physical strength and endurance. The performance began with Congolese rumba moves synchronized to BM's "Rosalina Remix" before transitioning to Ammy Virk's "Record Bolde," which set the pace of the energetic bhangra dance. In case the symbolism of the fusion dance had been lost on the audience during the performance, Major Ayush walked back onto the stage in front of the #LacKivu structure, reading off his script: "A power-packed performance indeed. This was, in a true sense, an amalgamation of two cultures, which forms an integral part of peacekeeping."

That amalgamation outlived the night of the event itself. A few weeks after the event, I went to an officer's farewell drink at a relatively upscale bar-restaurant popular among foreign interveners with some of the officers present at National Day. Dancers from the company approached our otherwise socially and physically isolated group. They shared that they had incorporated many of the bhangra moves into their performance repertoire and chatted with their new acquaintances from that night. The dancers who joined us projected a protective air around the Indian officers throughout the rest of that night, as other Congolese friends of theirs approached sporadically, offering services and seeking out different economic opportunities from them. The lead choreographer of the group worked to mediate and translate between his Congolese and Indian acquaintances in a nonconfrontational way that left everyone feeling relaxed enough to enjoy the rest of the evening together. The symbolism of the dance performance itself—of Indian soldiers and Goma citizens dancing each other's choreography—was meaningful enough for all involved that the exact same dance was performed at the following year's Republic Day celebration.

The fast tempo of National Day was brought down by a solo performance of John Denver's "Take Me Home, Country Roads"—Brigadier Rawat's favorite tune. The number was introduced with a discussion of the linguistic diversity of India, a diversity that includes the global language of English. The Gorkha regiment was by far the most involved in the evening, performing "Country Roads" as well as the subsequent *jhamré*. The *jhamré* is a dance for which the Gorkhas are particularly respected and celebrated in the Indian army. Performing *jhamré* for over three minutes as these soldiers do requires incredible strength, agility, and endurance. The troops of the brigade were treated to an encore performance by the Gorkhas the following night at a *bara khana*, enthusiastically cheering and filming the performance. The Congolese and Sikh

Rehearsal of the Indo-Congolese fusion dance number. (Photo by author)

regiment dancers were also invited to perform and by the end of the night, everyone was joining in a dance circle to try out the challenging *jhamré* dance.

Before the *jhamré* dancers marched off the lawn, two standard-bearers came out waving the UN and Indian flags behind the dancers. This was our cue. Major Raju, Vaani, and I climbed up into the *machan* to perform. The three of us traded off verses, choruses, and harmonies such that Major Ayush introduced the number as a "fusion of Hollywood and Bollywood." What he didn't mention is that "O Re Piya" is actually an Urdu song made famous by a Pakistani *qawwali* singer. Given the context of ongoing conflict between India and Pakistan and internal religious violence, our song brought another nuanced shade to the brigade's ideas about what it means to be Indian and what it means to be a part of one world. A combination of pipe and drum bands from different battalions concluded the evening. To be visible to the audience, they added cords of lights down their pants and jackets and around their hats and drums. The red and green lights auspiciously matched the colors of both of the regiments performing. Noting this last-minute costume change, I'm reminded of something Lieutenant Colonel Dev once said about the meaning of regiments in the Indian army. While the system is inherited from the British colonial army and relies profoundly on difference, Dev reduced those differences to lanyards and shoulder flashes: "I am not obscured by these colors to judge a man."

The expression "Unity in Diversity," which is mentioned in the program and found on various posters in different Indian peacekeeping camps, is a comment not only on the diversity of India as a nation but also of that diversity as it is translates and becomes visible within the military institution. The MCs concluded the program by thanking the audience for attending the "cultural feast":

[Major Ayush]: "Each country, ladies and gentlemen, is unique in its culture and traditions. And this evening, we hope we gave you a glimpse into ours."

[Captain Seema]: "Let us carry forward this evening with a message to spread a way of peace, love, and light all over the world. So keep recharging your glasses, and continue enjoying this lovely evening with us."

[Unison]: "Thank you and Jai Hind."⁹

Inscribing themselves into the world, the National Day acts displayed a unique blend of culturally specific performances and intercultural collaborations. The program both reified the Indian army's patriotic commitment to the nation-state through the displays of their martial qualities (Henry 2015) and intimated a context-specific cosmopolitanism through the integration of Congolese civilians and foreign nationals like myself as performers. The tone of the program artfully balanced songs with more nationalistic themes against performances of global, popular music with which the diverse audience could variably relate. Beyond the broad and international makeup of invited spectators, performers themselves came together in exceptional, global configurations to perform musical arrangements that cut across and expressed connection between different cultures within and beyond India, such as the Sikh anthem and John Denver tune performed by the musically inclined Gorkhas. From interregimental displays of unity to musical mash-ups and fusion dances, National Day was a highlight of many Indian officers' tenure in the mission, simultaneously encapsulating and articulating their brigade's ideas and ascribed meanings of being from India, being in Goma, and becoming part of an international environment and community.

National Day wasn't the first time that I had become part of a military drill or been more squarely perceived as part of the international environment to which peacekeepers seek exposure. Over the course of my research, I had to adjust to various officers' insistence that I be driven home after spending evenings in

Rehearsal of the *khukri* dance. (Photo by author)

any one of their camps. While I enjoyed my independence and felt safe with my *boda boda* drivers, many contingents felt responsibility for my protection as a foreign civilian and were not willing to accept the risk of something happening to me on my way from their camps at night. They were often resolute in organizing a vehicle and security detail to drop me home. As the frequency of invitations to one of the Indian camps picked up, I couldn't help but feel increasingly guilty and had become overly apologetic toward the *jawans* that would be called (and often woken up) to either pick me up or take me home. On one particular night, the Indian officers and I had gone to the URUBATT camp together for party. Even from URUBATT, Lieutenant Colonel Manoj, the most senior officer among our cohort, insisted that his boys drive me home. When I protested, he replied, "They must know there will be long nights. We have to test them to be ready to go in seven minutes. And they must respect women from other countries." My late nights at the camps provided ideal grounds, in their minds, to conduct a drill, the training value of which was partially rooted in my positionality as a white American woman—a feature of the international environment of Goma that, through inclusion in a musical ensemble, could performatively attest to India's ability to integrate and adapt to that space.

For the Indian brigade in particular, the international community living in Goma is multinational as well as transnational. The National Day invitation list made sure to invite many of the most prominent members and business leaders of the Indian diaspora, mentioned in the preceding chapter. One of the eldest and longest-standing members of the Indian diaspora, Irfan, was also in attendance at National Day. Over at his house a week before the patriotic holiday, he told me that he has met every Indian commander stationed in Goma since 2005. Irfan and his community have had a privileged relationship with the various rotations of peacekeepers from India, who are keen to take note of civilians of Indian origin or descent in Goma for their protection but also to privilege and patronize their shops, bars, and restaurants. For his part, Irfan's relationships with various officers enhances his understanding of the security situation (particularly observable during the 2018 general election) and gives him an added sense of assurance that the Indian contingent will help the community in case of an incident or crisis. Recognizing these social ties between Indian contingents and the small but economically significant diaspora in Goma recovers an important component of how some peacekeepers relate to and understand the constitution of the international environment. Indian peacekeepers' encounters with this transnational community in particular work to blur discrete framings of the "local" versus the "global."

One more group of people that the Indian peacekeepers invited to the event and that highlights variable degrees of proximity and distance within the international environment is constituted by officers from the Armed Forces of Pakistan. The ongoing Kashmir conflict in which both armies are engaged against each other, as well as their geopolitical histories, appear to impact encountering practices and intramilitary camaraderie only minimally. As a result of the copresence of regional adversaries in Goma, Indian army officers know to only exchange their temporary, local SIM card number with such military colleagues and to be cautious about how information circulates about which of their regiments are present in the DRC at any given time, lest another army is gathering intelligence on the operability of particular units. While officers exercise caution about phone numbers and add levels of classification to certain information, ongoing regional conflict back home does little to deter officers from each army from gathering and expressing feelings of closeness to one another relative to other colleagues and international interveners. Many Indian camps have overflow areas with extra tents for attached troops who may be transiting through Goma. Pointing to the tents, Lieutenant Colonel Shyam clarifies that in his base, this accommodation is available primarily for troops from neighboring countries—Pakistan and Bangladesh—as they would be more comfortable in an Indian camp based on certain shared cultural traits and tastes. Similarly, stories from Indian officers who have been guests in Pakistani bases have been marked by their positive impressions of the hospitality of the officers and the respect and subservience of the troops. Beyond sharing space in their camps, Indian and Pakistani officers who serve as military observers (MILOBs) or military staff officers and live in national houses frequently invite each other over for more informal gatherings. Major Siddharth's residence, one of three "Goma houses" inhabited exclusively by Indian MILOBS, is coincidentally or not located near the historical Quartier Asiatique in Goma. In preparation of his new year's brunch for his brigade friends (which I graciously tagged along to), Major Siddharth and his fellow MILOB housemates made sure to extend the invitation to Pakistani brigade officers passing through Goma, who joined for *idli sambar* and *dosa*. This type of sociality is foreclosed back on the subcontinent, whereas in Goma, and relative to other foreign interveners there, officers from these two armies share, recognize, and honor their commonalities through mutual inclusion at social functions.

The Indian Republic Day event instantiates peacekeepers' widespread practices of organizing social encounters and performing for other foreigners in Goma, the latter of which is a social practice particular to military contingents in the intervention space. Similar performances that celebrated national distinction and international ambit included the BANMP Victory Day celebration. The Victory Day program similarly contained both Bengali songs and popular English-language musical performances and included a melodrama depicting the liberation struggle. Lieutenant Colonel Janeeb concluded the Victory Day program, held in the neighboring Tanzanian camp's Kikweke Hall, by inviting Brigadier Rawat to the stage for a photo with his contingent of performers. The contingent's photographer and officers alike were keen to capture photographs with the variety of guests in attendance before they departed, snapping selfies or inviting attendees in front of the stage to give a national backdrop to photographs with their international audience.

As demonstrated in both the Indian Republic Day and Bangladesh Victory Day celebrations, performances by contingent peacekeepers are not limited to representations of (inter)national selves, but often contain elements meant to exhibit and impress on the audience their military prowess (Henry 2015),

A peacekeeper attending GUASFOR's Kaibil Day takes a video of troops helicasting. (Photo by author)

as a matter of connecting with their military peers. While projections of archival battle footage during both celebrations showcased each contingent's military fortitude and competence, neither could match the scale and extent of the performances at GUASFOR's Día del Kaibil. Kaibil Day celebrates the establishment of the Guatemalan Special Forces—akin to a regimental raising day. The early December day was structured around a "demonstration of the capabilities of a Kaibil soldier" (as per the written invitation). The capabilities displayed included how Guatemalan Special Forces are trained to handle hostage situations and extractions through inductions by water, rope (rappelling from a helicopter), and helicasting (jumping into the water from a helicopter). The day of the demonstration that I attended, Colonel Pablo leaned over to say that the helicopter pilots must be the South Africans; Ukrainian pilots would have known how to kick up less dirt when hovering so low to the ground.

Unlike at the other events detailed in this chapter, I was one of only a handful of Kaibil Day attendees in civilian dress, including the Congolese DJ who played during lunch. GUASFOR leadership had nearly exclusively invited members of other foreign forces that made up MONUSCO. Much like other performance events, however, the Kaibil Day guest list emphasized how en-camped peacekeepers enshrine their military colleagues as central members of the international environment and audiences for their performances. Like other gatherings of foreign militaries in each other's camps, the Kaibils' per-formance conveyed a desire for recognition by, and association with, a more international cohort of categorically military peers. The tension between indi-viduating one's national military identity and adopting a more global identity as a member of a multinational force is one that is most explicitly displayed in these types of performances. As the main stage for such productions, peace-keeping camps act as critical forums for expressing and attempting to reconcile these identity tensions.

Splitting Peaceland—Sharing Salt

In unpacking what constitutes the international environment for these par-ticular actors, this chapter has illustrated peacekeepers' experiences and un-derstandings of its social and geographic heterogeneity, fault lines, and fluidity. Importantly, contingent officers' experiences of the professional milieu of the mission and their encounters (or lack thereof) with humanitarian interveners call into question military peacekeepers' presumed inclusion in the metaphori-cal lifeworld that Autesserre (2014) has designated as Peaceland. Repeated discursive framings of the UN as an other and the challenges that have been highlighted by military personnel in their dealings and work relationships with civilians in the mission illustrate very different everyday experiences and un-derstandings of achieving peace. Beyond these social divisions within MO-NUSCO's workplace culture, the lack of a shared sociality between military peacekeepers and humanitarian workers mirrors professional distances that the latter professionals take from actors that they perceive as combatantlike (Sutton 2020), even in places like Goma that are more removed from active conflict zones.

I argue then that the socioprofessional world of Peaceland does not include (and in practice often excludes) contingent officers and troops, though some of their self-perceptions and experiences can be likened, partially, to those lived by civilian interveners. Sutton's theorization of foreign intervener's iden-tity transformation in similar contexts are helpful here. Her notion of the "ci-vilianness continuum" helps explain "the ways in which some civilians might compete to distinguish themselves from each other" and "the micro-strategies these actors engage in to negotiate their relative status in war" (2020, 1–2). While this spectrum is meant to account solely for the ways humanitarians distinguish themselves in the presence of other civilians (in particular members of a UN peacekeeping mission), military peacekeepers also understand themselves as traveling along this continuum during their deployment in a UN mission toward a novel, more civilian identity. Henry (2015, 379) understands peacekeepers' "bifurcated sense of themselves as citizen-warriors" as shaped by a responsibility to demonstrate their civilian competency to be sent on such a military-civic mission while still demonstrating their more martial identities. Rather than using their heightened sense of civilianness to validate their presence in the intervention space, this chapter has illustrated how relating to a more civilian identity helps them legitimate their charity and recognize similarities between themselves and the Congolese people they are mandated to protect. In relation to other nonmilitary interveners in Goma, however, this relative civilianness is not recognized nor translated into social practices of rapprochement between the two actor groups. Major Guru, who had strong feelings relative to these social differences and distances, blames his military uniform for obscuring his humanity in interactions with foreign civilians and humanitarians.

The "international community" proves to be an elusive actor group in political science (Heathershaw 2016). As this chapter has hoped to highlight in a more overt way, peacekeepers experience othering by members of this community, particularly in relation to their military profession but also along social and cultural axes of identity. If we understand their use of the term *international environment* to connote place and people—we can acknowledge that this environment is both grounded in Goma and partially existing elsewhere in a notional international community to which peacekeepers often feel that they do not belong. I say partially because I understand the "international environment" as a much wider framing than what has come to be associated with the term *international community*, with the former including local actors, other transnational communities like diasporas, and other foreign military actors. It is with these latter actors, specifically members of other contingents from the Global South, that military officers' curate a sense of belonging to something bigger than themselves.

Becoming part of a multinational peacekeeping force involves changes in how military personnel do their jobs, perceive themselves, and relate to the imagined community of their own nation and of a multinational United Nations (Anderson 2006). The professional adjustments necessary for military peacekeepers to be successful have not been lost on UN secretary-generals over the years. In his final remarks about the UN Emergency Force mission (the first UN mission with a military force), U Thant acknowledged that the peacekeeper is "faced with a concept of soldiering which is entirely foreign to anything taught him in his national service" (cited in Wills 2009, 8). Dag Hammarskjöld's quote on the matter has become famous: "Peacekeeping is not a job for soldiers, but only soldiers can do it." While MONUSCO's rules of engagement lead soldiers to denounce certain aspects of what "the olive green" means operationally, peacekeepers in Goma cling closely to several other meanings of wearing the national flag on one arm of their uniform while adding new meanings and experiences to their soldierly repertoire through the addition of the blue UN badge on the other.

Military sociologist Charles Moskos raised the question of peacekeepers' attitude formation relative to commitment and loyalty to the UN badge in his research on the UN Peacekeeping Force in Cyprus (UNFICYP) nearly fifty years ago.[10] Through interviews with officers, he found that "UN military service did not increase internationalist sentiments" overall, considered as "a commitment to political institutions transcending the nation-state" (1975, 395). Discourses among officers in MONUSCO reveal a similar lack of commitment to (or sense of inclusion in) the international political institution but not to the multinational community of their peers who, unlike those serving UNFICYP during Moskos's study, are overwhelmingly from the Global South.

As Benedict Anderson (2006) has argued, nations are imagined as limited, sovereign communities. As communities, Anderson writes, "ultimately, it is this fraternity that makes it possible, over the past two centuries, for so many millions of people, not so much to kill, as willingly to die for such limited imaginations" (7). Imaginations of community that surpass the limits of the nation are not automatic but have to be fostered in social encounters between those who are members of that community, particularly among those who need to be willing to lay down their life for it. For members of the peacekeeping force, that community is not the high-earning civilians running the mission, nor is it to be found across the numerous professional and sociocultural fault lines dividing humanitarian professionals from military servicemen and servicewomen. For peacekeepers to cultivate a sense of allegiance to the UN flag is to imagine a military community of other soldiers, carefully bring that community into specific encounters with the population that they serve to protect, and seek encounters with both groups through in-camp social events and spectacles. Sociality and celebration between militaries in each other's

Officers from different national contingents salute the Uruguayan Battalion.
(Photo by author)

camps reveal practices and performances that cultivate camaraderie between officers from different nations living in the same city as a matter of curating a more global sense of the peacekeeper self.

There is a guiding principle in the Indian army, Lieutenant Colonel Dev tells me over a cold coffee in his base: "Naam, Namak, Nishan." These also happen to be the three patches found on every uniformed soldier. *Naam,* or "name" in Hindi, stands for a multilevel understanding of reputation. It can be the name of the soldier but is more commonly understood as your regimental identity. *Namak* literally means "salt" and represents the loyalty of the soldier to those with whom he or she serves or "shares salt"—as in the act of eating together. The notion of *namak* helps realize the imagined community of the nation, for which soldiers risk their lives, in the soldier next to them. Last is the *Nishan*—the symbol or flag representing the higher purpose for which the soldier serves. *Naam, Namak, Nishan* as ethos thus captures the multiple subjectivities and relationships that make up a soldier, including the regiment to which one belongs, one's understanding of being part of a military community, and the mission or cause that unites them.

"When we wear this flag, we represent the nation," Lieutenant Colonel Dev says pointing to the Indian tricolor on his chest over his heart. He qualifies that "nationality should not determine how I behave with others," something Indian army officers evidenced time and time again in social interactions with military peers (including from hostile nations). I point to the UN emblem on his shoulder, asking what this represents. He concedes that, in a sense, the *nishan* has shifted to the blue beret for this particular tenure. Lieutenant Colonel Puneet, with whom I rode to Kiwanja after the National Day celebration, was quicker to acknowledge the *nishan* of the UN emblem on his own uniform but understood his ability to identify and serve the mission of peace as contingent on "the illustrious history back home." The stakes of upholding a strong national reputation is heightened in peacekeeping (Daugirdas 2019), while a soldier's pride and attachment to his nation tends to be strengthened by the relative distance of a UN deployment, copresence of troops from other nations, and foreign civilians to protect. In this way, the degree to which peacekeepers associate themselves or feel attachment to the cause represented by the UN emblem is ultimately dependent on the pride they have for their own national colors and loyalty to upholding a national reputation. "The blue badge is temporary," Lieutenant Colonel Puneet added on our ride north. "The olive green is forever."

When a soldier adds the *nishan* of the UN to his uniform, he is serving not only the mission and his nation's reputation in relation to that mission but also the national flags of others on the force. Attachment to the national *nishan* and curating a commitment to the UN *nishan* is an animating tension that activates peacekeeping camps as world stages—sites of spectacle directed at connecting with a multinational audience of military peers. The path to becoming a more "global" soldier is made not by curating a sense of loyalty to a supranational entity but through making interpersonal and international acquaintances. This is done in Goma by inviting those with other nations' flags on their uniform or passport into the camp, including Congolese institutional partners, assistants, and performers. The sociality of the camp is about more than simply throwing a party. It is about sharing salt.

Thinking back to the medal day ceremony that opened this chapter, I have to question Lieutenant Colonel Puneet's statement about the temporality of the UN emblem on a soldier's uniform. The medals being passed out that day at URUBATT were hung on a ribbon with two light blue bands representing the presence of the United Nations in the DRC. Moving toward the center of the ribbon, two thin yellow bands represent the dawn of an era of peace and

Distribution of the UN medal. (Photo by author)

prosperity. The dark blue in the middle of the ribbon represents the Congo River—understood as a symbol of unity in the DRC. On an individual level, the medal is a memento that marks a national soldier's service to UN peacekeeping and service to the DRC. On the collective level, medal ceremonies (like other camp-based festivities) provide opportunities for national groups to inscribe themselves with a more global identity as a blue helmet and member of a multinational peacekeeping force in a specific, foreign national context. It marks their mission tenure—a process of becoming part of the world as it is imagined to exist within the international environment of UN peacekeeping and their service to the mission of peace in the DRC on behalf of the world. The world, like home, is thus understood as both here and elsewhere.

Upon a soldier's return home and removal of the UN *nishan* from the armband, the ribbon of the medal is added to the left chest of the uniform as a badge of achievement. It is added to the olive green forever.

Conclusion

Camping the City

Rather than being one definite sort of thing—for example, physical, spiritual, cultural, social—a given place takes on qualities of its occupants, reflecting these qualities in its own constitution and description and expressing them in its occurrence as an event: places not only *are*, they *happen*.

—Edward Casey, "How to Get from Space to Place in a Fairly
Short Stretch of Time," 27 (emphasis in original)

Geographical philosopher Edward Casey shares a vision of place that is reflected in Ravish Kumar's *Ishq Main Shahar Hona*, translated by Akhil Katyal as *A City Happens in Love*. I picked up the book on one of my trips to India to visit officers and friends I had met in Goma. In one of the prologues to the book, Kumar (2018, xi) writes: "I have always seen the city from the lens of the village. Where people go and forget the village. The city came to my life as the city versus the village. Until then, the city was but a temporary address for me. In the column for 'permanent address' I always filled in my village address. Not where I had encamped in the city. On every occasion I found myself returning from the capital, Patna, to village Jitwarpur in district Motihari. All the time the difference between the home and the camp was intact. Home meant village, camp meant city."

The differences elaborated by Kumar disintegrate through love stories. The city comes to mean home though falling in love with, in, and through the city. Camping, I have argued, can also transform a place like a city into a home, though not necessarily at the expense of the camp, nor at the expense of experiences of the city as an elsewhere. As I have tried to demonstrate throughout this book and clarify here, peacekeeping camps *happen* in dwelling and movement, and a city also *happens* in, though, and with camps.

The east, faced with the brunt of civil conflict, is one of the least urban-
ized regions of the DRC yet boasts one of the highest urban growth rates,
led largely by Goma (Ranarifidy 2018). Forced displacement in the form of
conflict-driven rural to urban migration has been a defining feature of Goma's
rapid demographic growth and urbanization (Büscher 2011; Pech, Büscher, and
Lakes 2018). Yet relatively few people in Goma who have experienced internal
displacement enter the humanitarian regime as formally defined internally displaced persons (IDPs), preferring alternative settlement options to camps such
as renting, staying with family, or getting together with others from one's home
town to form a *gîte*. As the city has grown and welcomed a large international
aid and development presence, so have opportunities in the city, attracting
people to the city for economic, educational, or other personal reasons. What
I have tried to propose in this book, through an ethnographic detour into (and
out of) Goma's peacekeeping camps, is an approach to urban spaces of dwelling
that foregrounds how place and space is lived through dynamic and variegated
dislocations from other places and spaces that are tenaciously held, ruptured,
adapted, and transformed through human acts and affects of relocation. In this
way, understanding rapid urbanization as similarly rapid dislocation from a
home elsewhere opens up the possibility of thinking Goma through practices
of *camping*, not only among peacekeepers temporarily stationed in various barracks across the city but also among those urban dwellers who have left homes
elsewhere for Goma, bringing new worlds nearer while working to make new
homes within them.

Attesting to how these senses of newness work on urban identity formation, Koen Vlassenroot and Karen Büscher (2013, 3177–78) write that, in Goma
(compared to Kinshasa), "a shared history of inhabiting and making the city
together is largely lacking." Perhaps what contributes to this sense that a shared
history of making the city is lacking goes back to the broader idea intimated
in this book's opening line, "David is not from Goma." Indeed, when I comb
through my field notes and think about the Congolese people I met and with
whom I lived, most were not from Goma. They talked about home as elsewhere
and incorporated images and practices from these elsewheres into their homes
in Goma; elsewheres to which many had a desire to return but with no concrete
plans to do so. Perhaps across the many axes of human difference in Goma, including those between temporary peacekeepers and more permanent residents,
the most shared way of expressing the relationship between oneself and the city
is being-from-elsewhere.

Vlassenroot and Büscher are right. Goma's urban dwellers do not inhabit
the city together. The style of living in the *gîte* is typical of many individual

housing arrangements and reflected on a larger neighborhood scale. People in Goma frequently live together among kith and kin from the same hometown or territory or at least near them. People do, however, make the city together by embedding actual and aspirational elsewheres in it. This, from both sides of the peacekeeping camp gates. A shared history of dwelling in the city is only lacking in that it needs to be coupled with a shared history of coming and going, of dislocation, of journeying. There is a shared history of dwelling in the city by way of a journey that is characteristic of life in Goma. There is a shared history of making the city together through camping.

This last discussion positions the story of peacekeeping camps within the urban fabric of Goma and within the discipline of urban studies more squarely, demonstrating how the study of such camps can contribute to a new narration of urbanity and the making of the city. Theorizing that story builds on and repurposes Ananya Roy and Aihwa Ong's (2011) notion of worlding cities to understand how camps and camping can constitute a new kind of worlding practice. That practice, which I theorize as worlding home, is less about movement toward a center composed of "global regimes of value" (Roy and Ong 2011, 312) and more about how home is made into an unsettled and errant center through movement. Theorizing such making and moving, I argue for a shift in camp studies' analytical object away from *camp* as a noun and toward *camp* as a verb. In doing so, I develop *camping* as a concept-term in its own right and argue for its inclusion in a growing vocabulary of not only southern but also global urban practice (Bhan 2019).

Denominalizing the Camp

"Camping" as an urban practice/theory adopts a similar mode of theory building as "worlding" both in its use of the same grammatical transformation and with the conceptual implications that come with the "thinging" of things (Heidegger 1971). This mode, characterized by verbing nouns, attunes to a broader ontology of "becoming" in its emphasis on action, process, and the in-between (Deleuze 1998). While peacekeeping camps have been shown to exhibit many qualities of being-at-home, different camps and *gîtes* in Goma exhibit different paths toward revising and reproducing the notion of home. Accounting for such differences demands an equally unsettled grammar. Michael Jackson (1995, 6) echoes this sentiment thus: "Sometimes, the places where we feel most at home are like nouns in sentences. We are comforted by the way they appear to be sealed off from the world, complacent in their own definition. But sometimes it is imperative to unsettle that sense of being housed, to risk oneself in the world, to recognize the power of verbs, prepositions, and copulas." The term *camp* can already be understood as both a noun (place) and a verb (practice), allowing scholarly analysis to combine static territorialization with the fluidity of action. While the term can simultaneous be understood as a physical place or mode of practicing settlement (or dislocation), camping, as a progressive grammar, better conveys the sense of an indiscernible, multiple, and unfixed form and location, thereby retaining salient aspects of "worlding" as understood by Roy and Ong (2011).

In English, using anthimeria to change lexical categories of other types of urban settlements like the suburb and the ghetto has resulted in verbs like *suburbanize* or *ghettoize*, which are more ubiquitously used in their more static noun forms—*suburbanization* and *ghettoization*. This grammar relegates them to the subjective case in which they can only act on space and focuses our attention on results as the "thing" rather than the incremental, ongoing, unfinished processes that constitute its "thinging." While retaining camping's attention to the processual and constantly becoming, the suffix *-ize* implies external, often unlocatable agents acting on the object or the nexus of that object and the city. The gerund *camping*, on the other hand, places the conceptual location of its making back within the object itself, shifting focus to the agency of those who inhabit the object (in this case, the camp) and who engage, themselves, in the practice as its subjects—in other words, those who make the camp *happen*.

Urban scholarship as well as anthropological theory is familiar with the power of such a move to call attention to the agent of an activity (both in the grammatical and social theory sense). John F. C. Turner's (1972) chapter "Housing as a Verb" makes a distinction between the term's use as both a noun (a commodity) and a verb (an activity), pointing out the ways in which the latter better conveys the importance and centrality of users (as opposed to producers) in decision-making. With this grammatical and conceptual transformation, he advocates for a more open, plural housing system whose realization is grounded in the needs and demands of the housed themselves. Turner does not privilege the human experience of housing over material qualities, quantities, or outcomes on which housing standards, problems, and values are generally assessed by central planning authorities. Rather, his argument for approaching housing as an activity reconfigures the relationship between the ends of the housing user and material means. Similarly, the concept of camping that I seek to set forth is one that does not ignore the politics and apparatuses at work in making camp but understands them as a practice of processual relation.

Tim Ingold's conception of making (yet another verb in the progressive form) puts a finer point on this last idea. Just as Turner's critique of the housing sector lies in its conceptualization and centralized implementation, which operates solely on assessments of its material culture, Ingold's making recovers missing pieces of process. Ingold (2013, 7) reinserts "making" into the study of things that we can touch and see thus:

> In the study of material culture, the overwhelming focus has been on finished objects and on what happens as they become caught up in the life histories and social interactions of the people who use, consume or treasure them. In the study of visual culture, the focus has been on the relations between objects, images and their interpretations. What is lost, in both fields of study, is the creativity of the productive processes that bring the artefacts themselves into being; on the one hand in the generative currents of the material of which they are made; on the other in the sensory awareness of practitioners."

Making helps us recover these lost agentive and processual aspects of our visual and material world by leveraging what Ingold calls "correspondence." Correspondence goes beyond a simple interaction between a maker and an object to account for the relationship between people, objects, and the world. It not only helps account for human agency in the making of material forms (such as the camp in this case) but reminds us that in such movements, a beginning, end, or break between the two is indeterminable (Ingold 2013).

The camp is always becoming in ways similarly described by Heidegger as things "thinging"—a notion that Ingold (2013, 85) also relies on in to give "making" such rich theoretical content. If the camp is constantly camping in this sense, it is not only attuned to a Deleuzian becoming or the agentive aspects of a correspondence with the world through making but, as Heidegger (1971, 179) sees it, is already a matter of "the nearing of world." I posit that this nearing of world happens in the peacekeeping camp as in the gîte, through a dialectic of dwelling and journeying, though the latter is constantly moving the point of reference (that toward which the world is being neared) in its inherent errantry. I prefer to think of camping's correspondence with the world not solely through a process of bringing near but also through the casting out implied by the journey. Doing so allows me to conceptualize camping as a practice of worlding home.

Camping as Worlding Home

Worlding as urban theory seeks to capture the complex and dialectical relationship between the local and global forms of aspirational urban projects, assuming that there are places where we can study any single project and global spaces with which a certain practice might engage or through and to which it might travel (Simone 2001; Roy and Ong 2011). Similarly, the coming-into-being of peacekeeping camps relies on both a sense of place that is at once local and global but necessarily multiplies and reconfigures their meanings. As has been illustrated throughout, what is local to peacekeepers is simultaneously located in Goma and in the countries they come from. Similarly, the global is at once constituted by an international cohort of peers and their experience of Goma as the world. As such, peacekeeping camps challenge a basic assumption of worlding—namely, that there is something local and singular about the situated, something global and generic about the forces acting through or instigating the camp. The material environments, differing copresence of Congolese civilians, and peacekeeper discourses of these camp spaces avoid such a clear-cut binary, as the situated experience of the camp becomes an experience of "the international environment" for peacekeepers and their sense of gaining a more global identity is forged in performances that are relatively local to themselves and their experience of Goma as a locality and social sphere.

Second, the peacekeeping camp as object of study productively complicates and transcends many of the cleavages in postcolonial urban scholarship to date by holding together theoretical objects that have largely been treated in isolation by scholars—namely, global hegemony and postcolonial subjectivity. Worlding's theoretical power lies in its problematization of the marked divide in urban scholarship between a political economy approach focused on economic globalization and postcolonial studies' emphasis on subaltern agency (Roy and Ong 2011). Its use as a heuristic device is simultaneous reliant on place-based events and practices and an understanding of the complex processes, occurring in multiple elsewheres, into which and from which these practices write themselves. The existence of peacekeeping camps is predicated on the liberal internationalism underpinning the United Nations, a global governance institution that often intervenes to improve the national and urban conditions in which neoliberalism can flourish. The agents on the ground of that intervention, however, are less central to this global power structure and do not share its grand intentions. Many individuals participate in peacekeeping with socioeconomic and professional mobility in mind. Many countries participate seeking inclusion into groups of influential and powerful states within this global governance institution. We cannot overlook the fact that troops carrying out peacekeeping military operations today are overwhelmingly from countries in the Global South, with their attendant histories as subjects of

colonialism. Nor can we ignore the ways in which Congolese civilians participate in many of the professional and performative aspects of peacekeeping in
Goma. In such a tension, institutional and individual aspirations and anxieties
energize the camp as forces from above and from below converge in ways that
are difficult to disentangle into neat hegemonic and postcolonial categories.

It would be a mistake, however, to assume that those who are encamped are
always one presupposed category of social actors (notably a sort of subaltern
subject). While peacekeepers based in Goma overwhelmingly come from a
very specific set of elsewheres, and generally feel othered by Euro-American
civilians in the mission, their camps nonetheless retain a level of heterogeneity in the military composition of officers from more affluent segments of
their respective societies and troops with lower-middle-class backgrounds.
The military nature of such camps lends itself then to a multiplicity of power
structures from above and below, as peacekeepers juggle identities linked to
their combatantness, nationality, regiment, and rank as well as their newfound
cosmopolitanism. Taking seriously this heterogeneity within the peacekeeping
camp allows us to start from the situated and the global at once, exploring a
space of entangled engagements across geographies of power and subordina-
tion at various scales.

Third, camping forces us to consider new directionalities and previously
overlooked geographies of worlding occurring within, between, and beyond
camp space in the city. Drawing on Spivak's postcolonial critique, Roy (2011,
313–14) maintains that worlding is a practice of centering while acknowledging
that the center can shift from a global regime of value to the type of "self-world-
ing" exhibited in inter-Asian urbanism. This worlding reconfigures center and
periphery, remaps relationships of power, and yet maintains urban scholars'
focus on directional trajectories. Yet, to think of worlding through such itiner-
aries reinforces a commitment to a specific directional trajectory rather than
the multiple, potential relationships people and places can take up with the
world as it is conceived at various scales. Peacekeeping camps and the encountering and distancing practices that emerge within, through, and beyond them
with Congolese civilians, mission staff, diasporas, other foreign militaries, and
among encamped peacekeepers themselves, intimates the existence of multiple
centers and multiple peripheries.

The experiences of peacekeepers camping in Goma exhibit a much more
unstable and ever-shifting centering than the worlding at work in urban studies
today; one that questions the existence of a fixed center, a detectable periphery, and a unidirectional path between the two. Peacekeepers from the Global

South camping in Goma map and remap different relationships between home and world but allow neither to occupy a singular center or to remain fixed in and of themselves. To consider their camping as a new kind of worlding practice allows us to recover an important stage in Édouard Glissant's (1997, 29) poetic imagination—that of circular nomadism—which creates of every periphery a center to the point where such divisions and directions are abolished. To understand camping as a practice that "instantiate[s] some vision of the world in formation" and instantiates multiple visions of a center, of a home and a world in formation, expands the potential destinations and elsewheres toward which a worlding process can happen (Roy 2011, 312).

Glissant is increasingly being embraced by scholars of southern urbanism to come to term with cities' connections and disconnections with various elsewheres. Garth Myers (2018) considers Glissant's Relation as important to non-hierarchical comparative thought that "makes productive use of particularities and differences."[1] Similarly, Tariq Jazeel (2019) proposes Glissant's poetics to decolonize geographical knowledge toward the singular or the particular, taking comparison in other directions (toward the incomparable). Myers (2020) mobilizes a Glissantian approach to relationality to explore cultural translocalities in two Caribbean and two African cities in a chapter of his latest book, marking a creative departure from urban studies' typical agenda of thinking about relationality in political-economy terms. Camps, I argue, like the cities Myers studies, are also cultural translocalities, or places that people make in "the Here and the Elsewhere" to quote the subtitle of one of his chapters (105).

A specific and crucial contribution of Glissant's Relation that I take forward for thinking about the translocality of the peacekeeping camp itself and its connection to Goma is the demolition of directional trajectories—trajectories that "link the places of the world into a whole made up of peripheries, which are listed in function of a Center" (Glissant 1997, 28). "In Relation," Glissant writes, "every subject is an object and every object a subject." Telling the story of peacekeepers camping in Goma has necessarily required this type of analytical fluidity. The camp is at once a subject that works on the object of the city—altering its built environment throughout history, providing protection through its presence, and offering it new (albeit limited) economic opportunities—and the object on which the city works to induce peacekeepers' confinement, determine the locations of their camps, and add to aesthetic and sensory repertoires of inhabitation and being-at-home-in-the-world (Jackson 1995).

Camping then, might be thought of as an embodied reconciling of multiple spatial notions of here and elsewhere done in the space between dwelling and journeying—a making that finds its poetic correlative in Glissant's notion of "a thinking of errantry." Errant thought retains the idea of rootedness (a rooted errantry) but renounces it as a totality: "The root is not important. Movement is" (Glissant 1997, 14). If we think about the root as the nations that peacekeepers come from, for instance, multiple examples in this book illustrate that while it is retained in institutional practices, as an identity, and through aesthetic features of the camp, it is not overdetermining of the space. Movement, or the journeying aspect inherent in camping, changes and multiplies the root. In a word, it worlds them. Suggesting that camping be considered a practice of worlding *home* seeks to safeguard the particular by recognizing that that the root, or the center, will always already be relative to multiple heres and multiples elsewheres.

As peacekeepers engage in worlding home through camping, not only do they strive to bring the world into a new configuration of home, but their camps simultaneously instantiate a casting out of their homes into the world. In terms of movement, the process at work in camping is "an internal dialectic of experienced mobility and immobility" (T. Hendriks 2015, 156). Thomas Hendriks (2015, 168) goes on to elaborate on the dynamics of labor camps belonging to a foreign logging concession in the Congolese rainforest this way: "Ever-lurking sentiments of sadness, frustration, disappointment, neglect, and boredom tainted momentary flashes of excitement, joy, possibility, consumption, and distinction. This very contradiction between both sides of a particular camp atmosphere gave rise to what I would call a centrifugal work of the imagination: instead of focusing on the here and now of everyday camp life, people's imaginations were usually propelled outwards to 'another' place beyond camp borders." As this book has sought to illustrate, peacekeepers' understandings of their camps as home spaces in the world are the result not only of the "centrifugal work of the imagination" as Hendriks suggests. Such an imagination would, in my understanding, notionally locate and think of home as strictly elsewhere and more familiar, and of the world (represented by people from Congo and elsewhere) as overwhelmingly foreign. Peacekeeping camps, however, equally exhibit centripetal forces of the imagination that seek to bring other people and places into their experience of the camp. Intramilitary and civilian-military encounters during ceremonies and celebrations, decorations and materials made by Congolese artisans, and new practices related to food, for instance, pull people and things into the atmosphere of the camp. Peacekeepers' imaginations situate their camps as homes in the world as they are perceived to be in and part of Goma. Their camp cultures acknowledge the place from which they have arrived, but also the place to which they have come, drawing in the world beyond the national contingent that inhabits the camp and beyond the camp perimeter.

Roy and Ong (2011, 4) define worlding practices in cities as "projects that attempt to establish or break established horizons of urban standards in and beyond a particular city." Camping is a worlding practice that particularly attempts to establish *and* break established horizons of home. Urbanity forged through camping makes it imperative to identify moving and multiple homes as centers in unstable and variegated worlds to find correspondences between a single city and the multitude of elsewheres that contribute to its making.

While inextricably linked to the geopolitical motivations and financial will of European and North American powers consolidated in the United Nations, the encounters between today's peacekeeping camp space and city space demand a reinterrogation of what can count as worlding. I see worlding home as precisely encompassing this productive tension of the global order of peace and the peacekeeper from the Global South, of the peacekeeper and the peacekept population, and of camps and the cities that host them. This worlding adds new sources and directions to previous iterations of the concept that require a single notional direction, for instance of either centering or being cast out into the world. Worlding home offers new understandings of what it means to be at-home-in-the-world in the city, offering an analytical starting point at the translocality of place itself (Massey 1994), with an agenda that privileges the study of how different people inhabit (in the sense of living and tenaciously holding) the city in the space of Relation between here and elsewhere.

Adding Camping to a More Global Vocabulary of Urban Practice

This book puts forth an anthropological understanding of peacekeeping camps to argue that camping, as a becoming through the dialectical process of dwelling and journeying that worlds home, should join our growing vocabulary of urban practice. By conceptualizing practice in a broad sense as ways of moving, Gautham Bhan (2019) has begun the important work of building a vocabulary that is empirically rooted in southern places and that finds its theoretically generative power in the vocabulary building itself. Theorizing by building a vocabulary of camping joins Bhan in his quest for vocabulary of modes of practice that are attendant to the types of theory building proposed by Teresa Caldeira (2017) in exploring modes of making sociospatial forms. In addition, expanding our vocabulary of the urban to include camping responds to the theoretically generative demands of multiple disciplines. In urban studies, it "enable[s] an expansion of the lifeworlds under consideration" (Bhan 2019, 2) and "liberat[es] the city as a conceptual container of capitalism and subaltern agency" (Roy and Ong 2011, 9). The anthropology of becoming equally demands a resistance to binaries and emphasis on the processual and in-between by "choosing to look at how lives, rationalities, social fields, and power relations are inflected in one another and in the enclosures, impasses, thresholds, and breakthroughs that are the materials of lifeworld and subject construction" (Biehl and Locke 2017, 28). By imbuing camping with the theoretical bridging power of worlding, we surpass the persistent dichotomies through which we approach and increasingly understand the urban—such as global/subaltern (Roy and Ong 2011), encounter/distanciation (Förster 2013), modernity/development (Robinson 2006)—with an analytics of urban practice that is, itself, a mediation of simultaneously global and situated phenomenon.

Camping as a verb expands our reading of the city to consider not only the built environment of a seemingly static form of camp but also the lifeworlds of people living diverse dislocations, including deployment. It forces us to hold more closely together concepts as opposed as temporality and permanence, individual agency and institutional subjugation, open space and closed space, the ordinary and the extraordinary, and a homely and worldly sense of place in our understanding of urbanity. In a word, it forces us to study cities not *through* elsewhere but *as* elsewhere.

To think of the city as elsewhere, as proposed in the introduction, I have argued that camping be conceptually understood as a practice of worlding home—the urbanity of which is forged in a dialectic of centrifugal forces hurling outward and centripetal forces huddling inward. As a centrifugal space, peacekeeping camps are established to meet objectives beyond their confines and are acted on by forces outside of them. In the peacekeeping camp, those objectives can be concrete strategies and tactics based on the security situation in the DRC or more abstract ambitions to improve a nation state's international image. In both cases, realities beyond the camp work to shape the architectural culture within and the social identities of its inhabitants. Camps become a point from which patrols are launched, vehicles are dispatched, soft diplomacy toward other foreign contingents and the Congolese population is leveraged, and from which we might better understand certain urban geographies and socialities at and beyond their gates. Yet, they are also centripetal spaces in their confining of soldiering bodies, their importation of familiar products and images from near and far, and their ability to reproduce military cultures and assemble the materials that make soldiers feel at home. Shedding light on this productive tension, Goma's peacekeeping camps stand as a theoretically rich field for transforming not only how we think about what makes a camp but also how we understand what makes a city as a social, cultural, and architectural space.

Throughout the empirical exercise of thinking the city of Goma through its peacekeeping camps, movement and connectedness to myriad places at a plethora of scales have emerged as salient qualities of the camp space. To attune to movement and change in and between these camps is to recognize them as processes. I have argued for a more processual understanding of the camp by imbuing the term *camping* with the conceptual power of privileging camp as a practice rather than a particular form. While this may signal a shift from how camps have traditionally been approached in academic circles, it is not new in urban studies. Christian Schmid (2012) has pointed out, for example, a detectable shift in the evolution of Henri Lefebvre's body of work between focusing on the city as an object of analysis to urbanization as a process. Without drawing a conclusion parallel to Lefebvre's about a complete campification of society, what this book hopes to do is urge us to take inspiration from different forms of camping to inform the content of a theory and vocabulary or, as Bhan would have it, practice. To add camping to a vocabulary of urban practice attendant to theory-building then, is to attune to the ways that people live cities *as* elsewheres in a practice between dwelling and journeying. Like camping, the work of theorizing the city is necessarily unfinished, the possibilities as infinite as the types of errantry and elsewheres we can imagine.

Da Coda al Capo

Camping as urban practice and analytical lens restores focus to the agents and practitioners of the camp—the people making it happen. During a peacekeeping mission, one way that contingents make their camps into eventful happenings is through camp-based spectacles and gatherings that perform nationality and internationality. Wearing, representing, and being able to make the ultimate sacrifice under the *nishan* of the United Nations is not something that an individual UN peacekeeper simply adopts (or not) to a certain degree. Rather, it is one element that, when arranged with an individual peacekeeper's national *nishan* and a multinational cohort of peers and performers creates a new identity out of that relationality. Sociality in the camp and the sharing of salt across groups of encamped peacekeepers builds the energetic potential to curate a sense of belonging (at a near distance or far) to the world and mission inscribed in the ideals of the United Nations.

Questions of how to be a UN peacekeeper as opposed to a national sol-dier permeate the mission space as soldiers must learn to work with civilian counterparts, who are not always keen to be associated with them. Despite this dependence and the UN's promulgation of what they call an integrated approach to stabilization (requiring civilian and military cooperation), there is a palpable social rift in Goma between civilian humanitarian and develop-ment professionals and military men and women working within contingents, construed partially through the latter's encampment. The presence of soldiers in a humanitarian mission like MONUSCO induces transformations in the ways that professional humanitarians and professional soldiers alike relate to and appeal to their civilian identities. On the one hand, international civil staff tend to adopt practices of distinction based on notions of themselves as "civil-ian plus" figures (Sutton 2020). At the same time, military officers and troops working under the UN aegis also detect shifts in their "civilian-ness" as a matter of working among international civilians and encountering and engaging with Congolese civilians beyond the dictates of their mandate, becoming a sort of "civilian-warrior" (Henry 2015, 379).

In addition to expressing variable degrees of belonging to a multinational military force, peacekeeping camps reflect soldiers' home country aesthetics and cultures. Replicas, murals, and posters of national monuments, landscapes, and traditions turn certain rooms, walls, and fields in peacekeeping bases into something between symbols of national pride and tourism advertisements. Such imagery, as well as the importance of familiar flavors from their respec-tive countries, make peacekeepers feel at home in the camp. While some camp aesthetics work to situate notions of home among foreign peacekeepers else-where, in their countries of origin, other culinary, visual, and architectural features that contribute to senses of home come from images and imaginations of Africa, Congo, and Goma itself. For the Indian battalions, the presence of a diasporic community strengthens the familiarity of the city. For all battalions, camps made with familiar and novel, place-based features contribute to a sense of comfort relative to risks experienced in deployments and patrols further afield. The sense of home that peacekeeping camps engender, therefore lies in a balance and arrangement of spatial and temporal features between "here" and "elsewhere" at operational, national, and continental scales.

Peacekeeping camp space at once registers the power structures of liberal internationalism and the subalternity of peacekeeper soldiers; it becomes at once ordinary and extraordinary or, as I have argued, (extra-)ordinary. The ubiquity of messaging, discussion, and attention paid to camp curfew times and the UN's zero-tolerance policy on sexual exploitation and abuse exemplify the politicization of the natural life of peacekeepers and control of their bodies. Yet peacekeeping camps are also designed to care for the soldiers that dwell within them. Camps' recreational amenities stress the significance of keeping troops comfortable to enhance their operational performance. They combine infrastructures, utilities, and services that serve to maintain the troops' physical, spiritual, and intellectual well-being. Keeping consistent routines familiar to most modern militaries serves to strengthen the ordinariness of the camp. The theoretical power of the ordinary as it has been used to understand cities and to level the playing field of starting points for urban theory generation offers the possibility for the way of life inside the camp to burst out of itself, to go back outside (Robinson 2006). Only then can peacekeeping camps be included in "a world of camps" (Agier 2014). Only then can Goma be discussed in a world of cities. Only then can we begin to talk about contemporary urban life in Goma *with* camps.

Despite their boundedness and materially rigid exteriors, peacekeeping camp space and peacekeepers themselves interact with the urban environment in ways that generate new ways of life in the city. Congolese language assistants and community liaisons facilitate many of these interactions despite the precarities that come with the job. Often, MONUSCO's prolonged presence coupled with perceptions of inaction create frustrations among the local population that these assistants must translate. Some of these perceptions of inaction are born of the distinction for peacekeepers between "law and order problems" and their mandate to protect civilians. Protecting civilians in the relative security of Goma is mostly a matter of carrying out patrols across the city by vehicle and by foot. Peacekeepers' conduct in the city is itself patrolled as well, as BANMP circulates and surveilles the city to ensure and enforce the disciplinary and behavioral requirements of soldiers serving in a multinational force. Peacekeepers also undertake practices that seek to bridge the distances created between them and the local community by organizing different events outside of their camps or by inviting in Congolese civilians. Urakfiki Meetings, civil-military coordination activities, quick impact projects, and additional winning hearts and minds (WHAM) activities are critical complements to peacekeepers' operational strategies and tactics by enhancing opportunities for meaningful cooperation. Contingents' with operational responsibility for Goma focus many more resources on WHAM, since the city requires less attention on protecting civilians from armed groups than other parts of the eastern DRC. Spaces of encounter between peacekeepers and the peacekept are also spaces of opportunity. Working for MONUSCO, knowing civilian or contingent MONUSCO staff, or simply knowing one of their national languages is perceived as opening a literal and figurative world of opportunity to un-employed university graduates of Goma and even younger adolescents. The languages of troops leak out of the camps and are seized on by children who gather near their entrances. Life as it unfolds through encounters in the city and around camp gates complicates the notion of the camp as a bounded space. A mode of urbanity emerges between the city and the camp as various social, cultural, aural, and visual interactions between the two spaces.

The spatiality of peacekeeping camps in Goma, positioned to take advantage of various urban infrastructures, transnational connections, and economies of scale, extends over a much more expansive geography than is typically associated with humanitarian presence in the city. The situation of peacekeeping camps in Goma defies the idea that international interveners only live and work in privileged enclaves (primarily in the city center or in lush lakeside estates). Military bases are scattered throughout the city to fulfill diverse taskings, vehicle and foot patrols are conducted across Goma's eighteen neighborhoods, and company operating bases are strategically positioned on arterial roads into Goma at Munigi and in Mubambiro. Peacekeeping camps occupy the city's personified center—Mount Goma—and its flanks, creating bulwarks of defense on which the functioning of the humanitarian enclave and the every-day lives of Congolese civilians rely. Geographically, Peaceland as a concept term that can be applied to understand Goma through specific localizations of international interveners (Autesserre 2014), fails to acknowledge the broader territorial arrangement of peacekeeping camps across the city occupied by MONUSCO contingents.

MONUSCO installations in Goma occupy features in the city that have historically been seized on by former missions and other foreign actors as campsites, such as the downtown lakeshore area and Mount Goma. A wide array of camps have appeared in Goma throughout its history as a result of dynamics of imperial expansion, colonial subjugation of indigenous populations, genocide, incursion and capture of the city by insurgents, and armed conflict causing displacement toward the city. The protracted armed conflict in the eastern DRC not only has engendered several refugee and IDP camps in Goma's westernmost neighborhoods but has also been the catalyst for the significant peacekeeping camp footprint in the city in the late 2010s. Peacekeeping camps thus join over a century of encampments that have and continue to shape the urbanization and urbanity of Goma.

In Amanda Hammar's (2014, 9) efforts to broaden understandings of displacement as a relational concept, she defines dislocation as "enforced changes in interweaving spatial, social and symbolic conditions and relations." The generative space of the particular dislocation of deployment, while ultimately a voluntary change of location, nonetheless effectuates new connections and disconnections between times, places, and people along various axes and scales. Seeing human mobility as the vector that forges connections to endless elsewheres helps us productively unsettle camps, cities, and our study of urban settlements (Allen, Massey, and Pryke 1999). Attuning to how we live our cities in camping, between dwelling and journeying, between feeling at home and being in the world, reminds us of cities' "character as places of juxtaposed spaces and superimposed relational webs" (36). Looking at the ways in which dislocated populations beyond deployed soldiers live the city between journeying and dwelling and move and multiply their homes elsewhere as a matter of being-at-home-in-the-world stands to enrich not only our understandings of how people camp but also how people make their cities as social, cultural, and architectural spaces. This is the type of urban research agenda that I have sought to promote by starting and learning from the peacekeeping camp, as David's former roommate proposed at the *gîte* when he said that the men from Kindu lived their *gîte* like the men from MONUSCO live their camps.

To expand our vocabulary of urban practice, Gautham Bahn (2019) argues that we need to take into consideration a wider range of actors, modes, and ways of moving in the city that all seek to respond to the urban environment. Peacekeepers, camps, and the human experience of deployment as one particular mode of dislocation not only respond to an urban environment plagued by the threat of armed conflict and acting as a refuge for thousands of conflict-displaced people but *correspond* with it. The city joins the gathering that is the camping of the camp (as Heidegger would put it) while peacekeeping camps join in the becoming of the city—in its making (Ingold 2013). Camping, a mode of being between dwelling and journeying, emphasizes the undetermined space of the arrangement, where differences between binary thought-objects like the city and the camp, the local and the global, home and the world are reconfigured to provoke new meanings, including of urbanity. To focus on camping as a verb rather than the camp as a noun also works to unfetter camp studies from its preoccupation with camps as instantiations of variable states of exception (Agamben 1998), instead recognizing the ordinary joys and personal risks of the practice. Embracing and reconciling this meaning of camping with the predominant meaning of the camp as it has developed in scholarly literature dominated by refugee camps demonstrates that another understanding of the camp is not only possible but also exists within the spaces of peacekeeping.

Lastly, to theorize from the Global South is not only to seek out new starting points that allow for a broader diversity of empirics on which to build the

Camp Katindo viewed from Mount Goma with a UN warehouse in the foreground. (Photo by author)

interdiscipline of urban studies but to also "engage with distinctive intellectual formulations drawn from the diverse and not always well understood physical, social, and economic realities of cities in the South" (Parnell and Robinson 2012, 596). The peacekeeping camp is one such reality. While such camps may be empirically and geographically bound to conflict contexts in the Global South, East, and Northeast, the tensions they reveal in the human experience of dwelling have much wider purchase. I propose that attending to these contingent politics of inhabitation (pun intended) may help us trace the "elsewheres within here" that constitute urban spaces (Minh-ha 2011).

As of 2016, there were 170 cities where UN peacekeeping operations were taking place in sub-Saharan Africa alone (Shoshan 2016, 7). We still know far too little about these cities in relation to the presence of peacekeeping camps and in a world of ordinary cities. For a more global urban studies, I therefore propose not only thinking cities through elsewhere but also thinking cities *as* elsewheres, as places experienced by people living diverse dislocations. I also propose thinking cities with elsewhats—phenenoma happening in cities that have remained bound to specific disciplines beyond urban studies, such as UN peacekeeping. Like Jennifer Robinson, I too want to "keep conversations going about cities, always in a world of other cities, by opening more opportunities to think through elsewhere, and to build methodologies and practices which require that such conversations be intrinsically open to revision, making space for insights starting from anywhere" (Robinson 2016, 5). Goma opens many more opportunities to think through elsewhere; peacekeeping camps are but one practice to keep these conversations going.

Notes

Introduction

1. Paraphrased from field notes, original French
2. Theodore Trefon and Noël Kabuyaya's collection of portraits in their book *Goma: Stories of Strength and Sorrow* (2018) manages, in my reading, to escape an essentialization of conflict in the personal narratives they tell.
3. I distinguish peacekeeping camps from other UN administrative compounds and mission facilities as places where military personnel have nightly accommodation.
4. In the case of Goma specifically, the UN peacekeeping mission space is touched on and problematized in several anthropological accounts of the city (Oldenburg 2015; Trefon and Kabuyaya 2018; Büscher 2020).
5. One notable exception is journalist Linda Polman's (2004) description of the embassy base in Mogadishu; Polman offers a compelling portrait of the "tent city" of fourteen thousand troops that illustrates the modes of planning, dwelling, encountering, and distancing that this book seeks to emphasize (39).
6. The phrase *a world of camps* is a reference to the English translation of Michel Agier's compendium titled *Un Monde de Camps* (2014).
7. See, for example, "The World's Largest Refugee Camp Is Becoming a Real City," published by Bloomberg CityLab in September 2019; "How Bidibidi, a Refugee Camp in Uganda, Is Becoming a City," published by *National Geographic* in April 2019; or "Refugee Camp for Syrians in Jordan Evolves as a Do-It-Yourself City," published by the *New York Times* in July 2014.
8. The other way that our bodies are placialized is through "subjection"—whereby Casey (2001) understands the ways that we are still "in the places to

which we are subject because . . . they are in us." What we are, then, is an expression of the way a place is (688). This "incoming" process of place appears widely represented in structuralist approaches and is, of course, not entirely absent in how ethnographer's sense of self colludes with place.

9. In scholarly circles, it is also worth mentioning that there is equal mistrust generated through anthropologists' work with military institutions. The 1960s was a turning point for anthropology's relationship to militaries after the instrumentalization of anthropologists and anthropological knowledge to further the ends of the American national security state in its military operations abroad (Gusterson 2007). Beginning with the Vietnam War and continuing through the wars in Iraq and Afghanistan, the US Army has controversially employed anthropologists to develop knowledge around the concept of "human terrain." Human terrain as a concept in US military circles is underpinned by the idea that successful warfare against or among a population requires knowledge of that population, ultimately facilitating its control (González 2008). The inception of the Human Terrain System in counterinsurgency operations in Iraq and Afghanistan led the American Anthropological Association to speak out against the ethical dangers raised by the work of social scientists in these settings (American Anthropological Association 2007). This well-known example about the instrumentalization of anthropological knowledge to obtain military objectives makes it all the more necessary for this research to be understood not as anthropology for militaries (military anthropology) but rather as a type of urban anthropology with militaries.

10. The formalities of several institutions necessitated that initial interactions take the form of interviews. I conducted rounds of semistructured interviews with fourteen different military commanders at the levels of the contingent, battalion, brigade, and force. Semistructured interviews were also one of the ways that I engaged with civilian and military mission staff from over twelve different sections and offices in and affiliated with the MONUSCO mission as well as Congolese urban actors from provincial ministries, sections, or offices of urbanism, planning, housing, geography, and revenue; various institutional directors and faculty at UNIGOM; private security companies; architects; former mayors; provincial assembly members; cartographers; Congolese nongovernmental organizations; and prominent members of the Indian business community. Focus group discussions were less frequently employed but nonetheless valuable to gaining the perspectives of contingent troops, as rank soldiers and officer cadres "live" the base and the city differently. With the help of contingent officers and translators in the Spanish-speaking camps, I conducted two focus group discussions: one with a single company of GUASFOR and one with the noncommissioned officers of URUBATT. I conducted another four focus group discussions

on my own with gendarmes of the Senegalese Formed Police Unit (SEN-FPU), including one group exclusively composed of women. The groups I talked to across the camps were up to the discretion of the commanding officer, who also approved all questions proposed and discussed. A conversation with a group of language assistants and community liaison assistants working with the IN-DRDB also resembled a focus group discussion, though it had not been planned as such.

11. The "we" I speak of throughout the book includes a "we" of nearly one hundred peacekeeping officers. The majority of officers I engaged with most frequently were those living inside the camps at the heart of this book. These include the URUBATT, GUASFOR, SEN-FPU, RSA Aviation, and Central Sector Brigade camps; two camps of BANMP; and three camps of the INDRDB. All officers have been given pseudonyms that relate to the places they come from. I have retained their military titles but refrained from dating communications to protect their anonymity.

1. Urbanization and Encampment

1. Hailey's guidebook is structured by breaking the camp into three nonexclusive, overlapping types: autonomy, control, and necessity (2009). Inspired by this approach, I have adapted this typology to Goma's campscape, discussing camps of defense, control, and refuge.

2. That European was German army officer Gustav Adolf von Götzen, who would become the governor of German East Africa in 1901.

3. Kisenyi, Kissenji, and Kissenje are alternative spellings found on early maps for the city known today as Gisenyi in western Rwanda (BMA 97376, n.d.; Andree and Scobel 1906).

4. "Since it was obvious that news of our incursion would get through to Rutshuru pretty soon we trekked on all night and reached the top of a track across a spur running down from one of the Mufumbiro mountains. Here we looked down on Lake Kivu about 20 miles away: and here also I was astonished to learn that there was a German officer right on the shore of the Lake more or less on the spot where I had been told to stick up the Union Jack!" (Coote 1956, 106).

5. Kibumba was variously referred to by the British as Kikumba (War Office 1909; Coote 1956), Kivumba (War Office 1919) and Kiwumba (War Office 1911) and corresponds to the village known today as Kibumba in Nyiragongo Territory and is referred to here in its contemporary appellation.

6. It is worth noting that in the midst of this contention, the Congo Free State was handed over from King Leopold II's personal rule to Belgian rule in 1908.

7. Britain's position on Mufumbiro, along with its own struggles with Germany over Mpororo (southwestern Uganda), cannot be underestimated due to the negotiating positions into which they forced the Germans, ultimately leading to their willingness to concede the northern shore of the lake to Belgium.

8. This period of initial urbanization corresponds with the end of World War I, which had brought heavy fighting to Goma and Gisenyi, destroying the Belgian post and much of the small town around it. Only after the war did Belgians begin to settle in Goma in larger numbers (Büscher 2011).

9. *Birere*, in common parlance, refers to an area stretching across the administrative *quartiers* of Kahembe, Mapendo, and Mikeno (Büscher and Mathys 2013).

10. An overview and analysis of conflict in the Great Lakes Region, including its actors, dynamics, and consequences, is beyond the scope of this book. Only salient events and debates are discussed here as they relate to the emergence or closure of camps in relation to Goma's urban development. For a more thorough background of this regional crisis that delves into and analyzes this history of conflict, see Nzongola-Ntalaja 2002; Prunier 2010; Stearns 2011; Lemarchand 2012; Van Reybrouck and Garrett 2015; and Berwouts 2017.

11. Kituku, Mugunga, and Lac Vert were and still are the westernmost neighborhoods of the city of Goma.

12. Elements of the ex-Rwandan Armed Forces and Interahamwe regrouped under the Forces Démocratique pour la Libération du Rwanda (FDLR) in 2000 and are still active today (albeit fragmented) in the southern Lubero and Rutshuru territories, North Kivu ("Kivu Security Tracker," n.d.; Pole Institute 2017).

13. Juvénal Habyarimana was the former president of Rwanda (1973–94). He was assassinated when his plane was shot down under mysterious circumstances, an event that is regarded as a key trigger of the Rwandan genocide.

14. The AFDL was led by Laurent Desiré Kabila, who took control of Zaire in May 1997 (ending the First Congo War). He renamed the country the Democratic Republic of the Congo (DRC).

15. The CNDP militia was established in 2006 by Laurent Nkunda.

16. Personal communication, National Commission for Refugees Head of Office–Goma.

17. Personal communication, National Commission for Refugees Head of Office–Goma.

18. MONUC, it is worth mentioning, was preceded by nearly forty years by the United Nations Operation in the Congo (ONUC) mission, which began in 1960 (the same year Congo achieved independence) and marked the UN's first peacekeeping mission in Africa. However, given the geopolitical realities of this conflict, Goma, did not play a prominent role in hosting international forces during the ONUC mission (United Nations 1961). As Norrie MacQueen

(2002, 33) points out, though, issues and conflicts that remained unresolved after the complete withdrawal of UN troops from the Congo in 1964 continued to threaten peace in the country well into the late 1990s, several of which would go on to incite the inauguration of MONUC.

19. Any UN action was predicated, however, on coordination with the Organization of African Unity (OAU), the predecessor organization of the African Union.

20. Gérard Prunier (2010), Jason Stearns (2011), and René Lemarchand (2012) offer highly readable and comprehensive overviews of this period of history.

21. Jean Pierre Bemba signed the agreement on behalf of the armed opposition group Mouvement de Libération du Congo (MLC) on August 1, 1999. RCD–Goma, represented by its fifty founding members, signed on August 31, 1999. For more on the political situation surrounding the signing of the agreement see Georges Nzongola-Ntalaja (2002) and François Ngolet (2011).

22. It is worth mentioning that the UN had received requests to intervene with a peacekeeping force as early as 1996. Security Council resolutions 1078 (1996) and 1080 (1996) both determined that the humanitarian crisis in eastern Zaire constituted a threat to peace, but no action was taken to deploy a peacekeeping force (Kamanda wa Kamanda 1997).

23. This policy of disarmament, demobilization, repatriation, and resettlement has since evolved to include reintegration.

24. This agreement was the outcome of the Inter-Congolese Dialogue. On this process, see International Crisis Group (2001) and Ngolet (2011).

25. This discrepancy between contingents and bases reflects the fact that the camp of the Senegalese FPU shifted between 2017 and 2019 from a parcel owned by a coffee estate across from the airport to a former UN storage facility. The hospital also shifted from its downtown location in an old hotel to a new UN compound.

26. Similarly, this discrepancy reflects the consolidation of the Indian camps referred to by peacekeepers as "Old Saké" and "New Saké" into a single camp. My decision to reference these spaces as camps rather than bases aligns with the vocabulary used by most of my interlocuters in everyday speech and informs (and is informed by) my theoretical framework and findings.

27. "Level III," in military terms, refers to the highest level of care that can be provided in an area of operation.

28. Personal communication, field engineering officer.

29. *Jambaar* means "courage" in Wolof.

30. The following relies on a personal communication and is supported by short visits in and around the camp between 2017 and 2019 through personal, informal invitations from individual officers.

31. The term *Mai Mai* regroups a diverse set of militias with variable motives, aspirations, and areas of control within the DRC over time. For a thorough review of the diversity of these militias and their relationship to violent resistance, see Marta Iñiguez de Heredia (2017).

32. Personal communication, mission support officer.

33. The section of the RN2 from Saké through Goma to Kanyabayonga is considered part of a national priority network (Direction de la Planification 2016).

34. Translated from the original French: "temple de savoir," "usine à capital humaine," "centre stratégique de la province," "nerf de la modernité," and "Revolution de la Modernité."

35. Translated from original French: "On ne pouvait pas imaginer que Mugunga ferait parti de la ville un jour."

36. Translated from original Swahili: Our Lady of Peace.

37. In fact, several peacekeeping bases rent land from various religious organizations. Near the border, three camps forming a combined garrison occupy land owned by the international Focolare movement, while the base in Kiwanja is also the property of a local church group, where the officer's mess occupies the former place of worship.

38. Himbi is another adjacent administrative neighborhood in western Goma. The Himbi base was in fact located in the Keyshero neighborhood.

39. The Pinga base was closed in June 2017, followed by Buyampuri, Nyabiondo, Masisi Centre, and Walikale Center in August 2017 (MONUSCO 2018).

40. The mission's lakeside compounds go by different names depending on who you ask and depending on what offices are located in each site at any given time. While "Regional" denotes the site of the regional headquarters of MONUSCO, Lava Site is quite literally that—a plot of land that was covered by the lava flows of the 2002 volcanic eruption. The TMK base name refers to the corporate landowner, the Société de Transports et Messageries au Kivu.

41. In 2019, MONUSCO began to move into yet another easterly adjacent parcel. The TMK base was separated from these compounds by a large parcel that now hosts the Goma Serena Hotel built by prominent local hotelier and business man Vanny Bishweka.

42. Translated from Swahili and French: "Yeah, record, record. Yeah, Mr. [name redacted] said this: You ICs, I order you to leave. If you do not, I will give the order to fire on you. One. Two. Three. Fire."

43. Translated from Swahili and French: "Tomorrow. Eight o'clock. They are going to resolve the situation. It will be finished. We are opening the road back up."

44. In July 2022, violent protests targeting MONUSCO personnel and installations in the cities of Goma and Butembo left four peacekeepers and thirty-two civilians dead (Bukajera 2022).

2. Through the Gates

1. *Urafiki* is Swahili for "friendship."
2. Hindi term for soldiers below the rank of commissioned officers (literal meaning: "youngsters").
3. Translated from French: "S'ils ne veulent pas étudier, ils vont rester comme ça."
4. Translated from French: "Sans les Uruguayans, ils n'ont pas de vie" (personal communication).
5. *Mayibobos* is the colloquial Swahili appellation of street children.
6. QIPs, as they are described here, regroup projects that were not directly financed by this mechanism (but by other agencies like the United Nations Development Programme [UNDP] or UNOPS) that have a tangible, visible output; This reflects the way mission personnel speak of QIPs rather than the actual program.
7. In Goma in 2018, the only planned QIP project carried out by a contingent was a water harvesting system planned at a school in Mugunga by the Indian Rapidly Deployable Battalion.
8. In addition to the friendly soccer match, BANMP conducted medical campaigns and distributed books and writing materials to students and orphans during the period of study.
9. Several orphanages in Goma benefit from the support of different contingents. Some have had a privileged relationship with peacekeepers due, in part, to their situation near bases or the houses of different commanders.
10. Translated from Swahili: "Banditry is disturbing [us] a lot."
11. Translated from Swahili: "Kidnapping ina endalea sana."
12. The ways that national security forces contribute to insecurity through human rights violations and ties with armed groups are well documented in scholarly literature. For discussions of the PNC and FARDC as forces of insecurity in the DRC and Goma specifically, see OHCHR 2013; Pole Institute 2017; and M. Hendriks and Büscher 2019. For discussions of the dilemma of the UN working with these forces, see Hirschmann 2019.
13. This "closeness" and feelings of "similarity" between military peacekeepers and Congolese civilians is discussed in more detail in chapter 5.
14. *Sabzi* refers to an Indian vegetable dish, generally cooked in gravy.
15. Two different bodies enforce the UN curfews in Goma: military police for military personnel and the Department of Safety and Security for civilians. Small detachments from BANMP constitute the military police in both Goma and Saké and have been known to cause late-night panic at downtown nightclubs when they show up looking for the owners of the UN vehicles parked outside past curfew. BANMP's motto is plastered all over their camps: "Custodian of Discipline."

16. As of the end of 2018, there were also six out-of-bounds establishments in Saké (near the Mubambiro garrison).

17. Translated from French: "People drive however they want"; "Motorcycles pass left and right."

18. *Junoon* is an Arabic/Persian/Urdu/Hindi word meaning "mania" or "obsession."

19. ICVs are also referred to across the mission as APCs (armored personnel carriers), or BMPs (*boyevaya mashina pekhoty*—Russian for "infantry fighting vehicle").

20. Translated from French: "Go back to your country"; "You cannot occupy us."

21. Translated from Swahili: "Hey, kid, *morning* is *asubui* but right now it is *muchana*, so you should say *afternoon*."

22. Others include Local Protection Committees (composed of ten to fifteen influential and representative community members); Community Protection Plans (updated every three months with development-oriented recommendations), Community Early Warning systems (which operate through the Community Alert Network), and the Senior Management Group on Provincial Protection.

23. David uses the term *gîte* to describe a home in Goma that regroups people from his hometown of Kindu. I have recounted my visit to this *gîte* at the beginning of the introduction.

24. Translated from French: "J'ai dérangé les Uruguayens chaque jour."

25. Translated from French: "Tout Goma était là!"

26. Translated from Spanish and French: "Yes, my colonel." "Si tu me laisses, je meurs ici à Goma."

27. Translated from French: "J'ai connu deux guerres là-bas."

28. Translated from French: "Pour moi, c'était beaucoup d'argent et la porte d'entrée à la MONUSCO."

29. Insights from Focus Group Discussion with LAs and CLAs working with an Indian battalion.

30. Translated from Swahili: "Same, or one blood."

31. Bangla was famously added as one of the official languages of Sierra Leone as a sign of gratitude for the participation of Bangladeshi troops in the United Nations Mission in Sierra Leone (Bangladesh Army 2017).

3. The (Extra-)Ordinary Spaces of Peacekeeping

1. According to Williamson Murray (1999, 27), "Military culture represents the ethos and professional attributes, both in terms of experience and intellectual study, that contribute to a common core understanding of the nature of war within military organizations."

2. "If I advance, follow me. If I stop, urge me on. If I retreat, kill me. Kaibil!"

3. The year prior, the Congolese flag flying in GUASFOR had been replaced by the Honduran flag. Countries with smaller armies, and thus fewer troops to contribute to peacekeeping operations, often deploy with other, larger armies in the peacekeeping field area with more experience. This was the case at various moments during my research in and around Goma with a few Honduran troops serving with GUASFOR and a few Paraguayan troops serving with URUBATT.

4. In 2007, CORIMEC was banned from the United Nation's authorized list of vendors after an internal investigation uncovered an inappropriate relationship between the firm and a UN procurement officer. In 2014, CORIMEC became part of EDILSIDER S.p.A., which is currently listed as an authorized vendor.

5. Bed tea is one of three tea breaks in the daily routine of the Indian peacekeeper and soldier. The importance of tea in the life of a soldier is regarded by many peacekeepers I spoke to as a hangover from the British military tradition but also provides a constant and comfort in the ever-changing, highly mobile life of the Indian soldier.

6. The ration contractors for MONUSCO included ES-KO International (Monaco) and Hashi Energy (Kenya) during the period of study.

7. George Washington, "Instructions to Company Captains, 29 July 1757."

8. The subsequent chapter goes into greater detail about how peacekeepers negotiate time zone differences and how they materialize in the camp.

9. It was also in this space that multiple focus group discussions were held with GUASFOR troops and from which many of the insights throughout this chapter come.

10. This 2016 film, directed by Glenn Ficarra and John Requa, written by Robert Carlock, and starring Tina Fey is based on the memoir *The Taliban Shuffle: Strange Days in Afghanistan and Pakistan* by Kim Barker. The title of the film plays on the NATO phonetic alphabet spelling of WTF, the acronym for "what the fuck."

11. This divide and attendant socioeconomic inequality is reflected in not only military forces in Guatemala but also the Guatemalan security landscape more broadly. See Dickins de Girón (2011) for a discussion of these dynamics and politics.

12. Simić (2012) highlights her stance as an exception among other scholars of SEA in peacekeeping.

13. Nearly half of all SEA allegations waged against MONUSCO since 2010 have been deemed unsubstantiated (United Nations Peacekeeping 2020).

14. There was one SEA allegation being investigated in Goma and two in Mubambiro/Saké that I was aware of during my fieldwork.

15. If contingents want to receive the "self-sustainment reimbursement rate" for constructing their own ablution units, they must "account for adequate

gender separation for personnel if required" (UNGA 2017). It is unclear whether this system developed in Burundi proved adequate for reimbursement.

16. The UN has ambitious targets for women's participation in peacekeeping. As of March 2020, 5 percent of MONUSCO troops and 17 percent of police were women (United Nations Peacekeeping 2020). This discrepancy can be linked to the fact that many of the largest troop-contributing countries in MONUSCO, such as India, Pakistan, and Bangladesh, do not recruit female "active duty" soldiers, though women are allowed in officer ranks (and therefore eligible to become staff officers or MILOBs in UN peacekeeping missions).

17. Translated from French: "un peu étrange."

18. In the evening, the honorary officer attended a ritual and rare drink in the officers' mess.

19. Men and women in uniform view morale as a determinate factor for success as well as an outcome of victory on the battlefield. As famous British general Bernard Montgomery writes after the Second World War: "I call morale the greatest single factor in war. A high morale is based on discipline, self-respect and confidence of the soldier in his commanders, in his weapons and in himself. Without high morale, no success can be achieved, however good may be the very strategic or tactical plan, or anything else. High morale is a pearl of very great price. And the surest way to obtain it is by success in the battlefield" (Mace and Grehan 2014, 9). Morale may very well be the single greatest factor for organizing peacekeeping camp space as well. Obtaining and bolstering it, however, has required new and creative means and definitions of victory in peacekeeping and in Goma.

4. At Home in the Camp

1. The burgeoning literature in question refers to authors writing about resettlement and include Rogers and Wilmsen 2020; Wang 2020; Beier, Spire, and Bridonneau 2021; and Meth et al. 2022.

2. A review of this literature merits another book entirely, though Valentine 1999 and Petridou 2001 have provided important overviews on the literature that centers food. More recent compendiums on home, such as Lenhard and Samanani 2019 and Blunt and Dowling 2022 (particularly chapter 5 in that volume, "Transnational Homes"), also discuss the centrality of food to the notion of home.

3. Through the Indian battalion, I was able to meet many of these families and interview several elders, community leaders, and successful businessmen of the Indian diaspora in Goma, including Congolese people of Indian origin, dating as far back as four generations. Much of the insights in this paragraph come from participant-observation and interviews with this community.

4. Translated from Swahili, "welcome."

5. The *tchukudu* is a wooden scooter cum cart used for transporting cargo by foot. It is an important symbol of and for the city's hardworking and resilient residents and appears iconized in souvenirs and in a monument in the middle of the former Bralima roundabout in downtown Goma.

6. Translated from French: "On est venu pour aider un pays et ils nous mettent dans ces conditions!"

7. The Senegalese men's feelings about their living conditions were just one of many issues fueling the SEN-FPU's general sentiment that the UN treats their contingent worse than others in the mission.

8. When acquiring land for a base, the owner generally signs a statement of reception that stipulates the condition of the premise before the COB is built. When a COB closes, the landowner signs an environmental status certificate, testifying that solid waste, dangerous waste, oil, abandoned equipment, medical equipment and dirty water have all been removed and that the site has been returned in the same condition it was handed over (personal communication, Environmental Protection Unit officer).

9. These findings mirror current understandings about how migrant remittances are predominantly used, as well as the poverty reduction and development capacity of remittances invested in productive assets such as land and housing improvements (See Ratha 2007).

10. Translated from French: "Des terrains de 300 m^2 disponibles à hauteur de Diass" (a village near the new Blaise Diagne International Airport).

5. Being Global in Goma

1. Marsha Henry (2015) has also written about medal ceremonies but finds that peacekeeper's feelings toward these kinds of displays are more ambivalent. In his writing about the subject, Robert A. Rubinstein (2008) finds that the military ritual of awarding medals in peacekeeping serves to connect members of the mission.

2. Erin A. Weir (2006) acknowledges that professional communication gaps between militaries and humanitarians operate in both directions but represents military actors as perceiving themselves as indispensable to aid delivery and "better placed than the humanitarian actors to carry out humanitarian projects." My empirics and analyses challenge the suggestion of a sense of superiority among military actors in the mission while maintaining that they often do not feel recognized for the operational support they provide for the delivery of humanitarian aid.

3. MILOBs in Goma tend to encounter and socialize with UN civilians and INGO staff with more frequency due to the nature of their work and relative

freedom of movement compared to encamped contingent officers. Their office jobs and living arrangements in national houses also exude a lower level of combatantness compared to their colleagues living and working in armed military units, facilitating their sociality with humanitarians in Goma (Sutton 2020).

4. On "humanitarian space" see Brauman 1992. On its encroachment by peacekeepers, see Franke 2006; Sutton 2020.

5. Adding to the complexity of this spectrum on which peacekeepers understand themselves as more or less of a soldier or civilian is the fact that several contingents have brought civilian personnel with them on the mission, giving them some basic training and issuing them a uniform for their Goma tenure. "Major" Hari, for instance, is not a military major but works as a civilian Defense Accounts Officer back home. His professional grade has been deemed the equivalent of a major for his inclusion in the staff of the Central Sector Brigade. Similarly, in a rotation at GUASFOR, five civilians (three interpreters and two doctors) had joined the special forces exclusively for the UN mission.

6. Weir (2006) specifically discusses WHAM as humanitarian aid that puts "genuine humanitarians" at risk by blurring the line between military and humanitarian assistance—a line that humanitarian principles of work rely on. At the same time, Sandra Whitworth (2004, 18) acknowledges that "it is often the nonwarrior qualities of soldiering that leave an impact on local people's security: building a park, reopening a hospital, or repairing a local school."

7. Translated from Hindi: "Oh Mother, I salute you." The chorus of the song repeats the title of the National Song of India—"Vande Mataram" (Ode to the Motherland).

8. All songs mentioned in this chapter have been curated as a Spotify playlist available here: https://open.spotify.com/playlist/5CRkKrQLqaHsHRNuiUqAl3?si=2lqjvTKbQlShSYaW8Ekpxw.

9. "Jai Hind" is a salute meaning "Victory to India."

10. UNFICYP is a mission founded in 1964 that remains ongoing today.

Conclusion

1. The capitalization of *Relation* replicates Glissant's orthography, which seeks to valorize the term as a concept. When using the term in the sense that Glissant means it, I follow his style of geographical writing.

Bibliography

Abourahme, Nasser. 2020. "The Camp." *Comparative Studies of South Asia, Africa and the Middle East* 40 (1): 35–42. https://doi.org/10.1215/1089201X-8186016.

Abourahme, Nasser, and Sandi Hilal. 2012. "The Production of Space, Political Subjectification and the Folding of Polarity: The Case of Deheishe Camp, Palestine." Camus in Camps. http://www.campusincamps.ps/wp-content/uploads/2012/12/Nasser-Abourahme-and-Sandi-Hilal_Deheishe-Paper.pdf.

Adebajo, Adekeye. 2011. *UN Peacekeeping in Africa: From the Suez Crisis to the Sudan Conflicts*. A Project of the International Peace Institute. Boulder: Lynne Rienner.

Adelman, Howard, and Govind C. Rao, eds. 2004. *War and Peace in Zaire-Congo: Analyzing and Evaluating Intervention, 1996–1997*. Trenton, NJ: Africa World Press.

Agamben, Giorgio. 1998. *Homo Sacer: Sovereign Power and Bare Life*. Stanford: Stanford University Press.

Agier, Michel. 2002. "Towards an Urban Anthropology of Refugee Camps." *Ethnography* 3 (3): 317–41.

Agier, Michel. 2008. *On the Margins of the World: The Refugee Experience Today*. English ed. Malden, MA: Polity.

Agier, Michel. 2011. *Managing the Undesirables: Refugee Camps and Humanitarian Government*. Translated by David Fernbach. Cambridge: Polity.

Agier, Michel, ed. 2014. *Un monde de camps*. Paris: La Découverte.

Alchin, Angela, Amanda Gouws, and Lindy Heinecken. 2018. "Making a Difference in Peacekeeping Operations: Voices of South African Women Peacekeepers." *African Security Review* 27 (1): 1–19. https://doi.org/10.1080/10246029.2017.1406381.

Allen, John, Doreen B. Massey, and Michael Pryke, eds. 1999. *Unsettling Cities. Understanding Cities.* New York: Routledge.

American Anthropological Association. 2007. "American Anthropological Association Executive Board Statement on the Human Terrain System Project." https://americananthro.org/about/committees-and-task-forces/human -terrain-system-hts-project/?_gl=1*7a62n1*_ga*MTY3NzQ2OTg5NS4xNzQ xNzAyNDUz*_ga_NHVoY97DC9*MTcoNDI3MTA1MS4yLjAuMTcoNDI3 MTA1OS41Mi4wLjA.

Anderson, Benedict R. O'G. 2006. *Imagined Communities: Reflections on the Origin and Spread of Nationalism.* Rev. ed. New York: Verso.

Andree, Richard, and Albert Scobel. 1906. "Deutsch—Ostafrika. Okt. 1905. Bearb. v.H. Mielisch u. W. Berg. Lithogr. A. Wagner u. A. Soeder. Vermittelnder Azimutaler Entwurf (Hauptpunkt 6 (Degree) s. Br., 35 (Degree) o. L.). (Inset:Nebenkarte) Klima-Ndjaro Und Gebiete." Atlas Map. Leipzig, Germany: Velhagen & Klasing. David Rumsey Historical Map Collection.

Aning, Kwesi, and Fiifi Edu-Afful. 2017. "Peacekeeping in a Francophone Space: Experiences of Ghanaian Peacekeepers in Côte d'Ivoire." *Round Table* 106 (4): 375–91. https://doi.org/10.1080/00358533.2017.1352146.

Antippas, Georges. 2016. *Pionniers méconnus du Congo belge.* Neufchâteau, France: Weyrich éditions.

Appadurai, Arjun. 1996. *Modernity at Large: Cultural Dimensions of Globalization.* Public Worlds, vol. 1. Minneapolis: University of Minnesota Press.

Autesserre, Séverine. 2010. *The Trouble with the Congo: Local Violence and the Failure of International Peacebuilding.* Cambridge Studies in International Relations 115. New York: Cambridge University Press.

Autesserre, Séverine. 2014. *Peaceland: Conflict Resolution and the Everyday Politics of International Intervention.* Problems of International Politics. Cambridge: Cambridge University Press.

Avasthi, Lieutenant Colonel Aabhas. 2010. *Blue Bravehearts: The Saga of the 2nd Battalion the Jammu and Kashmir Rifles (BODYGUARD) in Their Quest for Peace in Democratic Republic of Congo.* India: Commanding Officer 2nd Battalion the Jammu and Kashmir Rifles.

Babunga, Benjamin. 2018. "Le 19 Janvier 2014, Olive Lembe Kabila Lance les Travaux de Construction de la Nouvelle Cathédrale de Goma." *Babunga Raconte* (blog), January 18, 2018. http://www.babunga.alobi.cd/2018/01/18/le -19-janvier-2014-olive-lembe-kabila-lance-les-travaux-de-construction-de-la -nouvelle-cathedrale-de-goma.

Bachmann, Jan, and Peer Schouten. 2018. "Concrete Approaches to Peace: Infrastructure as Peacebuilding." *International Affairs* 94 (2): 381–98. https://doi.org /10.1093/ia/iix237.

Bangladesh. 2019. "Inclusion of Equipment for Internet Access and Increment of Reimbursement Rate for Internet." Member States Issue Paper Bangladesh

Issue Paper 1. 2020 COE Working Group. UN Department of Operational Support. https://drive.google.com/file/d/1Qyur1L_WfwWLK4vvy_vvoqbl3 RHLYfhf/view?usp=sharing.

Bangladesh Army. 2017. *Bangladesh Army in Overseas Operations.* Dhaka, Bangladesh: Overseas Operations Directorate. www.army.mil.bd.

BANMP. 2018. "Welcome to Force BANMP-13, the City of Volcano Nyiragongo." Internal Powerpoint, Goma, DRC, October 25.

Bauman, Zygmunt. 2000. *Liquid Modernity.* Cambridge: Polity; Malden, MA: Blackwell.

Beeckmans, Luce. 2010. "French Planning in a Former Belgian Colony: A Critical Analysis of the French Urban Planning Missions in Post-Independence Kinshasa." Edited by Johan Lagae and Tom Avermaete. *OASE* 26 (82): 56–76.

Beeckmans, Luce, Alessandra Gola, Ashika Singh, and Hilde Heynen, eds. 2022. *Making Home(s) in Displacement Critical Reflections on a Spatial Practice.* Leuven, Belgium: Leuven University Press.

Beier, Raffael, Amandine Spire, and Marie Bridonneau, eds. 2021. *Urban Resettlements in the Global South: Lived Experiences of Housing and Infrastructure between Displacement and Relocation.* New York, NY: Routledge.

Beilstein, Janet. 1998. "The Expanding Role of Women in United Nations Peace-keeping." In *The Women and War Reader*, edited by Lois Ann Lorentzen and Jennifer E. Turpin, 140–47. New York: New York University Press.

Bellamy, Alex J., Paul D. Williams, and Stuart Griffin. 2010. *Understanding Peacekeeping.* 2nd ed. Cambridge: Polity.

Benthall, Jonathan. 2017. "Humanitarianism as Ideology and Practice." In *The International Encyclopedia of Anthropology*, edited by Hilary Callan, 1–12. Oxford, UK: John Wiley & Sons. https://doi.org/10.1002/9781118924396.wbiea2089.

Berger, John, and Mike Dibb, dirs. 1972. *Ways of Seeing.* Episode 1 (1972). London: BBC. https://www.youtube.com/watch?v=0pDE4VX_9Kk.

Berwouts, Kris. 2017. *Congo's Violent Peace: Conflict and Struggle since the Great African War.* African Arguments. London: Zed Books, in association with International African Institute, Royal African Society, World Peace Foundation.

Bhan, Gautam. 2019. "Notes on a Southern Urban Practice." *Environment and Urbanization*, January, 095624781881579. https://doi.org/10.1177/0956247818815792.

Biaya, T. K. 1994. "Mundele, Ndumba et Ambiance: Le Vrai 'Bal Blanc et Noir(e).'" In *Belgique/Zaire: Une Histoire en Quête d'Avenir; Actes des Rencontres de Bruxelles (ULB, 7-8-9 octobre 1993)*, 85–100. Paris: L'Harmattan.

Biehl, João Guilherme, and Peter Andrew Locke, eds. 2017. *Unfinished: The Anthropology of Becoming.* Durham, NC: Duke University Press.

Birhahwa, Sabihene Migabo. 1974. *Histoire du Centre de Goma.* Université Nationale du Zaire, Campus de Lubumbashi.

Bittner, Regina, Wilfried Hackenbroich, and Kai Vöckler, eds. 2010. *UN Urbanism: Post-Conflict Cities Mostar Kabul*. Berlin: JOVIS.

Björkdahl, Annika, and Susanne Buckley-Zistel, eds. 2016. *Spatialising Peace and Conflict: Mapping the Production of Places, Sites and Scales of Violence*. Basingstoke, UK: Palgrave Macmillan.

Blier, Suzanne Preston. 2011. "The African Urban Past: Historical Perspectives on the Metropolis." In *African Metropolitan Architecture*, by David Adjaye and Peter Allison, 14–18. New York: Rizzoli.

Blunt, Alison, and Robyn M. Dowling. 2022. *Home*. 2nd ed. Key Ideas in Geography. New York: Routledge; London: Taylor & Francis.

BMA 97376. n.d. "Die Missionsgebiete Der Evangel. Missionsgesellschaft Für Deutsch-Ost-Afrika. Ruanda." 97376. Basel Mission Archives. Accessed January 29, 2020. http://www.bmarchives.org/items/show/100202541.

Borton, John. 1996. "The Joint Evaluation of Emergency Assistance to Rwanda. Study III Principal Findings and Recommendations." Edited by Relief and Rehabilitation Network. Overseas Development Institute. https://www.files.ethz.ch/isn/121184/networkpaper016.pdf.

Bove, Vincenzo, and Andrea Ruggeri. 2016. "Kinds of Blue: Diversity in UN Peacekeeping Missions and Civilian Protection." *British Journal of Political Science* 46 (3): 681–700. https://doi.org/10.1017/S0007123415000034.

Bradol, Jean-Hervé, and Marc Le Pape. 2017. *Humanitarian Aid, Genocide and Mass Killings: Médecins sans Frontières, The Rwandan Experience, 1982–97*. Humanitarianism: Key Debates and New Approaches. Manchester, UK: Manchester University Press.

Brauman, Rony. 1992. "Introduction" In *Populations in Danger*, edited by François Jean, 3-9. London: John Libbey.

Britt, Thomas W., and Amy B. Adler, eds. 2003. *The Psychology of the Peacekeeper: Lessons from the Field*. Psychological Dimensions to War and Peace. Westport, CT: Praeger.

Bukajera, Stanis. 2022. "Congo to Reassess U.N. Withdrawal Plan after Deadly Protests." *U.S. News*, August 2, 2022. https://www.usnews.com/news/world/articles/2022-08-02/congo-to-reassess-u-n-withdrawal-plan-after-deadly-protests.

Bunce, Melanie, Suzanne Franks, and Chris Paterson, eds. 2017. *Africa's Media Image in the 21st Century: From the "Heart of Darkness" to "Africa Rising."* Communication and Society. New York: Routledge.

Burke, Róisín Sarah. 2014. *Sexual Exploitation and Abuse by UN Military Contingents: Moving Beyond the Current "Status Quo" and Responsibility under International Law*. International Humanitarian Law Series 42. Leiden, Netherlands: Brill Nijhoff.

Büscher, Karen. 2011. "Conflict, State Failure and Urban Transformation in the Eastern Congolese Periphery. The Case of Goma." PhD. diss., Ghent University.

Büscher, Karen. 2016. "Reading Urban Landscapes of War and Peace: The Case of Goma, DRC." In *Spatialising Peace and Conflict: Mapping the Production of Places, Sites and Scales of Violence,* edited by Annika Björkdahl and Susanne Buckley-Zistel, 79–97. Rethinking Peace and Conflict Studies. London: Palgrave Macmillan.

Büscher, Karen. 2019. *Urban Africa and Violent Conflict: Understanding Conflict Dynamics in Central and Eastern Africa from an Urban Perspective.* London: Routledge.

Büscher, Karen. 2020. "Violent Conflict and Urbanization in Eastern Democratic Republic of the Congo: The City as a Safe Haven." In *Cities at War: Global Insecurity and Urban Resistance,* edited by Mary Kaldor and Saskia Sassen, 160–83. Columbia University Press. https://doi.org/10.7312/kald18538-008.

Büscher, Karen, and Gillian Mathys. 2013. "Navigating the Urban 'In-Between Space': Local Livelihood and Identity Strategies in Exploiting the Goma/Gisenyi Border." In *Violence on the Margins: States, Conflict, and Borderlands,* edited by Benedikt Korf and Timothy Raeymaekers, 119–42. Palgrave Series in African Borderlands Studies. New York: Palgrave Macmillan.

Büscher, Karen, and Koen Vlassenroot. 2013. "The Humanitarian Industry and Urban Change in Goma." *openDemocracy,* March 21, 2013, sec. openSecurity. https://www.opendemocracy.net/en/opensecurity/humanitarian-industry -and-urban-change-in-goma/.

Caldeira, Teresa P. R. 2017. "Peripheral Urbanization: Autoconstruction, Transversal Logics, and Politics in Cities of the Global South." *Environment and Planning D: Society and Space* 35 (1): 3–20. https://doi.org/10.1177 /0263775816658479.

Casey, Edward S. 1996. "How to Get from Space to Place in a Fairly Short Stretch of Time: Phenomenological Prolegomena." In *Senses of Place,* edited by Steven Feld and Keith H. Basso, 13–52. Santa Fe, NM: School of American Research Press.

Casey, Edward S. 2001. "Between Geography and Philosophy: What Does It Mean to Be in the Place-World?" *Annals of the Association of American Geographers* 91 (4): 683–93.

CCCM DR Congo. 2016. "Les Activités de Gestion et de Coordination des Camps au Nord Kivu." Internal Document.

Center on International Cooperation. 2017. *Global Peace Operations Review: Annual Compilation 2016.* January 27, 2017. https://cic.nyu.edu/wp-content /uploads/1663/16/gpor_publication_2016_final-min.pdf.

Charles, Nickie, and Marion Kerr. 1988. *Women, Food, and Families*. Manchester, UK: Manchester University Press.

Clifford, James. 1997. "Spatial Practice: Fieldwork, Travel, and the Disciplining of Anthropology." In *Anthropological Locations: Boundaries and Grounds of a Field Science*, edited by Akhil Gupta and James Ferguson, 185–222. Berkeley: University of California Press.

Coleman, Simon, and Peter Collins, eds. 2006. *Locating the Field: Space, Place and Context in Anthropology*. ASA Monographs 42. New York: Berg.

Cooley, Alexander, and James Ron. 2002. "The NGO Scramble: Organizational Insecurity and the Political Economy of Transnational Action." *International Security* 27 (1): 5–39.

Coote, J. M. 1956. "The Kivu Mission, 1909–1910." Edited by Dr. A. W. Southall, J. W. Pallister, Major B. G. Kinloch, and Dr. K. P. Wachsmann. *Uganda Journal* 20 (2): 105–12.

Cresswell, Tim. 1996. *In Place/Out of Place: Geography, Ideology, and Transgression*. Minneapolis: University of Minnesota Press.

Cunliffe, Philip. 2013. *Legions of Peace: UN Peacekeepers from the Global South*. London: Hurst.

Dahrendorf, Nicola. 2006. "Sexual Exploitation and Abuse: Lessons Learned Study. Addressing Sexual Exploitation and Abuse in MONUC." Peacekeeping Best Practices. UN Department of Peacekeeping Operations.

Danielak, Silvia. 2022. "The Infrastructure of Peace: Civil–Military Urban Planning in Mali." *International Peacekeeping* 29 (1): 115–38. https://doi.org/10.1080/13533312.2021.1996236.

Danielsson, Anna. 2020. "The Urbanity of Peacebuilding: Urban Environments as Objects and Sites of Peacebuilding Knowledge Production." *Journal of Intervention and Statebuilding* 14 (5): 654–70. https://doi.org/10.1080/17502977.2020.1834257.

Darwin, Leonard, Alfred Sharpe, C. F. Close, and Major Bright. 1913. "The Mufumbiro Mountains: Discussion." *Geographical Journal* 41 (6): 547–50. https://doi.org/10.2307/1778079.

Daugirdas, Kristina. 2019. "Reputation as a Disciplinarian of International Organizations." *American Journal of International Law* 113 (2): 221–71. https://doi.org/10.1017/ajil.2018.122.

De Boeck, Filip, and Sammy Baloji. 2016. *Suturing the City: Living Together in Congo's Urban Worlds*. London: Autograph ABP.

De Maere d'Aertrycke, André. 2011. "Demeures Insolites 'Les Orchidées Rouges.'" *Mémoires du Congo et du Ruanda-Urundi*, No. 18. https://www.memoiresducongo.be/wp-content/uploads/2014/03/mdc_revue_18.pdf

De Meulder, Bruno. 1996. *De kampen van Kongo: Arbeid, kapitaal en rasveredeling in de koloniale planning*. Antwerpen Amsterdam: Kritak J. M. Meulenhoff.

De Meulder, Bruno. 2005. "OCA (Office des Cités Africaines 1952–1960) and the Urban Question in Central Africa." In *ArchiAfrika Conference Proceedings*, 141–48. Dar es Salaam, Tanzania. https://archnet.org/publications/4922.

De Roulet, Pablo. 2022. *International Aid and Urban Change: Humanitarian Presence in Bamako, Abidjan, Nairobi and Juba.* New York: Peter Lang.

De Waal, Alex. 2002. "Anthropology and the Aid Encounter." In *Exotic No More: Anthropology on the Front Lines*, edited by Jeremy MacClancy, 251–69. Chicago: University of Chicago Press.

Deleuze, Gilles. 1998. *Essays Critical and Clinical.* Translated by Daniel W. Smith and Michael A. Greco. London: Verso.

Department of Field Support. 2008. "MONUC November 2008." Map No. 4121. United Nations. https://reliefweb.int/sites/reliefweb.int/files/resources /1DABBCD897842F4AC12574FD00444DD4-uncs_PRG_cod081109.pdf.

Department of Peacekeeping Operations. 2006. "MONUC January 2006." Map No. 4121. United Nations. https://reliefweb.int/sites/reliefweb.int/files /resources/88472B7E810C195DC125710D0026D6C1-uncs_DEP_cod310106 .pdf.

Des Chene, Mary. 1997. "Locating the Past." In *Anthropological Locations: Boundaries and Grounds of a Field Science*, edited by Akhil Gupta, 66–85. Berkeley: University of California Press.

Dharmapuri, Sahana. 2013. "Not Just a Numbers Game: Increasing Women's Participation in UN Peacekeeping." Providing for Peacekeeping, No. 4, July, 32. *International Peace Institute.*

Dickins de Girón, Avery. 2011. "The Security Guard Industry in Guatemala: Rural Communities and Urban Violence." In *Securing the City Neoliberalism, Space, and Insecurity in Postwar Guatemala*, edited by Kedron Thomas and Kevin Lewis O'Neill, 103–26. Durham, NC: Duke University Press.

Direction de la Planification. 2016. "Réseau Routier Prioritaire." Office des Routes.

Doevenspeck, Martin. 2011. "Constructing the Border from below: Narratives from the Congolese–Rwandan State Boundary." *Political Geography* 30 (3): 129–42. https://doi.org/10.1016/j.polgeo.2011.03.003.

Douglass, Mary. 1991. "The Idea of a Home: A Kind of Space." *Social Research* 58 (1): 287–307. https://www.jstor.org/stable/40970644.

Doyle, Michael W., and Nicholas Sambanis. 2000. "International Peacebuilding: A Theoretical and Quantitative Analysis." *American Political Science Review* 94 (4): 779–801. https://doi.org/10.2307/2586208.

DPKO and DFS. 2014. "United Nations Civil-Military Coordination Specialized Training Materials (UN-CIMIC STM)." United Nations. https:// resourcehub01.blob.core.windows.net/training-files/Training%20Materials /023%20STM-UNCIMIC/023-001%20STM%20UNCIMIC.pdf.

DPKO and DFS. 2017. "Core Pre-Deployment Training Materials." United Nations. https://peacekeepingresourcehub.un.org/en/training/pre-deployment/cptm/intro.

DPKO and DFS. 2018. "Gender Responsive United Nations Peacekeeping Operations." United Nations. https://peacekeeping.un.org/sites/default/files/gender-responsive-un-peacekeeping-operations-policy-en.pdf.

"DR Congo: System Vulnerability of The Kivu Security Tracker." 2023. *Human Rights Watch.* https://www.hrw.org/news/2023/11/09/dr-congo-system-vulnerability-kivu-security-tracker.

Duffield, Mark. 2012. "Risk Management and the Bunkering of the Aid Industry." *Development Dialogue* 58: 21–36.

Duncanson, Claire. 2009. "Forces for Good? Narratives of Military Masculinity in Peacekeeping Operations." *International Feminist Journal of Politics* 11 (1): 63–80.

Edström, Håkan, and Dennis Gyllensporre. 2013. *Political Aspirations and Perils of Security: Unpacking the Military Strategy of the United Nations.* Basingstoke, UK: Palgrave Macmillan.

Egnell, Robert. 2010. "Winning 'Hearts and Minds'? A Critical Analysis of Counter-Insurgency Operations in Afghanistan." *Civil Wars* 12 (3): 282–303. https://doi.org/10.1080/13698249.2010.509562.

Elias, Norbert. 1956. "Problems of Involvement and Detachment." *British Journal of Sociology* 7 (3): 226. https://doi.org/10.2307/587994.

Eriksson Baaz, Maria. 2019. "Who's at Risk? Reflections on In/Security When Working With/Through Military Brokers in Conflict Settings." *Civil Wars* 21 (2): 286–95. https://doi.org/10.1080/13698249.2019.1631428.

Feldman, Ilana. 2015. "What Is a Camp? Legitimate Refugee Lives in Spaces of Long-Term Displacement." *Geoforum* 66 (November): 244–52. https://doi.org/10.1016/j.geoforum.2014.11.014.

Flick, Uwe. 2009. *An Introduction to Qualitative Research.* 4th ed. Los Angeles: Sage.

Förster, Till. 2013. "On Urbanity: Creativity and Emancipation in African Urban Life." In *Living the City in Africa: Processes of Invention and Intervention,* edited by Birgit Obrist, Veil Arlt, and Elísio Macamo, 235–52. Schweizerische Afrikastudien 10. Münster, Germany: LIT.

Foucault, Michel. 1978. *The History of Sexuality.* Volume 1. Translated by Robert Hurley. New York: Pantheon Books.

Foucault, Michel. 1995. *Discipline and Punish: The Birth of the Prison.* Translated by Alan Sheridan. 2nd ed. New York: Vintage Books.

France 2, dir. 1994. "Journée à Goma." Video. *F2 le Journal 20H.* Institut National de l'Audiovisuel. https://www.ina.fr/video/CAB94071674.

Franke, Volker. 2006. "The Peacebuilding Dilemma: Civil-Military Cooperation in Stability Operations." *International Journal of Peace Studies* 11 (2): 5–25.

Gallagher, Julia, ed. 2015. *Images of Africa: Creation, Negotiation and Subversion.* Manchester, UK: Manchester University Press.

Garrido, Maria Rosa. 2017. "Multilingualism and Cosmopolitanism in the Construction of a Humanitarian Elite." *Social Semiotics* 27 (3): 359–69. https://doi .org/10.1080/10350330.2017.1301800.

Geertz, Clifford. 1988. *Works and Lives: The Anthropologist as Author.* Stanford, CA: Stanford University Press.

George, Shona. 2017. *Musings in the Mist.* Kolkata, India: Power Publishers.

Ghosh, Amitav. 1994. "The Global Reservation: Notes toward an Ethnography of International Peacekeeping." *Cultural Anthropology* 9 (3): 412–22.

GIS MONUSCO. 2013. "Out-of-Bounds Premises in Goma." Goma, DRC: United Nations.

Glissant, Édouard. 1997. *Poetics of Relation.* Translated by Betsy Wing. Ann Arbor: University of Michigan Press.

González, Roberto J. 2008. "'Human Terrain': Past, Present and Future Applications." *Anthropology Today* 24 (1): 21–26. https://doi.org/10.1111/j.1467-8322 .2008.00561.x.

Grabli, Charlotte. 2019. "La Ville des Auditeurs : Radio, Rumba Congolaise et Droit à la Ville dans la Cité Indigène de Léopoldville (1949–1960)." *Cahiers d'études Africaines*, no. 233 (March): 9–45. https://doi.org/10.4000 /etudesafricaines.25229.

Græger, Nina. 2019. "'Brothers in Arms': Kinship, Gender and Military Organizations." In *Kinship in International Relations*, edited by Kristin M. Haugevik and Iver B. Neumann, 81–100. New International Relations. London: Routledge; New York: Taylor & Francis Group.

Graham, Stephen. 2009. "Cities as Battlespace: The New Military Urbanism." *City* 13 (4): 383–402.

Graham, Stephen. 2011. *Cities under Siege: The New Military Urbanism.* London: Verso.

Grayson, Catherine-Lune. 2017. *Children of the Camp: The Lives of Somali Youth Raised in Kakuma Refugee Camp, Kenya.* New York: Berghahn Books.

Griffith, James. 2010. "When Does Soldier Patriotism or Nationalism Matter? The Role of Transformational Small-Unit Leaders." *Journal of Applied Social Psychology* 40 (5): 1235–57. https://doi.org/10.1111/j.1559-1816.2010.00617.x.

Gupta, Akhil, and James Ferguson, eds. 1997. *Anthropological Locations: Boundaries and Grounds of a Field Science.* Berkeley: University of California Press.

Gusterson, Hugh. 2007. "Anthropology and Militarism." *Annual Review of Anthropology* 36 (1): 155–75. https://doi.org/10.1146/annurev.anthro.36.081406 .094302.

Guyer, Julián González. 2013. "Punching above Its Weight: Uruguay and UN Peace Operations." In *South American and Peace Operations: Coming of Age,* edited by Kai Michael Kenkel, 244. Cass Series on Peacekeeping. London and New York: Routledge.

Hackenbroich, Wilfried, and Kai Vöckler. 2010. "The Re-urbanisation of Kabul by the International Community or What Can We Learn from Kabul?" In *UN Urbanism: Post-Conflict Cities Mostar Kabul.,* edited by Regina Bittner, Wilfried Hackenbroich, and Kai Vöckler, 79–93. Berlin: JOVIS.

Hailey, Charlie. 2008a. *Campsite: Architectures of Duration and Place.* Baton Rouge: Louisiana State University Press.

Hailey, Charlie. 2008b. "More Notes on Camp: A Formulary for a New (Camping) Urbanism." *Thresholds* 33 (Summer): 27–33.

Hailey, Charlie. 2009. *Camps: A Guide to 21st-Century Space.* Cambridge, MA: MIT Press.

Hammar, Amanda, ed. 2014. *Displacement Economies in Africa: Paradoxes of Crisis and Creativity.* London: Zed.

Hannerz, Ulf. 2003. "Being There . . . and There . . . and There! Reflections on Multi-Site Ethnography." *Ethnography* 4 (2): 201–16.

Hassan, Ismae'l Sheikh. 2010. "Reconstructing the Oxymoron: The Palestinian Refugee Camp of Nahr El Bared, North Lebanon." In *Human Settlements: Formulations and (Re)Calibrations,* edited by Viviana D'Auria, Bruno de Meulder, and Kelly Shannon, 134–41. UFO 2. Amsterdam: SUN Academia.

Hastrup, Kirsten. 2010. "Emotional Topographies: The Sense of Place in the Far North." In *Emotions in the Field: The Psychology and Anthropology of Fieldwork Experience,* edited by James Davies and Dimitrina Spencer, 191–212. Stanford: Stanford University Press.

Heathershaw, John. 2016. "Who Are the 'International Community'? Development Professionals and Liminal Subjectivity." *Journal of Intervention and Statebuilding* 10 (1): 77–96. https://doi.org/10.1080/17502977.2015.1137395.

Heer, Barbara. 2019. *Cities of Entanglements.* Bielefeld, Germany: Transcript Verlag.

Heidegger, Martin. 1971. *Poetry, Language, Thought.* Translated by Alfred Hofstadter. His Works. New York: Harper & Row.

Heinecken, Lindy, and Rialize Ferreira. 2012. "'Fighting for Peace': The Experiences of South African Military Personnel in Peace Operations in Africa (Part II)." *African Security Review* 21 (2): 36–49. https://doi.org/10.1080/10246029.2011.641687.

Helfrich, Kim. 2013. "Exclusive: Rooivalk Is Going to DRC." *defenseWeb,* October 11, 2013, sec. SANDF Portal. https://www.defenceweb.co.za/sa-defence/sa-defence-sa-defence/exclusive-rooivalk-is-going-to-drc/.

Hellmüller, Sara. 2018. *The Interaction between Local and International Peacebuilding Actors. Partners for Peace.* London: Palgrave Macmillan.

Helphand, Kenneth, and Henk Wildschut. 2019. "Displaced Gardens." https://rooted.nu/#1559025885541-fba7ee34-784a.

Henckaerts, Jean-Marie, Louise Doswald-Beck, Carolin Alvermann, and International Committee of the Red Cross, eds. 2005. *Customary International Humanitarian Law.* Cambridge: Cambridge University Press.

Hendriks, Maarten, and Karen Büscher. 2019. "Insecurity in Goma: Experiences, Actors and Responses." London: Rift Valley Institute.

Hendriks, Thomas. 2015. "Ethnographic Notes on 'Camp': Centrifugality and Liminality on the Rainforest Frontier." In *Borderities and the Politics of Contemporary Mobile Borders,* edited by Anne-Laure Amilhat Szary and Frédéric Giraut, 155–70. London: Palgrave Macmillan UK. https://doi.org/10.1057/9781137468857_9.

Hendriks, Thomas. 2017. "A Darker Shade of White: Expat Self-Making in a Congolese Rainforest Enclave." *Africa* 87 (4): 683–701. https://doi.org/10.1017/S0001972017000316.

Hendriks, Thomas. 2022. *Rainforest Capitalism: Power and Masculinity in a Congolese Timber Concession.* Durham, NC: Duke University Press.

Henry, Marsha. 2015. "Parades, Parties and Pests: Contradictions of Everyday Life in Peacekeeping Economies." *Journal of Intervention and Statebuilding* 9 (3): 372–90. https://doi.org/10.1080/17502977.2015.1070021.

Herz, Manuel. 2013. "Refugee Camps of the Western Sahara." *Humanity: An International Journal of Human Rights, Humanitarianism, and Development* 4 (3): 365–91. https://doi.org/10.1353/hum.2013.0029.

Herz, Manuel, and ETH Studio Basel, eds. 2013. *From Camp to City: Refugee Camps of the Western Sahara.* Zurich: Lars Müller Publishers.

Higate, Paul, and Marsha Henry. 2009. *Insecure Spaces: Peacekeeping, Power and Performance in Haiti, Kosovo and Liberia.* New York : Zed Books.

Hilal, Sandi, and Alessandro Petti. 2018. *Permanent Temporariness.* Edited by Maria Nadotti and Nick Axel. Stockholm, Sweden: Art and Theory Publishing.

Hirschmann, Gisela. 2019. "Cooperating with Evil? Accountability in Peace Operations and the Evolution of the United Nations Human Rights Due Diligence Policy." *Cooperation and Conflict,* February, 001083671982840. https://doi.org/10.1177/0010836719828406.

Hoffman, Danny. 2007. "The City as Barracks: Freetown, Monrovia, and the Organization of Violence in Postcolonial African Cities." *Cultural Anthropology* 22 (3): 400–28.

Holt, Kate. 2004. "DR Congo's Shameful Sex Secret." *BBC News,* June 3, 2004. http://news.bbc.co.uk/2/hi/africa/3769469.stm.

Holt, Victoria, Glyn Taylor, and Max Kelly. 2009. "Protecting Civilians in the Context of UN Peacekeeping Operations." New York: DPKO and OCHA. https://reliefweb.int/sites/reliefweb.int/files/resources/B752FF2063E282 B08525767100751B90-unocha_protecting_nov2009.pdf.

Hunt, Nancy Rose. 1999. *A Colonial Lexicon of Birth Ritual, Medicalization, and Mobility in the Congo.* Durham, NC: Duke University Press.

India. 2019. "Revision of Internet Access Claim." Member States Issue Paper India Issue Paper 1. 2020 COE Working Group. UN Department of Operational Support. https://drive.google.com/drive/folders/1gne_1DRDNhLU6BODulF A5l434iD6Fc8m.

Indian Air Force. 2019. "Indian Aviation Contingent—II (IAC-II)." Government of India. Indian Aviation Contingent—II (IAC-II). September 12, 2019.

INDRDB. 2019. "Goma City Map." Goma, DRC.

Ingold, Tim. 2013. *Making: Anthropology, Archaeology, Art and Architecture.* New York: Routledge.

Iñiguez de Heredia, Marta. 2017. *Everyday Resistance, Peacebuilding and State-Making.* Manchester: Manchester University Press.

International Crisis Group. 2001. "The Inter-Congolese Dialogue: Political Negotiation or Game of Bluff?" ICG Africa Report No. 37. Brussels: International Crisis Group. https://www.crisisgroup.org/sites/default/files/37-the-inter-congolese-dialogue-political-negotiation-or-game-of-bluff.pdf.

IRIN. 2014. "Chaotic Closure of a North Kivu IDP Camp." December 18, 2014. UNHCR, Refworld. https://www.refworld.org/docid/549401f54.html.

Jack, E. M. 1913. "The Mufumbiro Mountains." *Geographical Journal* 41 (6): 532. https://doi.org/10.2307/1778078.

Jackson, Michael. 1995. *At Home in the World.* Durham, NC: Duke University Press.

Jackson, Michael. 2002. *The Politics of Storytelling: Violence, Transgression, and Intersubjectivity.* Copenhagen, Denmark: Museum Tusculanum Press, University of Copenhagen.

James, Myfanwy. 2020. "Instruments of Identity: Médecins Sans Frontières and Humanitarian Negotiations for Access in the Democratic Republic of the Congo." Oxford, UK: St. John's College, University of Oxford.

Jansen, Bram. 2016. "The Protracted Refugee Camp and the Consolidation of a 'Humanitarian Urbanism.'" *IJURR*, Spotlight On. https://www.ijurr.org /spotlight-on/the-urban-refugee-crisis-reflections-on-cities-citizenship-and-the-displaced/the-protracted-refugee-camp-and-the-consolidation-of-a-humanitarian-urbanism/.

Jansen, Bram. 2019. *Kakuma Refugee Camp: Humanitarian Urbanism in Kenya's Accidental City.* Politics and Development in Contemporary Africa. New York: Zed Books.

Jazeel, Tariq. 2019. "Singularity. A Manifesto for Incomparable Geographies: Singularity." *Singapore Journal of Tropical Geography* 40 (1): 5–21. https://doi .org/10.1111/sjtg.12265.

Jennings, Kathleen M. 2008. "Protecting Whom?: Approaches to Sexual Exploitation and Abuse in UN Peacekeeping Operations." Oslo, Norway: Fafo. https://gsdrc.org/document-library/protecting-whom-approaches-to-sexual -exploitation-and-abuse-in-un-peacekeeping-operations/.

Jennings, Kathleen M. 2015. "Life in a 'Peace-Kept' City: Encounters with the Peacekeeping Economy." *Journal of Intervention and Statebuilding* 9 (3): 296–315. https://doi.org/10.1080/17502977.2015.1054659.

Jennings, Kathleen M. 2016. "Blue Helmet Havens: Peacekeeping as Bypassing in Liberia and the Democratic Republic of the Congo." *International Peacekeeping* 23 (2): 302–25. https://doi.org/10.1080/13533312.2016.1141055.

Jennings, Kathleen M. 2019. "Conditional Protection? Sex, Gender, and Discourse in UN Peacekeeping." *International Studies Quarterly* 63 (1): 30–42. https://doi.org/10.1093/isq/sqy048.

Johnston, Paul. 1997. "No Cloak and Dagger Required: Intelligence Support to UN Peacekeeping." *Intelligence and National Security* 12 (4): 102–12. https://doi .org/10.1080/02684529708432450.

Kahn, Clea. 2010. "Engaging with Communities: The Next Challenge for Peacekeeping." Oxfam International Briefing Paper, November 2010. https:// reliefweb.int/sites/reliefweb.int/files/resources/A79CD21B498DAA3AC 12577E6004DC7B9-Full_report.pdf.

Kamanda wa Kamanda, Gerard. 1997. "Position of the Government of the Republic of Zaire on the Non-Implementation of Security Council Resolution 1080 (1996) of 15 November 1996." United Nations Security Council, January 6, 1997. S-1096-0302-07-00004. https://search.archives.un.org/uploads/r/united -nations-archives/3/a/9/3a94915868f6788885f6e78db50f6308504cb13cca707445 ff48b70215d65a9d/S-1096-0302-07-00004.pdf.

Kanetake, Machiko. 2010. "Whose Zero Tolerance Counts? Reassessing a Zero Tolerance Policy against Sexual Exploitation and Abuse by UN Peacekeepers." *International Peacekeeping* 17 (2): 200–214. https://doi.org/10.1080 /13533311003625092.

Karim, Sabrina, and Kyle Beardsley. 2017. *Equal Opportunity Peacekeeping: Women, Peace, and Security in Post-Conflict States.* Oxford Studies in Gender and International Relations. Oxford, UK: Oxford University Press.

Karim, Sabrina. 2019. "Balancing Incentives Among Actors: A Carrots and Sticks Approach to Reputation in UN Peacekeeping Missions." *AJIL Unbound* 113: 228–32. https://doi.org/10.1017/aju.2019.52.

Khair, Tabish. 2009. *The Gothic, Postcolonialism and Otherness: Ghosts from Elsewhere.* New York: Palgrave Macmillan.

Kniknie, Sam. 2022. "'A Playground for Colonial Forces': Unpacking the Anti-UN Protests in DR Congo." *New Humanitarian*, August 23, 2022. https://www.thenewhumanitarian.org/opinion/2022/08/23/MONUSCO-Rwanda-Congo-M23.

Kniknie, Sam. 2023. "Performing Political Stories of the Self: Subverting Identities in the City of Goma, DR Congo." *Ethnography*. https://doi.org/10.1177/14661381231186003.

Kovatch, Bonnie. 2016. "Sexual Exploitation and Abuse in UN Peacekeeping Missions: A Case Study of MONUC and MONUSCO." *Journal of the Middle East and Africa* 7 (2): 157–74. https://doi.org/10.1080/21520844.2016.1192978.

Kronsell, Annica. 2012. *Gender, Sex, and the Postnational Defense: Militarism and Peacekeeping*. Oxford Studies in Gender and International Relations. New York: Oxford University Press.

Kumar, Ravish. 2018. *A City Happens in Love (Ishq Mein Shahar Hona)*. Translated by Akhil Katyal. New Delhi: Speaking Tiger.

Kusenbach, Margarethe, and Krista E. Paulsen, eds. 2013. *Home: International Perspectives on Culture, Identity, and Belonging*. Frankfurt am Main, Germany: Peter Lang.

Lamarque, Hugh. 2013. "Fuelling the Borderland: Power and Petrol in Goma and Gisenyi." *Articulo*, no. 10 (February). https://doi.org/10.4000/articulo.2540.

Lancione, Michele, and AbdouMaliq Simone. 2020. "Bio-Austerity and Solidarity in the COVID-19 Space of Emergency." *Society+Space*, March 19, 2020. https://www.societyandspace.org/articles/bio-austerity-and-solidarity-in-the-covid-19-space-of-emergency.

Lemarchand, René. 2012. *The Dynamics of Violence in Central Africa*. Philadelphia: University of Pennsylvania Press.

Lenhard, Johannes, and Farhan Samanani, eds. 2019. *Home: Ethnographic Encounters*. Encounters: Experience and Anthropological Knowledge. New York: Bloomsbury Academic.

Loscalzo, Yura, Marco Giannini, Alessio Gori, and Annamaria Di Fabio. 2018. "The Wellbeing of Italian Peacekeeper Military: Psychological Resources, Quality of Life and Internalizing Symptoms." *Frontiers in Psychology* 9 (February). https://doi.org/10.3389/fpsyg.2018.00103.

Louis, W. M. Roger. 1963. *Ruanda-Urundi 1884–1919*. Oxford, UK: Clarendon Press.

Mace, Martin, and John Grehan. 2014. *Liberating Europe: D-Day to Victory in Europe 1944–1945*. Barnsley, South Yorkshire, UK: Pen & Sword Military.

MacQueen, Norrie. 2002. *United Nations Peacekeeping in Africa since 1960*. Postwar World. London: Routledge.

Maertens, Lucile, and Malkit Shoshan. 2018. "Greening Peacekeeping: The Environmental Impact of UN Peace Operations." *International Peace Institute, Providing for Peacekeeping* no. 17: 40.

Mahmoud, Youssef. 2019. "Transitioning from Stabilization to Peace: An Independent Strategic Review of the United Nations Organization Stabilization Mission in the Democratic Republic of the Congo." United Nations Security Council. https://reliefweb.int/sites/reliefweb.int/files/resources/S_2019 _842_E.pdf.

Malkki, Liisa H. 1995. *Purity and Exile: Violence, Memory, and National Cosmology among Hutu Refugees in Tanzania*. Chicago: University of Chicago Press.

Mampilly, Zachariah. 2014. "Indian Peacekeeping and the Performance of the United Nations Mission in the Democratic Republic of Congo." In *Peacekeeping in Africa: The Evolving Security Architecture*, edited by Thierry Tardy and Marco Wyss, 113–31. CSS Studies in Security and International Relations. New York: Routledge/Taylor & Francis Group.

Marcus, George E. 1995. "Ethnography in/of the World System: The Emergence of Multi-Sited Ethnography." *Annual Review of Anthropology* 24 (1): 95–117. https://doi.org/10.1146/annurev.an.24.100195.000523.

Martin, Diana. 2015. "From Spaces of Exception to 'Campscapes': Palestinian Refugee Camps and Informal Settlements in Beirut." *Political Geography* 44 (January): 9–18. https://doi.org/10.1016/j.polgeo.2014.08.001.

Martin, Diana, Claudio Minca, and Irit Katz. 2019. "Rethinking the Camp: On Spatial Technologies of Power and Resistance." *Progress in Human Geography* 44 (4): 743–68.

Massey, Doreen. 1994. "Double Articulation: A Place in the World." In *Displacements: Cultural Identities in Question*. Theories of Contemporary Culture. Bloomington: Indiana University Press.

Massey, Doreen. 2005. *For Space*. Thousand Oaks, CA: SAGE.

Mathys, Gillian. 2021. "Questioning Territories and Identities in the Precolonial (Nineteenth-Century) Lake Kivu Region." *Africa* 91 (3): 493–515. https://doi .org/10.1017/S0001972021000267.

Mbembe, Achille, and Sarah Nuttall. 2004. "Writing the World from an African Metropolis." *Public Culture* 16 (3): 347–72. https://doi.org/10.1215 /08992363-16-3-347.

McCann, Colum. 2008. "An Imagined Elsewhere: The City of Cities." In Matteo Pericoli, *World Unfurled*. San Francisco: Chronicle Books.

McFate, Montgomery. 2018. *Military Anthropology: Soldiers, Scholars and Subjects at the Margins of Empire*. New York: Oxford University Press.

Médecins sans Frontières. 2013. "Rwandan Refugee Camps in Zaire and Tanzania 1994–1995." Case Study. MSF Speaks Out. Médecins Sans Frontières. https://www.msf.org/sites/msf.org/files/2019-04/MSF%20Speaking%20 Out%20Rwandan%20Refugee%20camps%201995-1995.pdf.

Meier, Prita. 2016. *Swahili Port Cities: The Architecture of Elsewhere*. African Expressive Cultures. Bloomington: Indiana University Press.

Meth, Paula, Metadel Belihu, Sibongile Buthelezi, and Fikile Masikane. 2022. "Not Entirely Displacement: Conceptualizing Relocation in Ethiopia and South Africa as 'Disruptive Re-Placement.'" *Urban Geography*, 1–26. https://doi.org/10.1080/02723638.2022.2042067.

Mills, Kurt. 2006. "The Postmodern Tank of the Humanitarian International." *Peace Review* 18 (2): 261–67. https://doi.org/10.1080/10402650600692466.

Minca, Claudio. 2015. "Geographies of the Camp." *Political Geography* 49 (November): 74–83. https://doi.org/10.1016/j.polgeo.2014.12.005.

Minear, Larry. 1997. "Humanitarian Action and Peacekeeping Operations." *Journal of Humanitarian Assistance* 4 (1–2): 7–18. https://doi.org/10.1163/187541197X00034.

Minh-Ha, Trinh T. 2011. *Elsewhere, within Here: Immigration, Refugeeism and the Boundary Event*. London: Routledge.

Misselwitz, Philipp, and Eyal Weizman. 2003. "Military Operations as Urban Planning." In *Territories: Islands, Camps and Other States of Utopia*, edited by Anselm Franke and Eyal Weizman, Kunst-Werke Berlin, 272–81. Berlin: KW, Institute for Contemporary Art, Verlag der Buchhandlung Walther König.

Mitchell, W. J. T. 2012. "Image, Space, Revolution: The Arts of Occupation." *Critical Inquiry* 39 (1): 8–32. https://doi.org/10.1086/668048.

Mobekk, Eirin. 2009. "Security Sector Reform and the UN Mission in the Democratic Republic of Congo: Protecting Civilians in the East." *International Peacekeeping* 16 (2): 273–86. https://doi.org/10.1080/13533310802685844.

Moncrief, Stephen. 2017. "Military Socialization, Disciplinary Culture, and Sexual Violence in UN Peacekeeping Operations." *Journal of Peace Research* 54 (5): 715–30. https://doi.org/10.1177/0022343317716784.

MONUSCO. 2018. "Overview of the impact of the base closures on POC / Goma FO (April 2018)." Unpublished report.

Moore, Sally Falk. 1993. "Changing Perspectives on a Changing Africa: The Work of Anthropology." In *African and the Disciplines: The Contributions of Research in Africa to the Social Sciences and Humanities*, edited by Robert H. Bates, V. Y. Mudimbe, and Jean O'Barr. Chicago: University of Chicago Press.

Moskos, Charles C. 1975. "UN Peacekeepers: The Constabulary Ethic and Military Professionalism." *Armed Forces & Society* 1 (4): 388–401. https://doi.org/10.1177/0095327X7500100402.

Mosse, David, ed. 2011. *Adventures in Aidland: The Anthropology of Professionals in International Development*. Studies in Public and Applied Anthropology, vol. 6. New York: Berghahn Books.

Mumford, Lewis. 1937. "What Is a City?" *Architectural Record* 82:93–96.

Murray, Williamson. 1999. "Does Military Culture Matter?" *Orbis* 43 (1): 27–42. https://doi.org/10.1016/S0030-4387(99)80055-6.

Mwenyemali, Maréchal. 2017. "Rapport de la Fermature Du Site de Déplacement de Mugunga 3." Commission Nationale pour les Réfugiés. Goma, DRC.

Myers, Fred R. 1991. *Pintupi Country, Pintupi Self: Sentiment, Place, and Politics among Western Desert Aborigines.* Berkeley: University of California Press.

Myers, Garth. 2018. "The Africa Problem of Global Urban Theory: Re-Conceptualising Planetary Urbanisation." *Revue Internationale de Politique de Développement,* 10: 231–53. https://doi.org/10.4000/poldev.2739.

Myers, Garth. 2020. *Rethinking Urbanism: Lessons from Postcolonialism and the Global South.* Bristol, UK: Bristol University Press.

Neudorfer, Kelly. 2015. *Sexual Exploitation and Abuse in UN Peacekeeping: An Analysis of Risk and Prevention Factors.* Lanham, MD: Lexington Books.

Newbury, David S. 1980. "Lake Kivu Regional Trade in the Nineteenth Century." *Journal des Africanistes* 50 (2): 7–30. https://doi.org/10.3406/jafr.1980.2001.

Newbury, David S. 1991. *Kings and Clans: Ijwi Island and the Lake Kivu Rift, 1780–1840.* Madison: University of Wisconsin Press.

Newton, Adam Zachary. 2005. *The Elsewhere: On Belonging at a Near Distance: Reading Literary Memoir from Europe and the Levant.* Madison: University of Wisconsin Press.

Ngolet, François. 2011. *Crisis in the Congo: The Rise and Fall of Laurent Kabila.* New York: Palgrave Macmillan.

Nguya, Gloria. 2019. "'We Are All IDPs': Vulnerability and Livelihoods in Mugunga 3 Camp, Goma, Democratic Republic of the Congo." Working Paper 77. Researching Livelihoods and Services Affected by Conflict. Secure Livelihoods Research Consortium, Overseas Development Institute. https://securelivelihoods.org/wp-content/uploads/We-are-all-IDPs-vulnerability-in-Mugunga-camp-online.pdf.

Northrup, David. 1988. *Beyond the Bend in the River: African Labor in Eastern Zaire, 1865–1940.* Monographs in International Studies, No. 52. Athens: Ohio University Center for International Studies.

Novosseloff, Alexandra, Adriana Erthal Abdenur, Thomas Mandrup, and Aaron Pangburn. 2019. "Assessing the Effectiveness of the United Nations Mission in the DRC / MONUC—MONUSCO." Oslo, Norway: Norwegian Institute of International Affairs. https://reliefweb.int/sites/reliefweb.int/files/resources/Assessing-the-effectiveness-of-the-United-Nations-Mission-in-the-DRC-MONUC-%E2%80%93-MONUSCO.pdf.

Nzongola-Ntalaja, Georges. 2002. *The Congo from Leopold to Kabila: A People's History.* New York: Zed Books.

Oesch, Lucas. 2017. "The Refugee Camp as a Space of Multiple Ambiguities and Subjectivities." *Political Geography* 60 (September): 110–20. https://doi.org/10.1016/j.polgeo.2017.05.004.

OHCHR. 2010. "Report of the Mapping Exercise Documenting the Most Serious Violations of Human Rights and International Humanitarian Law Committed within the Territory of the Democratic Republic of the Congo between March 1993 and June 2003." United Nations. https://www.ohchr.org/sites/default /files/Documents/Countries/CD/DRC_MAPPING_REPORT_FINAL _EN.pdf.

OHCHR. 2013. "Report of the United Nations Joint Human Rights Office on Human Rights Violations Perpetrated by the Soldiers of the Congolese Armed Forces and Combatants of the M23 in Goma and Saké, North Kivu Province, and in and around Minova, South Kivu Province, From 15 November to 2 December 2012." United Nations. https://reliefweb.int/sites/reliefweb.int/files /resources/UNJHRO%20-%20HRVs%20Goma%20and%20Minova%20 -%20May%202013.pdf.

Oka, Rahul. 2011. "Unlikely Cities in the Desert: The Informal Economy as Causal Agent for Permanent 'Urban' Sustainability in Kakuma Refugee Camp, Kenya." *Urban Anthropology and Studies of Cultural Systems and World Economic Development* 40 (3/4): 223–62.

Oldenburg, Silke. 2015. "The Politics of Love and Intimacy in Goma, Eastern DR Congo: Perspectives on the Market of Intervention as Contact Zone." *Journal of Intervention and Statebuilding* 9 (3): 316–33. https://doi.org/10.1080/17502977 .2015.1054660.

Oldenburg, Silke. 2016a. *À Goma on Sait Jamais: Jugend Im Ganz Normalen Ausnahmezustand in Goma, DR Kongo.* Beiträge Zur Afrikaforschung, Band 69. Zürich: Lit.

Oldenburg, Silke. 2016b. "'I Am an Intellectual'. War, Youth and Higher Education in Goma (Eastern Congo)." *AnthropoChildren*, no. 6. https://doi.org/10 .25518/2034-8517.2489.

Oldenburg, Silke. 2018. "Agency, Social Space and Conflict-Urbanism in Eastern Congo." *Journal of Eastern African Studies* 12 (2): 254–73. https://doi.org/10.108 0/17531055.2018.1452552.

Oldenburg, Silke. 2019. "Dead End? Young Mototaxi Drivers between Being Stuck, Bridging Potholes and Building a Future in Goma, Eastern Congo." *Cadernos de Estudos Africanos*, no. 37 (July): 63–87. https://doi.org/10.4000 /cea.3692.

Oldenburg, Silke. 2020. "Maisha Ni Kuvumiliya—Patrimonialism, Progress and the Ambiguities of Waiting in Goma, DR Congo." *Critical African Studies* 12 (1): 37–51. https://doi.org/10.1080/21681392.2019.1697314.

Oldfield, Sophie. 2023. *High Stakes, High Hopes: Urban Theorizing in Partnership.* Athens: University of Georgia Press.

Parnell, Susan, and Sophie Oldfield, eds. 2014. *The Routledge Handbook on Cities of the Global South.* Routledge Handbooks. London: Routledge.

Parnell, Susan, and Jennifer Robinson. 2012. "(Re)Theorizing Cities from the Global South: Looking Beyond Neoliberalism." *Urban Geography* 33 (4): 593–617. https://doi.org/10.2747/0272-3638.33.4.593.

Pech, Lisa, Karen Büscher, and Tobia Lakes. 2018. "Intraurban Development in a City under Protracted Armed Conflict: Patterns and Actors in Goma, DR Congo." *Political Geography* 66 (September): 98–112. https://doi.org/10.1016/j.polgeo.2018.08.006.

Petridou, Elia. 2001. "The Taste of Home." In *Home Possessions: Material Culture behind Closed Doors*, edited by Daniel Miller, 87–104. Oxford, UK: Berg.

Pierre, Jemima. 2013. *The Predicament of Blackness: Postcolonial Ghana and the Politics of Race*. Chicago: University of Chicago Press.

Pole Institute. 2017. "Analyses Croisées de Conflits à l'est de la République Démocratique du Congo: Pool d'appui à la Stabilisation des Experts de la Société Civile Congolaise." Goma, DRC: Pole Institute. https://www.peace workafrica.net/wp-content/uploads/2017/09/Publication_pool_4.pdf.

Polman, Linda. 2004. *We Did Nothing: Why the Truth Doesn't Always Come out When the UN Goes In*. London: Penguin.

Porch, Douglas. 2010. "Bugeaud, Galliéni, Lyautey: The Development of French Colonial Warfare." In *Makers of Modern Strategy from Machiavelli to the Nuclear Age*, edited by Peter Paret, 376–407. Princeton, NJ: Princeton University Press. https://doi.org/10.2307/j.ctv8xnhvw.

Pouligny, Béatrice. 2006. *Peace Operations Seen from below: UN Missions and Local People*. The CERI Series in Comparative Politics and International Studies. London: Hurst.

Powel, Brieg. 2017. "The Soldier's Tale: Problematising Foucault's Military Foundations." *Review of International Studies* 43 (5): 833–54. https://doi.org/10.1017/S0260210517000171.

Prunier, Gérard. 2010. *Africa's World War: Congo, the Rwandan Genocide, and the Making of a Continental Catastrophe*. Oxford, UK: Oxford University Press.

Rabinow, Paul. 2011. *Reflections on Fieldwork in Morocco*. 30th anniversary ed. Berkeley: University of California Press.

Radio Okapi. 2018. "Nord-Kivu: 26 armes récupérées après le bouclage de l'armée au camp Katindo." *MONUSCO*, June 27, 2018. https://www.radiookapi.net/2018/06/27/actualite/securite/nord-kivu-26-armes-recuperees-apres-le-bouclage-de-larmee-au-camp.

Ramadan, Adam. 2013. "Spatialising the Refugee Camp." *Transactions of the Institute of British Geographers* 38 (1): 65–77.

Ranarifidy, Dina, ed. 2018. *Democratic Republic of Congo Urbanization Review: Productive and Inclusive Cities for an Emerging Democratic Republic of Congo*. Directions in Development Environment and Sustainable Development. Washington, DC: World Bank Group.

Ratha, Dilip. 2007. "Leveraging Remittances for Development." Policy Brief. Washington DC: Migration Policy Institute. https://www.migrationpolicy.org /research/leveraging-remittances-development.

Rawlence, Ben. 2017. *City of Thorns: Nine Lives in the World's Largest Refugee Camp.* New York: Picador.

Richards, Paul, ed. 2005. *No Peace, No War: An Anthropology of Contemporary Armed Conflicts.* Athens: Ohio University Press.

Robinson, Jennifer. 2002. "Global and World Cities: A View from off the Map." *International Journal of Urban and Regional Research* 26 (3): 531–54. https://doi .org/10.1111/1468-2427.00397.

Robinson, Jennifer. 2005. "Urban Geography: World Cities, or a World of Cities." *Progress in Human Geography* 29 (6): 757–65. https://doi.org/10.1191/0309132 505ph582pr.

Robinson, Jennifer. 2006. *Ordinary Cities: Between Modernity and Development.* Questioning Cities. New York: Routledge.

Robinson, Jennifer. 2016. "Thinking Cities through Elsewhere: Comparative Tactics for a More Global Urban Studies." *Progress in Human Geography* 40 (1): 3–29. https://doi.org/10.1177/0309132515598025.

Robinson, Jennifer. 2023. *Comparative Urbanism: Tactics for Global Urban Studies.* IJURR Studies in Urban and Social Change Book Series. Hoboken, NJ: John Wiley & Sons.

Rogers, Sarah, and Brooke Wilmsen. 2020. "Towards a Critical Geography of Resettlement." *Progress in Human Geography* 44 (2): 256–75. https://doi.org /10.1177/0309132518824659.

Rokhideh, Maryam. 2019. "Transnational Networks on the Goma-Gisenyi Border." Paper presented at the African Studies Association Annual Meeting, Boston, MA, November 22, 2019.

Roy, Ananya. 2011. "Postcolonial Urbanism: Speed, Hysteria, Mass Dreams." In *Worlding Cities: Asian Experiments and the Art of Being Global,* edited by Ananya Roy and Aihwa Ong, 307–35. Studies in Urban and Social Change. Malden, MA: Wiley-Blackwell.

Roy, Ananya, and Aihwa Ong, eds. 2011. *Worlding Cities: Asian Experiments and the Art of Being Global.* Studies in Urban and Social Change. Malden, MA: Wiley-Blackwell.

Rubbers, Benjamin. 2019. "Mining Towns, Enclaves and Spaces: A Genealogy of Worker Camps in the Congolese Copperbelt." *Geoforum* 98 (January): 88–96. https://doi.org/10.1016/j.geoforum.2018.10.005.

Rubinstein, Robert A. 2008. *Peacekeeping under Fire: Culture and Intervention.* Boulder, CO: Paradigm Publishers.

Ruffa, Chiara. 2018. *Military Cultures in Peace and Stability Operations: Afghanistan and Lebanon.* Philadelphia: University of Pennsylvania Press.

Rutanga, Murindwa. 2011. *Politics, Religion, and Power in the Great Lakes Region.* Dakar, Senegal: Fountain Publishers.

Sanyal, Romola. 2014. "Urbanizing Refuge: Interrogating Spaces of Displacement: Urbanizing Refugee Spaces." *International Journal of Urban and Regional Research* 38 (2): 558–72. https://doi.org/10.1111/1468-2427.12020.

Schmid, Christian. 2012. "Henri Lefebvre, the Right to the City, and the New Metropolitan Mainstream." In *Cities for People, Not for Profit: Critical Urban Theory and the Right to the City*, edited by Neil Brenner, Peter Marcuse, and Margit Mayer, translated by Christopher Findlay, 42–62. New York: Routledge.

Shoshan, Malkit. 2016. "BLUE: The Architecture of UN Peacekeeping." In *BLUE: The Architecture of Peacekeeping Missions. The Dutch Submission to the 15th Edition of the Venice Architecture Biennale.* Het Nieuwe Instituut. https://issuu.com/hetnieuweinstituut/docs/blue_architecture_of_un_peacekeepin.

Simić, Olivera. 2010. "Does the Presence of Women Really Matter? Towards Combating Male Sexual Violence in Peacekeeping Operations." *International Peacekeeping* 17 (2): 188–99. https://doi.org/10.1080/13533311003625084.

Simić, Olivera. 2012. *Regulation of Sexual Conduct in UN Peacekeeping Operations.* New York: Springer.

Simone, AbdouMaliq. 2001. "On the Worlding of African Cities." *African Studies Review* 44 (2): 15. https://doi.org/10.2307/525573.

Sion, Liora. 2008. "Peacekeeping and the Gender Regime: Dutch Female Peacekeepers in Bosnia and Kosovo." *Journal of Contemporary Ethnography* 37 (5): 561–85. https://doi.org/10.1177/0891241607309988.

Smirl, Lisa. 2012. "The State We Are(n't) in: Liminal Subjectivity in Aid Worker Autobiographies." In *Statebuilding and State-Formation: The Political Sociology of Intervention*, edited by Berit Bliesemann de Guevara, 230–45. London: Routledge. https://doi.org/10.4324/9780203123935.

Smirl, Lisa. 2015. *Spaces of Aid: How Cars, Compounds and Hotels Shape Humanitarianism.* London: Zed Books.

Stearns, Jason. 2011. *Dancing in the Glory of Monsters: The Collapse of the Congo and the Great War of Africa.* New York: PublicAffairs.

Stearns, Jason. 2012. *From CNDP to M23: The Evolution of an Armed Movement in Eastern Congo.* Usalama Project. London: Rift Valley Institute.

Stearns, Jason. 2015. "The Attack on Goma Airport: Big Fish or Small Fry?" *Congo Siasa* (blog). June 5, 2015. http://congosiasa.blogspot.com/2015/06/the-attack-on-goma-airport-big-fish-or.html.

Stockton, Nicholas. 1998. "In Defence of Humanitarianism." *Disasters* 22 (4): 352–60. https://doi.org/10.1111/1467-7717.00098.

Sun Tzu. 1910. *Sun Tzu on the Art of War: The Oldest Military Treatise in the World.* Translated by Lionel Giles. Classic Etexts Series. Allandale Online Publishing. https://sites.ualberta.ca/~enoch/Readings/The_Art_Of_War.pdf.

Sutton, Rebecca. 2020. "Enacting the 'Civilian Plus': International Humanitarian Actors and the Conceptualization of Distinction." *Leiden Journal of International Law* 33 (2): 429–49. https://doi.org/10.1017/S092215651900075X.

Tardy, Thierry, and Marco Wyss, eds. 2015. *Peacekeeping in Africa: The Evolving Security Architecture.* CSS Studies in Security and International Relations. New York: Routledge; London: Taylor & Francis.

Thomassen, Bjørn. 2014. *Liminality and the Modern: Living Through the In-Between.* Burlington, VT: Ashgate.

Trefon, Theodore, and Noël Kabuyaya. 2018. *Goma: Stories of Strength and Sorrow from Eastern Congo.* London: Zed Books.

Tuan, Yi-Fu. 2012. "Epilogue: Home as Elsewhere." In *Heimat: At the Intersection of Memory and Space,* edited by Friederike Eigler and Jens Kugele, 226–40. Berlin, Boston: De Gruyter.

Turner, Edith L. B. 2012. *Communitas: The Anthropology of Collective Joy.* Contemporary Anthropology of Religion. New York: Palgrave Macmillan.

Turner, John F. C. 1972. "Housing as a Verb." In *Freedom to Build: Dweller Control of the Housing Process,* edited by Robert Fichter and John F. C. Turner, 148–75. New York: Macmillan.

Turner, Simon. 2009. "Suspended Spaces–Contesting Sovereignties in a Refugee Camp." In *Sovereign Bodies,* edited by Thomas Blom Hansen and Finn Stepputat, 312–32. Princeton, NJ: Princeton University Press. https://doi.org/10.1515/9781400826698.312.

Turner, Victor W. 1977. *The Ritual Process: Structure and Anti-Structure.* Symbol, Myth, and Ritual Series. Ithaca, NY: Cornell University Press.

UNEP and Totalförsvarets Forskningsinstitut. 2012. *Greening the Blue Helmets: Environment, Natural Resources and UN Peacekeeping Operations.* UN Environment Programme. https://wedocs.unep.org/bitstream/handle/20.500.11822/8840/UNEP_greening_blue_helmets.pdf?sequence=3&amp%3BisAllowed=

UNGA. 2005. "A Comprehensive Strategy to Eliminate Future Sexual Exploitation and Abuse in United Nations Peacekeeping Operations." United Nations. https://reliefweb.int/report/world/comprehensive-strategy-eliminate-future-sexual-exploitation-and-abuse-united-nations.

UNGA. 2017. "Manual on Policies and Procedures Concerning the Reimbursement and Control of Contingent-Owned Equipment of Troop/Police Contributors Participating in Peacekeeping Missions." United Nations, August 4, 2017. https://undocs.org/a/72/288.

UNHCR. 2000. "The Rwandan Genocide and Its Aftermath." In *The State of the World's Refugees 2000: Fifty Years of Humanitarian Action.* United Nations High Commissioner for Refugees, 245–75. https://www.unhcr.org/sites/default/files/legacy-pdf/3ebf9bb60.pdf.

UNHCR. 2017. "Statistiques par Zone de Retour—Regroupement et Fermature des Sites de Déplacement au Nord-Kivu 2017." Camp Coordination and Camp Management. Unpublished manuscript.

UN Secretariat. 2003. "Secretary General's Bulletin on Special Measures for Protection from Sexual Exploitation and Sexual Abuse." United Nations Secretariat, October 9, 2013. https://undocs.org/ST/SGB/2003/13.

United Nations. 1961. "Report No. 10 on United Nations Civilian Operations in the Congo : First Year of Operations, July 1960 to June 1961." New York: United Nations. ST/ONUC/PR.10. United Nations Digital Library. https://digitallibrary.un.org/record/766519?ln=en.

United Nations and Inter-Agency Standing Committee. 2008. "Civil-Military Guidelines & References for Complex Emergencies." New York: UN Office for the Coordination of Humanitarian Affairs. https://digitallibrary.un.org/record/697614?ln=en&v=pdf.

United Nations Peacekeeping. 2020. "Sexual Exploitation and Abuse." Conduct in UN Field Missions. May 14, 2020. https://conduct.unmissions.org/sea-data -introduction.

UNSC. 1999. "Resolution 1234 (1999): The Situation Concerning the Democratic Republic of the Congo." United Nations Security Council, April 9, 1999. http://unscr.com/en/resolutions/doc/1234.

UNSC. 2000a. "Resolution 1291 (2000): The Situation Concerning the Democratic Republic of the Congo." United Nations Security Council, February 24, 2000. http://unscr.com/en/resolutions/doc/1291.

UNSC. 2000b. "Resolution 1325 (2000)." United Nations Security Council, October 31, 2000. https://undocs.org/S/RES/1325(2000).

UNSC. 2013. "Resolution 2098 (2013): The Situation in Democratic Republic of the Congo." United Nations Security Council, March 28, 2013. http://unscr .com/en/resolutions/doc/2098.

UNSC. 2014. "Report of the Secretary-General of the United Nations Organization Stabilization Mission in the Democratic Republic of the Congo." United Nations Security Council, March 5, 2014. https://monusco.unmissions.org /sites/default/files/n1424637.pdf.

UNSC. 2021. "United Nations Organization Stabilization Mission in the Democratic Republic of the Congo: Report of the Secretary-General." United Nations Security Council, September 17, 2021. https://monusco.unmissions.org/sites/default/files/s-2021-807_-_sg_report _on_monusco_in_english.pdf.

Urry, John. 2005. "The Place of Emotions within Place." In Emotional Geographies, edited by Joyce Davidson, L. Bondi, and Mick Smith, 77–83. Burlington, VT: Ashgate.

Valentine, Gill. 1999. "Eating In: Home, Consumption and Identity." *Sociological Review* 47 (3): 491–524. https://doi.org/10.1111/1467-954X.00182.

Van Melkebeke, Sven. 2016. "Coerced Coffee Cultivation and Rural Agency: The Plantation-Economy of the Kivu (1918–1940)." In *On Coerced Labor: Work and Compulsion after Chattel Slavery*, edited by Marcel van der Linden and Magaly Rodríguez García, 25:187–207. Studies in Global Social History. Leiden, Netherlands: Brill.

Van Melkebeke, Sven. 2020. *Dissimilar Coffee Frontiers: Mobilizing Labor and Land in the Lake Kivu Region, Congo and Rwanda (1918–1960/62)*. African History, vol. 9. Leiden, Netherlands: Brill.

Van Reybrouck, David, and Sam Garrett. 2015. *Congo: The Epic History of a People*. New York: Ecco.

Verhoeve, Anne. 2004. "Conflict and the Urban Space: The Socio-Economic Impact of Conflict on the City of Goma." In *Conflict and Social Transformation in Eastern DR Congo*, edited by Koen Vlassenroot and Timothy Raeymaekers, 103–22. Ghent, Belgium: Academia Press Scientific Publishers.

Verweijen, Judith. 2019. "Violent Cities, Violent Society: Analyzing Urban Violence in the Eastern Congo." Usalama Project. Insecurity in the City. London: Rift Valley Institute.

Vinck, Patrick, Phuong Pham, and Anupah Makoond. 2017. "Peacekeeping and Reconstruction Polls (Data from September-October 2017)." Report 12. Voices of Congo. Cambridge, MA: Harvard Humanitarian Initiative. https://www .peacebuildingdata.org/_files/ugd/02fbdb_069e0f72d4dc4dc898f21e0d309d e5e7.pdf.

Vlassenroot, Koen, and Karen Büscher. 2009. "The City as Frontier: Urban Development and Identity Processes in Goma," *Cities and Fragile States* Working Paper 61 (2). Crisis States Research Centre, London School of Economics and Political Science, London.

Vlassenroot, Koen, and Karen Büscher. 2013. "Borderlands, Identity and Urban Development: The Case of Goma (Democratic Republic of the Congo)." *Urban Studies* 50 (15): 3168–84. https://doi.org/10.1177/0042098013487772.

Wainaina, Binyavanga. 2005. "How to Write About Africa." *Granta*, Winter 2005. https://granta.com/how-to-write-about-africa/.

Wang, Zheng. 2020. "Beyond Displacement—Exploring the Variegated Social Impacts of Urban Redevelopment." *Urban Geography* 41 (5): 703–12. https:// doi.org/10.1080/02723638.2020.1734373.

Wangermée, Émile Antoine Marie. 1909. *Grands lacs africains et Katange: Souvenirs de voyages*. Bruxelles: J. Lebègue & Cie.

War Office. 1909. "Routes between Lakes Kivu & Mutanda." Blueprint with manuscript additions. WOMAT/AFR/BEA/207/1. Geographical Secretary General Staff. British Library Digitized Manuscripts. https://commons

.wikimedia.org/wiki/File:Routes_between_Lakes_Kivu_%26_Mutanda _-_War_Office_ledger_(WOMAT-AFR-BEA-207-1).jpg.

War Office. 1911. "Rutschuru to Lake Kivu." Blueprint, with a minor manuscript addition. Geographical Secretary General Staff. British Library Map Collections. https://commons.wikimedia.org/wiki/File:Rutschuru_to_Lake_Kivu ._(WOMAT-AFR-BEA-218-2).jpg.

War Office. 1919. "Ruanda and Urundi 'Index with Maps.'" Printed, with manuscript additions in coloured ink, pencil and crayon; 65 x 56cm. Geographical Sec. Gen. Staff. WOOS/4/4. British Library Digitised Manuscripts. https:// commons.wikimedia.org/wiki/File:Africa._1-1.000.000._Ruanda_and _Urundi_-_btv1b530646712.jpg.

Washington, George. 1757. "Instructions to Company Captains, 29 July 1757." *Founders Online*, National Archives. https://founders.archives.gov/documents /Washington/02-04-02-0223

Weir, Erin A. 2006. "Conflict and Compromise: UN Integrated Missions and the Humanitarian Imperative." Kofi Annan International Peacekeeping Training Centre monograph no. 4, June 2006. https://reliefweb.int/sites/reliefweb.int /files/resources/1EE897418FD9945CC12571CE003EB9F8-KAIPTC-Jun2006 .pdf.

Westendorf, Jasmine-Kim. 2023. "Sex on Mission: Care, Control and Coloniality in Peacekeeping and Humanitarian Operations." *International Affairs* 99 (4): 1653–72. https://doi.org/10.1093/ia/iiad119.

White, Anne-France. n.d. "The Spectrum of Expat Facial Hair in Eastern Congo." Accessed June 4, 2020. https://livingingoma.com/miscellaneous /#jp-carousel-367.

Whitworth, Sandra. 2004. *Men, Militarism, and UN Peacekeeping: A Gendered Analysis*. Critical Security Studies. Boulder, CO: Lynne Rienner.

Wills, Siobhán. 2009. *Protecting Civilians: The Obligations of Peacekeepers*. Oxford, UK: Oxford University Press.

Wirth, Louis. 1938. "Urbanism as a Way of Life." *American Journal of Sociology* 44 (1): 1–24.

Young, Eoin. 2007. "RD Congo: Redéploiement des Effectifs Militaires de la MONUC à l'ouest Du Pays." MONUC Press Release, January 9, 2007. https:// reliefweb.int/report/democratic-republic-congo/rd-congo-red%C3 %A9ploiement-des-effectifs-militaires-de-la-monuc-%C3%A0o.

Index

Maren Larsen is Senior Lecturer in Urban Studies at the University of Basel.

For Indiana University Press

Sabrina Black *Editorial Assistant*

Tony Brewer *Artist and Book Designer*

Anna Garnai *Production Coordinator*

Sophia Hebert *Assistant Acquisitions Editor*

Samantha Heffner *Marketing and Publicity Manager*

Katie Huggins *Production Manager*

Darja Malcolm-Clarke *Project Manager/Editor*

Bethany Mowry *Acquisitions Editor*

Dan Pyle *Online Publishing Manager*

Michael Regoli *Director of Publishing Operations*

Pamela Rude *Senior Artist and Book Designer*

www.ingramcontent.com/pod-product-compliance
Lightning Source LLC
Chambersburg PA
CBHW022305280326
41932CB00010B/990